The Human Tradition in Modern Britain

The Human Tradition around the World Series
Editors: William H. Beezley and Colin M. MacLachlan

The Human Tradition in Modern Britain

Edited by
Caroline Litzenberger
and
Eileen Groth Lyon

ROWMAN & LITTLEFIELD PUBLISHERS, INC.
Lanham • Boulder • New York • Toronto • Plymouth, UK

ROWMAN & LITTLEFIELD PUBLISHERS, INC.

Published in the United States of America
by Rowman & Littlefield Publishers, Inc.
A wholly owned subsidary of The Rowman & Littlefield Publishing Group, Inc.
4501 Forbes Boulevard, Suite 200, Lanham, Maryland 20706
www.rowmanlittlefield.com

Estover Road, Plymouth, PL6 7PY, United Kingdom

British Library Cataloguing in Publication Information Available

Library of Congress Cataloging-in-Publication Data

The human tradition in modern Britain / edited by Caroline Litzenberger and Eileen
Groth Lyon.
    p.   cm.—(The human tradition around the world)
    Includes bibliographical references and index.
    ISBN-13: 978-0-7425-3734-7 (cloth : alk. paper)
    ISBN-10: 0-7425-3734-X (cloth : alk. paper)
    ISBN-13: 978-0-7425-3735-4 (pbk. : alk. paper)
    ISBN-10: 0-7425-3735-8 (pbk. : alk. paper)
    1. Great Britain—History—Biography.   2. Great Britain—Civilization.   3. Great
Britain—Social conditions.   I. Litzenberger, C. J.   II. Lyon, Eileen Groth.   III. Series.
DA30.H86   2006
941.009′9—dc22

                        2006009576

Printed in the United States of America

∞ ™ The paper used in this publication meets the minimum requirements of American
National Standard for Information Sciences—Permanence of Paper for Printed Library
Materials, ANSI/NISO Z39.48-1992.

Contents

Acknowledgments

In the course of editing this set of essays, we benefited from the generous assistance of many individuals. In particular, we would like to thank William H. Beezley and Colin M. MacLachlan for their judicious comments and support of the project from its inception. Susan McEachern, Jessica Gribble, and Janice Braunstein at Rowman & Littlefield have helped to guide it to completion. We are grateful to Maggie Bryan-Peterson and Cathe Kilpatrick in the Grants Administration and Research Services Office at SUNY Fredonia and Paul Schwartz, Dean of Arts and Humanities at SUNY Fredonia, for their assistance in providing resources for the final preparation of the manuscript. One of the best pieces of advice we were given with respect to the preparation of the manuscript was to seek help from Joanne Foeller. Her attention to detail and knowledge of the intricacies of different word processing packages saved us many frustrations. We are also grateful to colleagues in the departments of history at Portland State University and SUNY Fredonia for all that they have contributed to creating intellectual communities that foster active scholarship. Finally, we thank our families, especially Jane Larsen, Gordon Lyon, and James Lyon for their love and encouragement.

Introduction

Survey courses on modern Britain often give very little attention to the examination of specific people, events, and movements involved in making that history. Time is of the essence, and so readers are given an introduction to the broad sweep of events that seldom slows down long enough to allow them to gain a sense of what life was really like between c. 1700 and c. 2000, or what was involved in creating new ideas—about God, education, colonialism, and the like. This book is intended to serve as a kind of "sampler" of those neglected topics by providing readers with the stories of individuals, events, and movements that serve as "gateways" to the larger themes in modern British history. In many cases, essays focus on individuals who have a unique place in Britain's history. They give us a glimpse of their time through their personal narratives or through what they reveal about the political, social, or cultural frameworks. In other essays, significant events or movements form the focal point. The collective narrative provided in these events or movements also has much to tell us about the human tradition in modern Britain.

Modern Britain was forged through the tumults of the sixteenth and seventeenth centuries. During the period from c. 1530 to c. 1688 England emerged as a force with which to be reckoned on the European stage. Government became increasingly centralized, albeit with much contention between the monarch and parliament as to which institution should dominate and indeed what form of government England should have. Wales officially came under the political control of England. Meanwhile, religious change profoundly transformed the country, as did increasing population and concomitant levels of poverty. There were also growing commitments to colonial interests in Ireland and North America. The latter, in turn, created a mercantilist economy that created new financial demands. Additionally, science and reason were emerging as alternatives to a religiously centered cosmos, and constructions of gender were becoming particularly unstable.

The year 1688, generally regarded as the turning point in British history, was the beginning of Modern Britain. In that year, the Protestant William of Orange and Mary, his wife and eldest daughter of the reigning but Catholic English king, James II, claimed the English throne and forced James II into exile in what has been called "The Glorious Revolution." This was a key step in the construction of a self-consciously Protestant national identity by the English government. However, this was also a time of transformation in other aspects of English life. The Scientific Revolution and the Enlightenment in England and Scotland brought challenges to the political, religious, and social order which would fully mature in the early part of the nineteenth century. Similarly, High Churchmen would seek to reinvigorate the Church through the Oxford Movement in the 1840s. Despite these movements and the deep cultural roots of religion in the Victorian age, strong secular currents manifested themselves by the latter half of the nineteenth century.

During the eighteenth century, England became Great Britain through the unions with Scotland and Ireland. These unions brought with them new challenges for governance through the creation of a much more complex and varied nation in terms of the economy, religion, and politics. Scotland's textile and shipbuilding industries were crucially important to the British economy. The influx of poor Irish laborers to England and the west coast of Scotland intensified the difficulties of poor relief and urbanization. Nineteenth-century parliamentary politics became deeply entangled in Irish questions. Early in the century, Catholic Emancipation caused deep divisions within the Tory party and helped to initiate more comprehensive reforms, including greater religious tolerance, and franchise and educational reforms. Later, efforts to achieve Irish Home Rule and assert a distinctive national identity apart from Britain were frequently debated at Westminster.

In the late-eighteenth and early-nineteenth centuries, Great Britain underwent profound social and cultural changes associated with the transition from a rural to an urban society. As the first nation to experience an "industrial revolution," Britain dominated world markets and celebrated her technological and economic achievements in the Great Exhibition of 1851. This sense of national pride was carried over into a desire to acquire control over more markets, and by extension, people across the globe. At the height of her empire, Britain ruled some 372 million people over 11 million square miles. Her political system evolved from one rooted in aristocratic privilege and patronage to one dominated by middle-class interests reflected in the Reform Act of 1832. The nineteenth century saw greater moves toward popular democracy through the Reform Acts of 1867 and 1884 and the Ballot Act of 1872. For women, full participation in the democratic process finally came in the aftermath of World War I through the Representation of the People Act (1918) and the Equal Franchise Act (1928).

The modern period in British history is also marked by conflict both at home and abroad. The sociopolitical reforms of the nineteenth century were born of much popular agitation and periodic unrest. Britain's trading and diplomatic interests overseas drew her into wars with France and the American colonies, and later, two world wars. The Second World War merely confirmed a process already begun that would reveal the twilight of a great power. As superpowers moved to the center of the world stage, great European states of an earlier age found themselves focusing on domestic woes and quickly relinquishing those overseas territories that they had so eagerly sought a century before.

The book begins with two essays that serve as a bridge to modern Britain. W. J. Sheils examines John Locke, an immensely influential figure both in the early modern and modern periods. His *Two Treatises on Government* posited a contractual view of political relations that would lie at the root of England's Revolution in 1688 and many subsequent revolutions seeking less hierarchical forms of government. Locke's writings greatly influenced modern thought on religion, moral behavior and formation, the management of public life, and the organization of trade and economic affairs.

Amy Froide's essay provides a fascinating glimpse into the social complexion of early modern England. She examines the Zaines sisters of Southampton. Although neither Alice nor Jane Zaines married, they lived rich and purposeful lives, defying stereotypes of spinsters and old maids. Jane and Alice purchased property and set up a household of their own; they started a linen drapery business becoming the first never-married women in Southampton to practice a trade with town officials' approval. Later, they passed this business down to their niece. The Zaines sisters are representative of the large number of singlewomen who lived in the villages and towns of seventeenth-century England. Through the Zaines sisters, we can gain a perspective on the lives of the one-third of adult women who were single in early modern England.

The eighteenth century was marked by great intellectual and diplomatic ferment. Andrew Thompson examines the career of Charles, 2nd Viscount Townshend, a prominent whig politician and statesman whose career offers keen insight into the persistence of party, aristocratic faction, and diplomacy in the eighteenth century. Townshend's diplomatic contacts and the changing alliances during his tenure as secretary of state offer the opportunity to consider the relationship of Britain with Europe, especially with respect to the king's German holdings and the character of British foreign policy.

The eighteenth century also saw the beginnings of modern evangelical Christianity, a topic that Grayson Carter explores. Often referred to as the first "Great Awakening," this movement in which John Wesley, his brother Charles Wesley, and George Whitfield prominently figured, led to the development of Methodism. Perhaps more significantly, however, the movement inspired a wide variety of reform campaigns, including abolitionism and the Sunday School Movement.

During the first half of the nineteenth century there was a groundswell of interest in political and social reform in both England and Ireland. Michael Huggins examines this phenomenon in his essay on the opposing forces of popular rebellion and political radicalism, which he points out were often at odds with one another. Huggins depicts the conflict as a class struggle, where those involved in popular rebellion—that is rebellion of the common folk—tended to unite against the radical leaders who at first glance seemed to be working to promote the causes for which the common fold was fighting.

Frances Knight explores the impact that the high church revival known as the Oxford Movement or Tractarianism had in Wales during the mid- and late-nineteenth century. In doing so, it provides an introduction to one of the major religious movements in Britain of the period. Wales, one of the most culturally and linguistically distinctive parts of the United Kingdom, might appear to be an unpromising soil for the Oxford Movement to take root, yet it had made its presence felt in Wales by the 1860s. The Welsh movement was far more anti-Roman and antipapal than its English counterpart, taking as its inspiration the "pure" and "undefiled" ancient Celtic Church that had existed before Augustine's mission to Canterbury in 597.

The opening of the Great Exhibition of 1851 is often cited as a central event in the Victorian age. John Davis's essay examines the precarious negotiations over the opening ceremony, revealing what amounted to a standoff between anti- and promodernizing forces. Eventually, an interesting compromise was reached. Davis reveals how conventional and attractive forms of ceremony were borrowed and assimilated into the day's events, and old and new ceremonial forms woven together to create a new, modern pattern of behavior.

Just six years after the celebration of Great Britain's dominant position in the world, her authority came under attack in India, the richest and most populous of Britain's imperial possessions, the "Jewel in the Crown." According to London newspapers, on June 9, 1857, some native soldiers had mutinied against their British officers. In his essay, David Savage tells the story of this uprising from two perspectives: that of newspaper readers in England and that of the British Army in India. Rumors on the ground in India were transformed into at best, inaccurate reporting, and more often myths by the English newspapers, revealing much about British attitudes toward indigenous peoples.

The Victorian age is most commonly associated with deep religiosity. At the start of the nineteenth century, a public declaration of atheism was virtually unheard of. Moreover, a Christian profession of faith was a requirement to participate in numerous aspects of civic life, from providing evidence in court to serving as a Member of Parliament. By the end of the century, however, there was a public, organized, atheist community that had gone a long way toward securing its rights. Timothy Larsen explores the career of Charles Bradlaugh, the leader of the movement that produced this change. Bradlaugh's critique of religious faith in general and Christianity in particular illuminates the nature and spread of skeptical ideas in Victorian Britain and the eventual transformation of religious unbelievers in Britain from a marginalized and persecuted group to one that was able to participate fully in civic life.

Debates over education in the nineteenth century were integrally linked to the movement for parliamentary enfranchisement. On one hand, there were movements such as utilitarianism and Parliamentary reform that pointed to the necessity of providing a better standard of education for all members of society, including the lower orders. Yet, standing as obstinate sentries to defend against such trends were traditions and institutions such as laissez-faire political economy and the Established Church. Eric Tenbus examines Sir James Kay-Shuttleworth, a former poor law commissioner who became the first secretary of the Committee of Council on Education in 1839. Through such a study, much is revealed about the nature of British education from its inchoate stirrings in post-Napoleonic Britain to its eventual evolution into an antagonistic dual system of state-supported board schools and subsidized denominational schools in the last decades of the century.

The women's suffrage movement became increasingly important in the years prior to the First World War. June Hannam and Myriam Boussahba-Bravard explore this movement by examining the political careers of three individuals: Annie Kenney, Teresa Billington-Greig, and Helena Swanwick. By focusing on three women of very different backgrounds and temperaments, Hannam and Boussahba-Bravard are able to provide a nuanced, multifaceted depiction of the struggle undertaken by women (and some men) to gain the right to vote in Great Britain.

The nineteenth century was marked by continued debate about Home Rule for Ireland. Organizations such as *Sinn Fein*, the Gaelic League, and the United Irishwomen sought to foster Irish identity and demand political change. James MacPherson focuses on Mary E. L. Butler, an Irish nationalist and writer, in his exploration of the changing economic and social position of women in Ireland at the turn of the twentieth century. An examination of Butler's writings reveals how the domestic role of women was crucial to the construction of Irish national identity.

National identity was also a concern in the next century as two world wars profoundly changed Britain's political, social, and cultural landscape. Susan Hanssen explores the writings of G. K. Chesterton as he looked back on the experience of World War I or "The Great War" as it was known. He was one of a number of writers who saw that struggle as a challenge to the nation's identity and sought to construct a new identity for Britain. Chesterton, however, seems to have been particularly uncomfortable with the racial themes of this analysis. Hanssen traces the evolution in Chesterton's thinking from his prewar political radicalism, through his wartime renegotiation of Great Britain's cultural relationship with her allies, to his postwar emphasis on Britain's singular position as the last of the Roman provinces to have been created and therefore as the standard bearer of republicanism and Christian liberalism.

In his depiction of an Air Raid Warden named Barbara Nixon in World-War-II London, Matthew Clarcq takes the reader into the nitty-gritty reality of wartime London. Nixon is shown grappling with challenges and a world she never imagined. In this essay, Clarcq helps the reader to see how the experience of the Second World War forged a new national culture, including some blurring of class distinctions.

Britain's hold on parts of her empire had been precarious in the interwar period as nationalist movements grew stronger and resources to be spent on colonial administration grew more meager. While the process of decolonization varied considerably from place to place, the loss of empire after World War II confirmed the decline of Britain as a great power. Anene Ejikeme examines the political activism of women in Onitsha, an Igbo-speaking community in southeastern Nigeria during this transitional period of decolonization. In the years just prior to independence and again shortly afterwards, women in Onitsha organized wide-scale demonstrations protesting new educational initiatives by the regional governments. Such a study demonstrates the impact of post-1945 British imperialism on the Nigerian experience.

Debates about disarmament in the 1960s and 1970s and difficult economic times further highlighted Britain's retreat from the status of a great power. The election of Margaret Thatcher in 1979 seemed to mark a decisive shift. Thatcher became the first politician in the modern era to win three consecutive general elections. Her economic policies gave rise to intense debate and her involvement in the Falklands War was just one of several moves to reassert Britain's power on the world stage. Mark Garnett's essay explores

Thatcher's personal background, whether or not her views reflected popular attitudes, and her legacy.

This collection of essays, then, is intended to provide the reader with selected glimpses into life in modern Britain. It will offer brief portraits of key individuals and analyze important events and movements from the perspective of the localities or the people involved. It is hoped that such stories will help to enliven the historical narrative of modern Britain.

Chapter One

John Locke: Politics, Philosophy, and Public Service

W. J. Sheils

Uncovering the interior intellectual and emotional history of individuals in the past is a notoriously difficult task for the historian, but in our case study we are fortunate to have abundant material. As a result of his extensive correspondence, his diary, and his wide-ranging manuscript and printed works on political, philosophical, religious, and economic questions, John Locke (1632–1704) is one of the best documented of seventeenth-century thinkers. Given the very important influence that his ideas have had on shaping the modern Western world, we are fortunate that he was such a careful recorder of his own activities. His surviving writings provide us with an excellent source for locating his intellectual life within the contours of his own experience and the sometimes dramatically shifting political, religious, and cultural climate of the years through which he lived.

These years were eventful ones. Locke's youth was dominated by the Civil Wars, and his early manhood witnessed the constitutional experiments under Cromwell and the Interregnum. Apparently destined for an academic career, in 1667 he was unexpectedly thrust into the center of politics through his association with the charismatic Earl of Shaftesbury, one of the chief ministers to King Charles II until 1673. Locke's role was that of secretary and advisor to his patron who, after 1673, was forced out of office and became, in effect, the leader of the opposition. The years in opposition included periods of exile in France and Holland, during which time Locke developed his philosophical and political ideas. These ideas were to prove influential during and after the Revolution of 1688 that saw the removal of King James II. His empirical philosophy, based on the use of reason as applied to experience, his advocacy of religious toleration, and his understanding that political power was justified by the consent of those governed, have combined to identify Locke as a key intellectual figure in the making of the modern world. This chapter will examine Locke's life and the way in which events shaped his ideas, consider the contemporary significance of those ideas, and assess the ways in which later generations have interpreted them.

A SCHOLARLY LIFE IN EVENTFUL TIMES

Locke was born on August 28, 1632, at Wrington in Somerset to a minor landowner and lawyer who supplemented his income through posts in local government and by acting as attorney to his more substantial neighbors. Locke's father, also called John, was a Puritan who was active on Parliament's side during the Civil Wars, serving as a captain in a regiment raised by Alexander Popham, a substantial Somerset gentleman who was elected Member of Parliament (MP) for Bath in 1645. This Puritan background was a significant factor in Locke's early intellectual development and reminds us that, for all the influence that his ideas were to have in the centuries following, Locke's views owed much to the religious and ideological upheavals of the English Civil Wars. Through the influence of Popham, Locke gained a place at Westminster School, the leading English school of the day, and from there he proceeded to Christ Church, Oxford, where he graduated with a BA in 1656 and an MA in 1658. Locke held a fellowship at Christ Church, which could have put him in line for a successful career in the Church and, indeed, his first known theoretical works date from his time as tutor there and are concerned with Church affairs. Following the Restoration of the monarchy in 1660 and the reestablishment of the Church of England, which had been abolished under Cromwell, questions of authority in religious matters and on the character of the restored church were at the heart of political debate. These issues eventually led to the departure of over 2,000 puritan clergy from the Church in 1662.

As a junior academic, Locke was not party to these discussions, but was clearly interested in them, and wrote two manuscripts on church-state relations. One of these argued that rulers had the right to determine matters of religious observance in order to maintain public peace, and the other was concerned with scriptural interpretation. Although his views of church-state relations were such as would commend themselves to the newly established Anglican authorities, and his notebooks reveal a sophisticated engagement with Anglican theology, his work on scriptural authority provides some clue as to why he did not pursue a clerical career. In that tract he argued that it was not necessary for the Church to have an infallible interpreter of Scripture, an early indication perhaps of the importance he was later to place on individual conscience in questions of belief.[1] His view of conscience was not uncritical, however, for conscience had to be based on reason and experience, a view he was shortly to develop in another manuscript, completed in 1664, and now known as the *Essays on the Laws of Nature*.[2] This text also provided an early statement of his empirical approach to questions of knowledge, in contrast to the theoretical deductive approach of the great French philosopher Rene Descartes (1596–1650), whose writings had originally attracted Locke to philosophical enquiry.

Locke's empiricism probably owed something to his interests in medicine, a career that he may already have intended to follow, and in science, especially chemistry. He had met the great chemist Robert Boyle (1627–1691), whose "mechanical philosophy" and scientific method, which allied observation and experiment to hypotheses, were to influence Locke's approach to questions of knowledge.[3] He was appointed Censor in Moral Philosophy at Oxford in 1664, but his university career was interrupted the following year by engagement as secretary to the ambassador, Sir Walter Vane, on a diplomatic mission to Brandenburg. Locke may have sought this position as a means of getting out of Oxford while he reviewed his future, but in any case, it was at this time that he abandoned any ambitions he may have had to follow a clerical career and formally committed himself to medicine. This enabled him to retain his Oxford fellowship, which was important as a source of income to a man of relatively modest means. In 1666 Locke met for the first time the man who was to become his most significant patron, Anthony Ashley Cooper, Lord Ashley, and later Earl of Shaftesbury (1621–1683), while the latter was visiting Oxford to take the spa waters at nearby Astrop.[4]

Within a year Locke had joined Ashley's household in London, principally as physician, and in 1668 he supervised a major operation on his patron, with the support of an old Oxford friend, Thomas Sydenham (1624–1689). Locke continued to act in a medical capacity to the household, supervising the births of children. While there he also copied out, or shared in the composition of, a treatise, *De Arte Medica*, advocating the superiority of observation and experience over hypothesis in the treatment of illness, a work primarily composed by his friend Sydenham.[5] Stimulated by the political excitement that surrounded the houschold and his experience of seeing government at close quarters after Ashley's appointment to the "cabal," the inner council of Charles II in 1667, Locke's interests soon extended beyond medicine, and he began to write about political, philosophical, and economic affairs, often representing the views of his patron in public. He also gained practical experience of government: helping to draw up orders for the newly founded colony of Carolina, and serving as registrar for the commissioners of excise between 1670 and 1675, as secretary for the extensive ecclesiastical patronage that Shaftesbury acquired on his appointment as Lord Chancellor in 1672, and as secretary and treasurer to the Council of Trade and Plantations. Through these posts Locke gained a wide experience of policy, chiefly in religious and economic spheres.

The years between 1667 and 1673 were also productive intellectually. His experience in government led him to write a lengthy essay on economics concerning the wisdom, or rather the futility, of governmental attempts to control interest rates.[6] This concern resurfaced in the 1690s when, after the Glorious Revolution and the removal of the Catholic James II from the throne and the coronation of William and Mary, Locke was once again at the center of public life. He advised the government on monetary policy and served for four years on the Board of Trade, for which he received the substantial salary of £1,000 a year. Shaftesbury's other major political interest was in religion, and his commitment to toleration for dissenters was subsequently to emerge in the late 1680s and 1690s as a central concern of Locke, who gradually cast aside his earlier more cautious views. Locke also turned his attention to more general philosophical questions, producing in 1671 extensive drafts for discussion among his scientific and political friends. These introduced the main arguments that were later to appear in his famous *Essay Concerning Human Understanding*, addressing issues in the theory of knowledge, political authority, religious toleration, and ethics.[7] These concerns, which remain his greatest legacy to the modern world, go back to his time at Oxford, but there is no doubt that his experience in London radically altered the shape and scope of his enquiries.

Locke's patron was the most powerful figure in Charles II's government in the years up to 1673, but following the Anglican backlash of that year the earl was out of favor with a court and government whose Catholic proclivities and close engagement with France made it the object of suspicion in many Protestant circles. Shaftesbury became their chief spokesman, and his commitment to toleration for dissenters and to the Protestant succession made him, in effect, the leader of the opposition. Locke's fortunes followed those of his master and in 1675, following Shaftesbury's fall, he moved to France. He began his diary at this time and remained in France until April 1679, pursuing his philosophical interests and meeting with doctors, scientists, and theologians, including the Jansenist theologian, Pierre Nicole (1625–1693), whose moral writings were translated by Locke.[8]

Locke returned to an England caught up in feverish political tension; the Popish plot, fabricated by Titus Oates who claimed a nationwide conspiracy of Catholics, had resulted in a number of executions of priests and laymen.

Additionally, the question of the succession by James, the Catholic brother of the king, led to a breakdown of relations between Charles and Parliament over the attempts of the latter to exclude the king's Catholic brother, James, from the throne. Charles dissolved Parliament in 1681, Shaftesbury was involved in planning rebellion, and Locke wrote two lengthy pieces in support of his patron. The first set out the grounds for James's exclusion from the throne and was an answer to the royalist theory of government set out by Robert Filmer (d.1653) in his *Patriarcha*, first published in 1680. The second was a justification for rebellion on the grounds that all political sovereignty was morally, and therefore constitutionally, ultimately dependent on the support of the elected representatives of those governed. These tracts were subsequently revised and published anonymously in 1689–1690 as the *Two Treatises of Government*, part of the theoretical justification of the Glorious Revolution, but in the context of the early 1680s they were potentially life threatening to their author.

Shaftesbury went into exile in the Netherlands in 1682, dying shortly after arriving there, but in 1683 three of Locke's other associates, Algernon Sidney, Lord William Russell, and the Earl of Essex were implicated in the Rye House Plot to kidnap the king.[9] Essex committed suicide, and the other two were executed. Locke, though a much less prominent figure, was under close scrutiny by the government. In September 1683 he fled to the Netherlands from where the government attempted to extradite him. Locke, now in his fifty-second year, had been removed from his Oxford fellowship and branded a political outcast, and had published very little. Had he died at this time, Locke would have appeared as little more than a footnote to the political and intellectual history of the period, albeit an interesting one. Exile was to prove an opportunity, however. Not only did he meet and converse with prominent Dutch theologians, such as Philip van Limborch (1633–1712), but also with Huguenot refugees fleeing from France after the Revocation of the Edict of Nantes in 1685. Freed from the daily thrust of English politics, Locke found time to write, and it was during his exile that he completed two of his most significant and enduring works, the *Essay Concerning Human Understanding* and the *Letter on Toleration,* as well as a substantial review of Isaac Newton's *Principia Mathematica* published in 1687.

The abdication of James II and the accession of William and Mary in 1688 represented a vindication of the causes which Locke and Shaftesbury had represented in the years since 1667. The Protestant succession was secured and Parliament became an integral part of the government. Locke returned to London the following year[10] and was quickly offered the post of ambassador to Brandenburg. He declined this in order to publish the works he had written while abroad, and the following decade saw the full flowering of his mature thought. In 1689 and 1690 Locke published those works for which he is chiefly remembered. His *Letter Concerning Toleration* was published at Gouda in Holland under a pseudonym. It appeared in Latin, the international language of the intelligentsia, and an English translation by William Popple (d.1708), a Unitarian minister, was published in September of that year. Also published anonymously were his *Two Treatises of Government*, which had been drafted at the height of the Exclusion Crisis. However, he continued to deny authorship publicly, even though his identity was well known, and he supervised the printing of a second edition in 1694. The only work which he publicly acknowledged at this time was his philosophical *Essay Concerning Human Understanding*, published in December 1689, in which he placed reason before revelation and experience before deduction as "the last judge and guide in everything," including questions of morality and religion.[11] The ideas which Locke developed in these works established his reputation in his own time and among later generations down to our own time, and they will be discussed more fully later.

More immediately, Locke used his growing influence to address other issues facing government in the 1690s. On religious policy his *Letter on Toleration* was followed by a second and a third on the same topic, published anonymously in 1690 and 1692 respectively.[12] These were written in reply to criticisms of the original by the Anglican divine, Jonas Proast. In 1691 he challenged parliamentary economic policy in a tract on interest rates based on his earlier work. His views on the economy held sway, and in 1695 he was made a member of a committee advising the Chancellor of the Exchequer, an appointment that led to an important post in the Council for Trade and Plantations. In 1693 he published an influential work on education, and in 1694 a second edition of the *Essay on Human Understanding* was published, as were the *Two Treatises*.

In the following year another anonymous publication, *On the Reasonableness of Christianity*, issued from his pen. This work combined his writings on epistemology[13] with his writings on religion to advocate a minimalist view of Christian doctrine, which stated that the only essential truth was that Christ was the Messiah, promising forgiveness to those who repented and lived according to his moral precepts. It said nothing of Christ's divinity and thus laid the author open to the charge of Socinianism, or the denial of Christ's divinity, thus placing him beyond orthodox Trinitarian Christianity. Locke defended himself against these charges, which were taken up by an old Anglican adversary, Edward Stillingfleet (1635–1699), by now bishop of Worcester, whose case rested not on Locke's anonymous writings on religion but on the theory of knowledge that he had publicly expounded in his *Essay*. Locke defended himself in a series of tracts, and Stillingfleet's criticisms caused him to make some changes to a later edition of the *Essay* published in 1700.

By this date Locke was a sick man. He resigned his public offices and retired to Oates, in Essex, the home of the Masham family, with whom he had lived since 1691. In the course of his public life, he had published on almost all aspects of public life and framed his views within a comprehensive empirical theory of knowledge. In his retirement, he was revered, along with Newton, as one of the intellectual giants of a nation that had come through the social and political upheavals of a troubled century and was in the process of laying the institutional and intellectual foundations for what its leaders considered to be a modern and balanced form of constitutional government. His life and writings had played a significant part in those developments, but in retirement he returned to his earlier interest in biblical scholarship and to the question of divine revelation. He wrote several volumes on the Pauline epistles that were published immediately after his death and discussed divine revelation in his *Discourse of Miracles* of 1702,[14] where miracles are described as beyond human comprehension but compatible with natural law. Locke died in October 1704 while his host, Lady Damaris Masham, read to him from the Psalms.

THOUGHT AND ACTION: PHILOSOPHICAL IDEAS AND PUBLIC EVENTS

If Locke's life was closely integrated into the political events of the years between 1667 and 1700, his writings transcended the time in which they were written. Most of them, it is true, were prompted by an engagement with contemporary public concerns on a wide range of topics from religion through education to economics. However, their enduring importance lies in the philosophical foundations on which Locke based his ideas. It is therefore best to begin any discussion of Locke's work with a consideration of his theory of knowledge, as set out in the *Essay concerning Human Understanding*, one of the major works he was happy to acknowledge publicly as his own during his lifetime. In Locke's words the principal aims of the *Essay* were to "consider the discerning Faculties of Man, as they are employ'd about the Objects which they have to do with" so that we can come to know "the ways, whereby our Understandings come to attain the Notions of Things we have."[15] Knowledge of the world was therefore acquired through experience, that is to say through observation by the senses of the material, the moral, and the spiritual objects and events with which humanity comes into contact. Our ability to order and make sense of those experiences depends on our use

of reason. It establishes the relations between the "simple" ideas that we
receive through our senses and enables us to form them into more "complex"
or abstract ideas through which we come to understand the world for ourselves and to interpret it for others. In Locke's analysis, experience informed
by reason provided the foundation of our understanding. As such his
approach owed much to his contact with the scientific and medical communities, which were emerging as a force in the public life of the capital and the
court in the years after 1660. This development is best exemplified in the
careers of his friends, the chemist, Robert Boyle, and the mathematician,
Isaac Newton (1642–1727). In fact Locke modestly described his philosophical work as "removing some of the Rubbish, that lies in the way of Knowledge" uncovered by these two great scientists.

In stressing the essentially experiential nature of knowledge, Locke
departed from the Cartesian notion that humanity possessed knowledge of
innate truths, whether religious or deductive, at birth; for him the minds of
the newborn were like blank sheets of paper, a view which, we shall see, had
important implications for his view of education. By making reason the final
test of understanding, Locke did not claim that all truths rested on reason
alone but that reason provided us with the necessary understanding for salvation, which was the ultimate goal of humanity: God gave "all mankind so
sufficient a light of Reason, that they to whom this written Word [the Bible]
never came, could not either doubt of the being of a GOD, or of the Obedience due to him."[16] Reason therefore provided us with sufficient, if not full,
understanding of spiritual truth, and our understanding would advance as we
applied our rational faculties to the world around us. Knowledge was progressive and the faculties which humanity possesses were not to be explained by
accident or by somatic processes: they were God-given. In spiritual terms
careful reading of the scriptures would advance our understanding, so long as
it was directed by reason and not by what Locke called "enthusiasm," which
today we might interpret as an uncritical credulity or as literal fundamentalism. In scientific terms Locke knew that contemporary understanding of the
world was incomplete, and in some cases he doubted that full understanding
would be attainable, especially in the relationship between the mental and the
physical world. He asserted, "How any Thought should produce a motion in
Body is as remote from the nature of our Ideas, as how any Body should
produce any Thought in the Mind,"[17] but as our experience increases and we
apply our reason to it, so our understanding will increase also. In this respect
Locke's confidence in reason was both modern and optimistic and required
constant effort from all. The reward for that effort was greater understanding,
and its purpose was to make the world a better place, for as Locke concluded

in his *Essay*, "Morality is the proper Science, and Business of Mankind in general."[18]

It was that purpose which directed Locke to the consideration of political and social questions. Consideration of right government and the true basis upon which political authority should rest could hardly have escaped the attention of any serious thinker in a period which saw the Civil Wars, the Cromwellian Protectorate, the Restoration of the monarchy, the attempt by Charles II to rule without Parliament, the accession and removal of a Catholic king in James II, and the construction of a constitutional settlement which might stabilize the hitherto unstable relationship between the two key elements in political life, Crown and Parliament. Locke's interest in political ideas was of long duration, and we are still unsure as to when his mature statement, published in 1689 as the *Two Treatises of Government*, was written. It appears that he had written large parts of the work over a number of years prior to his flight to Holland in 1683, and that by that time, most of the text was complete. The book asserts the right of the governed to resist unjust government, a right founded on two principles; firstly, the theory of consent, which is the origin of the relation between governors and governed and legitimizes the form in which that relation is expressed; and secondly, the theory of trust, by which the authority of governors is sustained once they have been entrusted with power. It was the services that rulers provided for their subjects—peace, prosperity, and justice—which legitimized their authority, and not any God-given ordinance. As such, the work was a direct attack upon divine right monarchy and set firm limits to the constitutional powers of any rulers—in the immediate case, those of the King of England. Those monarchical powers had been expounded most forcefully by Sir Robert Filmer in his *Patriarcha* and in confronting the arguments set out in that book, Locke moved in a radical direction. Firstly, it was the responsibility of all men, and in Locke's case he meant men, to use their reason to judge the best means of preserving good government and not to leave that responsibility to the rulers. Political participation was, therefore, based on man's responsibility to use his reason to discern the best means of preserving society. Thus, politics, properly understood, was a duty, not a right, and one that embraced both ruler and ruled. Secondly, Locke's understanding of property imposed restrictions on the rights of governors over the material possessions of their subjects.[19]

For Locke, property originated as the result of human labor and was God-given, but, as such, was valued for the purposes to which it was put, since the link between human labor and God implied stewardship rather than ownership. More recently with the invention of money, which "being little useful to the Life of Man in proportion to Food, Rayment, and Carriage, has its value only from the Consent of Man,"[20] property had become more morally contentious. Locke never quite resolved the potential conflicts between rights to property acquired through labor and those acquired through speculation, a conflict which still resonates in today's world, but his clear recognition of the first as a right of all humans and of the second more guardedly so made private ownership a further check on the power of government. The stability and prosperity of a property-owning society depended upon a constitutional form of government and could not be guaranteed by absolute monarchy. Prosperity resulted from human endeavor in which the historical progression from a labor to a money economy benefited every member of society as wealth created by the market filtered down to the least well off. These benefits were accompanied by difficulties in that, as property became more complex, so disputes arose over competing rights. The stability of the system therefore depended upon law, which was maintained by "balancing the Power of Government by placing several parts of it in different hands."[21] Thus the case for an elective legislature was based on experience and reason.

Experience and reason were the foundation of Locke's view of education also. He held an unsentimental view of child development and regarded the proper object of education as the cultivation of virtue, an end that was to be achieved not by discipline but by fostering the innate rational powers of children. This could be a strenuous undertaking, as was Locke's requirement that all adults should place their experience under the scrutiny of their intellect. However, he also recognized the needs of children to be allowed to develop their minds at a pace consistent with their other needs and "not be hindered from being Children, or from playing." With such a positive attitude to the capacities of children, and a sympathetic understanding of their needs, Locke's *Some Thoughts Concerning Education* was an important watershed in changing attitudes to childhood in the eighteenth century. Indeed, unlike many contemporary writers on childhood, Locke did not think that the chief obstacle to the development of reason in the young was to be found in their obstinacy but in the credulous falsehoods told to them by adults.[22]

Some of these falsehoods were founded on a misunderstanding of religious truth, a subject on which Locke wrote extensively. His arguments centered on the role of reason in discerning religious truth, leading to a discussion of the relationship between knowledge and belief, the conclusions of which produced the famous argument for toleration. Locke's views had not always favored toleration and his mature position, published in 1689, was formed in part by the political events in England during Charles II's reign. Nonetheless, it was also consistent with his more general philosophical position, which he had developed over many years.

Throughout his life Locke did not doubt that human beings had a duty to God, but the source of that knowledge was not easy to explain. There were four ways of knowing: inscription, through which knowledge of the law was written on mankind's heart; tradition, through which the custom and practice of the churches passed on truth; reason and experience, by which humans came to an understanding of truth; and divine revelation. To Locke the first two were demonstrably false by virtue of the fact that individuals and churches had in the past, and in his own days, held different views concerning truth. Nor could revelation lead to knowledge. Locke accepted its existence but, almost by definition, it was beyond human comprehension and thus, insofar as divine revelation transmitted spiritual truths to the world, and Locke accepted that it did, these were not a matter of knowledge but of belief. The only source of religious knowledge was, as in other spheres of human activity, reason. Knowledge of God's existence was susceptible to reason. That God was the Christian God as indicated in the scriptures was also reasonable, its truth being required by natural law, a law that is just as amenable to human understanding as the laws of mathematics. This view he maintained throughout his life, returning to the study of the scriptures in his last years and writing his *Reasonableness of Christianity* in 1695 with further editions in the following years.[23]

A chief consequence of his concern to stress the reasonableness of the Christian religion was, however, to strip it down to its essentials: acknowledgement of the existence of God and our duties towards him, and recognition of Christ as the Messiah. This minimalist view of the essential truths of religion led his Anglican opponents to accuse him of Socinian, or Unitarian views, which denied the divinity of Christ. Locke denied this, but his understanding of religious truth, insofar as it could be based on knowledge, left this issue, at best, an open question. Beyond these truths all else was, in theology, a matter of belief, and in ecclesiastical arrangements, a question of custom and convenience. It was in this context that Locke's arguments for toleration were constructed. In theology Locke argued the essential irrationality in governments attempting to use coercive means to enforce belief. Not only was this futile, but belief being beyond the scope of reason, it was also unjust. So long as individuals accepted those aspects of religion susceptible to reason, there was no way of knowing that their beliefs were wrong. On matters of ecclesiastical order, Locke was deeply influenced by the current state of religious affairs in England and thus addressed the problems involved in attempting to reconcile liberty of conscience with the necessary authority of the state. In this context toleration could not be extended to everyone; Roman Catholics were excluded because they were still thought to represent a political threat to the stability of the government and because their own beliefs refused toleration to others. Locke and many of his contemporaries excluded atheists for denying the rational basis of Christianity as understood.

LOCKE'S INFLUENCE ON THE MODERN WORLD

As a result of his insistence on the primacy of reason in human understanding, his argument that political authority should be answerable to the people through an electoral system, and his advocacy of religious toleration, Locke has been thought of as a herald of the Enlightenment and a champion of liberalism. As such he has been considered one of the key influences in forming the modern world, but before considering the impact of his thought on subsequent generations, we should return briefly to the immediate context of post-Revolutionary Britain. If his long-term reputation has been associated with the rights of the individual, his actions and writings in the 1690s identified him closely with a state that was rapidly extending the power of government, especially in the social and economic realms. He was active in government financial regulation and advised on colonial policy, and the most recent scholarship has concluded that the 1690s saw the most ambitious program of state building undertaken in England. Divine right monarchy was replaced by a strong executive, in which ministers controlled policy and were answerable to, though they often dominated, Parliament. Notwithstanding his subsequent reputation, it is clear that, in the context of his time, Locke was a supporter of what we might today term "big government," so long as it commanded the support of those governed.[24]

It is Locke's philosophical work that was to have the most profound influence. He wrote at a time when scientific enquiry was beginning to replace religious understanding as the means through which humanity described the world in which we live, and his was the most significant philosophical contribution to that process. He has long been recognized as a key thinker in what historians have described as "the disenchantment of the world," ever since the German sociologist Max Weber (1864–1920) first coined the phrase a century ago. This Locke did by freeing intellectual enquiry from the burden of tradition and authority through a method of enquiry that has become known as empiricism. It was this that established his lasting reputation, and it did so rapidly. Many of his published works had been translated into French before he died, and Voltaire (1694–1778) referred to him as the "Hercules of metaphysics" for his theory of knowledge.[25] In England the novelist Laurence Sterne (1713–1768) attributed any genius he had to his reading of Locke, and as early as 1717 Locke's works were being read in America, influencing the young Jonathan Edwards (1703–1758) at New Haven. The indices of books written by most major eighteenth-century thinkers reveal the pervasive influence which Locke had on philosophy at the time, and his empirical approach directly influenced major Enlightenment figures like the Scotsman David Hume (1711–1776) and the German Immanuel Kant (1724–

1804). The Enlightenment was also associated with political change and especially with revolutionary change in France and America.[26] Locke's writings on politics and religion have long been identified as one of the fundamental influences on the American Constitution, especially on the rights of the individual and on the separation of Church and State, and thus on liberal democracy. However, in the aftermath of the French Revolution his works were less valued. His reputation declined during the nineteenth century until the publication in 1894 of Leslie Stephen's *English Thought in the Eighteenth Century,* which placed Locke at the heart of Enlightenment thought. Contemporaneous to this, and following the nation building after the Civil War, interest in Locke was revived in American political and scholarly circles. More recently, since the 1970s, there has been a reconsideration of Locke's influence: work on Locke's manuscripts has revealed him to have held a more complex position on political issues than previously thought, and concentration on the role of other traditions, and in particular the republican one expressed by Machiavelli, has led to a reconsideration of Locke's influence on modern liberal democracy.[27] That debate still continues, but that fact in itself is evidence for the continuing influence that Locke has on the way we view the modern world, and testifies to the importance of ideas in human experience. Locke lived in eventful times. Moving from an academic environment to become the secretary and advisor of a leading politician, his life was subject to the vagaries of politics and patronage typical of the *ancien régime*, and he had to flee his homeland before returning to serve it as a busy and conscientious public official. During that humdrum if busy life, Locke engaged with and observed the world around him with such clarity and insight that his attempts at making sense of it still resonate with us today. He was formed by his puritan background and retained some of its intellectual inheritance, but Locke's ideas mark a critical point in the shift from the post-Reformation world of confessional states to the modern pluralistic democracies in which most of the inhabitants of the developed world live at present. His convictions, set out in a letter to a friend in 1698, resonate with us today: "I know there is truth opposite to falsehood, that it may be found if people will, and is worth the seeking, and is not only the most valuable, but the pleasantest thing in the world."[28]

SUGGESTED READINGS

The best recent introductions to the history of the period are J. Hoppit, *A Land of Liberty? England 1689–1727* (Oxford, 2000) and J. Scott, *England's Troubles, 17th-Century English Political Instability in European Context*

(Cambridge, 2000). For Locke the best general introduction remains J. Dunn, *Locke* (1984) in the Oxford Past Masters series; he and I. Harris have collected a series of key articles on his political thought in *Locke*, 2 volumes (Cheltenham, 1997). A lively if contested account that places Locke's thought in the context of his political activity is in R. Ashcraft, *Revolutionary Politics and Locke's Two Treatises of Government* (Princeton, NJ, 1986); he has also edited a four-volume collection of key articles, *John Locke. Critical Assessments* (London, 1991), which looks at all aspects of Locke's thought. These are also treated in a series of articles in V. Chappell, *The Cambridge Companion to Locke* (Cambridge, 1994), which includes chapters on his life and his subsequent influence. The best introduction to his religious thought is found in J. Marshall, *John Locke: Resistance, Religion and Responsibility* (Cambridge, 1994); J. W. Yolton's early study, *John Locke and the Way Of Ideas* (Oxford, 1950) remains an accessible and short introduction to the intellectual background of Locke's ideas. M. Hunter, *Science and the Shape of Orthodoxy: Intellectual Change in Late 17th-Century Britain* (Rochester, NY, 1996) is a more recent account of the scientific background. The only full-length biography of Locke, M. Cranston, *John Locke: A Biography* (Reprinted Oxford, 1985) is rather dated, and there is a full political biography of his patron, K. H. D. Haley, *The First Earl of Shaftesbury* (Oxford, 1968), which provides a detailed account of the politics of the period.

Locke's own writings remain indispensable, and the introductions to the scholarly editions of those texts, most of which have been published by the Clarendon Press, Oxford, and are referenced in the article, also provide important background and context. In addition to the texts themselves, the excellent edition of his letters by E. S. de Beer, *The Correspondence of John Locke*, 8 volumes (Oxford, 1976 to date) is indispensable. These form the basis for a more accessible volume, M. Goldie, *The Selected Correspondence of John Locke* (New York, 2002). Finally, Locke's reputation in the century and a half after his death is considered in M. Goldie, *The Reception of Locke's Political Thought, 1690 to 1830* (London, 1999), six volumes of contemporary writings indebted to or contesting Locke's ideas. His continuing importance is best recognized by the fact that he has his own journal, *Locke Studies*, founded in 2001 from the *Locke Newsletter*, where the most recent scholarship on his life and thought can be found.

NOTES

1. Published as *Two Tracts on Government,* P. Abrams, ed. (Cambridge: Cambridge University Press, 1967) and in J. C. Biddle, "John Locke's Essay on Infallibility: Introduction, Text and Translation," *Journal of Church and State* 19 (1977): 301–27.

2. Modern edition edited and translated by R. Horwitz, J. Strauss, and D. Clay, *Questions Concerning the Law of Nature* (Ithaca, NY: Cornell University Press, 1990).

3. Michael Hunter, *Robert Boyle, 1627–91: Scrupulosity and Science* (Rochester, NY: Boydell & Brewer, Ltd., 2000).

4. K. D. Haley, *The First Earl of Shaftesbury* (Oxford: Clarendon Press, 1968).

5. The text is printed in K. Dewhurst, *Dr. Thomas Sydenham (1624–1689): His Life and Original Writings* (London: Wellcome Historical Medical Library, 1966), 79–84.

6. Published in 1692, modern edition in P. H. Kelly, ed., *Locke on Money* (Oxford: Clarendon Press, 1991).

7. Printed in P. H. Nidditch and G. A. J. Rogers, eds., *Drafts for the Essay Concerning Human Understanding, volume 1, Drafts A and B* (Oxford: Clarendon Press, 1990).

8. Jansenist theology emphasized predestination, denied free will, and maintained that human nature was incapable of good. The Roman Catholic Church condemned it as heretical.

9. P. Milton, "John Locke and the Rye House Plot," *Historical Journal* 43 (2000), 647–68.

10. See L. G. Schwoerer, ed., *The Revolution of 1688–1689* (Cambridge: Cambridge University Press, 1992).

11. P. H. Nidditch, ed., *An Essay Concerning Human Understanding* (Oxford: Clarendon Press, 1975), ref. at page 704.

12. For the Latin text and translation, J. W. Gough, ed., *A Letter Concerning Toleration* (Oxford: Clarendon Press, 1968); modern editions of Popple's translation are J. Tully, ed., *A Letter Concerning Toleration* (Indianapolis, IN: Hackett Publishing Company, 1983); and J. Horton and S. Mendus, eds., *A Letter Concerning Toleration* (London: Routledge, 1991), which also contains critical essays.

13. This is the branch of philosophy that studies the nature of knowledge, its presuppositions and foundations, and its extent and validity.

14. Printed in *The Works of John Locke*, vol. 9 (London: C. and J. Rivington, 1824); extracts in V. Nuovo, *John Locke, Writings on Religion* (Oxford: Clarendon Press, 2002), 44–52.

15. P. H. Nidditch, ed., *An Essay Concerning Human Understanding* (Oxford: Clarendon Press, 1975), 44.

16. Nidditch, *Essay Concerning Human Understanding,* 289.

17. Nidditch, *Essay Concerning Human Understanding,* 629.

18. Nidditch, *Essay Concerning Human Understanding,* 64.

19. P. Laslett, ed., *Two Treatises of Government* (Cambridge: Cambridge University Press, 1989 revised ed).

20. Laslett, *Two Treatises of Government,* 301–2.

21. Laslett, *Two Treatises of Government,* 338.

22. J. W. Yolton and J. S. Yolton, eds., *Some Thoughts Concerning Education* (Oxford: Clarendon Press, 1989), quote at page 156.

23. J. Higgins-Biddle, ed., *The Reasonableness of Christianity* (Oxford: Clarendon Press, 1998), prints the second edition.

24. M. Goldie, ed., *Locke, Political Essays* (Cambridge: Cambridge University Press, 1997), introduction, xxvi–xxvii.

25. Quoted by H. Aarsleff, "Locke's Influence," in *The Cambridge Companion to Locke,* ed. V. Chappell, 252 (Cambridge: Cambridge University Press, 1994).

26. For American politicians of the revolutionary period and their use of Locke, see M. Goldie, ed., *The Reception of Locke's Politics,* 5 vols. (London: Pickering & Chatto, 1999), vol. 1, introduction xlix–lix; volume 3 is devoted to American texts from 1760 to 1780 which refer to Locke's ideas.

27. D. Wootton, ed., *John Locke, Political Writings* (Harmondsworth: Penguin Books, 1993), 9–11.

28. E. S. de Beer, *The Correspondence of John Locke,* vol. 6 (Oxford: Clarendon Press, 1976–2000) 295.

Chapter Two

Sisters, Shopkeepers, and Dissenters: Singlewomen in Britain at the Turn of the Eighteenth Century

Amy M. Froide

When we think of British women three centuries ago, we think of them as wives and mothers; but in actuality as many as one-third of adult women in the later seventeenth century had never married. In the port town of Southampton, 34.2 percent of adult women were single according to the Marriage Duty tax of 1696, which is the closest we have to an early modern census. Add to this the 18.5 percent that were widowed, and it means that less than half, or 47.3 percent, of adult women were wives.[1] And yet, most of women's history has so far focused on married women. This essay will provide a much-needed look at the one-third of adult women whom British contemporaries termed "singlewomen" or "spinsters."[2] It will do so by examining the lives of two never-married sisters, Jane and Alice Zaines, who lived in Southampton at the turn of the eighteenth century. The lives and experiences of Jane and Alice Zaines illuminate many of the key themes in early modern British history, among them family and kinship, women's work, the urban Renaissance of provincial towns, and religious dissent. Their story was not unique even though the evidence that we have for the lives of these two sisters—who were not wealthy, famous, or titled—is.

Southampton's Record Office yields fifteen references to Jane and Alice Zaines and their niece Elizabeth Wheeler.[3] While this may sound like very little historical evidence, it is in fact quite a good amount for an average townswoman of the time. The Zaines sisters also appear in various sorts of sources—court documents, tax records, church parish registers, and wills.

From these sources it is possible to piece together the outlines of the Zaines sisters' lives.

ETHNICITY AND FAMILY ORIGINS

Jane and Alice Zaines were born into a large and prosperous family in seventeenth-century Southampton. Their ancestry, however, was continental, for the Zaines family was part of an influx of Huguenots from France and Walloons from the Low Countries. Southampton had been a prominent home for Protestant refugees since the early reign of Elizabeth I. The refugees came in three waves: 1567, 1627, and 1685, the latter being after Louis XIV's revocation of the Edict of Nantes (which ended toleration for non-Catholic Christians in France). The Zaines family had already begun to appear in the records from Southampton before 1685, so it appears they were part of one of the earlier migrations. The English first names of the siblings might also indicate the family had lived in Britain for some time. Jane and Alice had at least two other sisters and one brother. Their sister Sarah married Richard Sharp, and their sister Elizabeth married into the Wheeler family. These two sisters are prime examples of the type of intermarriage that often occurred between Huguenot and English families in Southampton. The religious immigrants by no means remained isolated; rather they quickly integrated themselves into the social, economic, and political life of the port town. It is not clear whom their brother Robert Zaines married, but he also was well integrated into the urban community. Alice Zaines's will also mentions a "brother Thomas Rouse" (also spelled Thomas Rowse), who could have been a stepsibling or a brother-in-law due to the different surname; but we know little about him.

It is unclear in what year Jane and Alice Zaines were born. Nevertheless, we can make some estimates since their sister Sarah appears in the 1678 Poll Tax as a servant of William Porter's family in Holy Rood parish. Girls usually went into service in their midteens and worked until marriage (the average age of first marriage for seventeenth-century women was 26).[4] This means that Sarah Zaines was probably born somewhere between the early 1650s and 1660s. Her sisters would have been born sometime around this period as well. Jane and Alice do not begin to appear in Southampton's civic or legal records until 1691. In this year the sisters began to be listed among those who rented houses and paid local taxes in All Saints Infra parish. This was an important turning point. Jane and Alice Zaines never married and yet by the 1690s they began to appear as independent women, renting property and engaging in a business. We can date their social adulthood to this period.

Jane and Alice Zaines illustrate two things that were very common about singlewomen in the early modern period. First, spinsters often had another never-married sister; it seems that singlewomen ran in pairs. For instance, the Zaines sisters might well have known Elizabeth and Johanna Shergold, who ran a boarding school for young ladies in Southampton, or Elizabeth and Mary Rowte, who both worked in the family ironmongery business. These spinster pairs in effect formed an alternative to the married couple. While the norm was for an adult woman to marry and create a family and household economy with a husband, singlewomen substituted a sister in place of a spouse. Second, in the early modern period women achieved social adulthood upon marriage; but for women who never married it was not always clear when the transition from daughter to matron occurred. In Southampton, singlewomen became independent when their parents died and when they reached their late thirties or early forties (the two events often occurred around the same time). Seventeenth-century wisdom held that a woman who had reached the age of forty without marrying was no longer viewed as marriageable, especially because marriage was for procreation and a woman in her forties was past her childbearing years in this time period.[5] It is most likely then that Jane and Alice Zaines began to appear in Southampton's documentary record when their parents died and as they reached middle age. This means that in 1691 they were probably near the age of 40, which would put their birth dates somewhere around 1650.

As middle-aged women, Jane and Alice Zaines lived together in Southampton's All Saints Infra parish (Infra or "inside" was opposed to the "Extra" part of the parish which was outside the city walls). This part of town was very demographically mixed. It included some of the poorest people in Southampton as well as a core of prosperous inhabitants. It was here that the Zaines sisters began to rent property in the 1690s. Renting was not necessarily inferior to owning, since most burgage (inside the borough) land was leased by the town's governing body, the Corporation. Alice is listed as paying rent and local taxes in 1691, and two years later Jane is also recorded. By 1697 "Jen and Elles Zaines" are listed together. At this point they seem to have moved to a bigger house, perhaps a sign of their growing prosperity in trade. For this house they paid £4 annually, a typical rent for a householder of middling status. In 1698, Alice appeared in the rental records again, but now alone. Since tax collectors commonly listed one head of household (usually the father), listing only one sister's name does not necessarily mean that she was living on her own. This is supported by the Poll tax of 1692, a document that did have to list all the inhabitants in a house, where both Jane and Alice are recorded as living together. Despite never marrying, these records tell us that the Zaines sisters were able to establish a home for themselves once they left the parental household.

URBAN WOMEN'S WORK

Jane and Alice Zaines not only resided together, they were also partners in business. It was common for never-married women in the early modern period to set up a trade with another single (or sometimes widowed) sister. In Southampton alone, Elizabeth and Joanna Shergold ran a school together, Ann Faulkner and her widowed sister Mary Stotes took over their mother's business when she died, and Mary Smith kept an alehouse with her single sisters. Southampton was not unique. Mary and Anne Hogarth, sisters to the famous engraver, ran a "frock shop" together on Long Walk in London.[6] And the author Fanny Burney's spinster aunts, Rebecca and Ann, established both a coffee shop and a lodging house in the metropolis.

Like the majority of Huguenot immigrants in Britain, the extended Zaines family was active in the clothing trades. Jane and Alice's brother Robert was a hatter, for example. But instead of working as seamstresses or hatters themselves, the Zaines sisters established themselves as linen drapers. Their choice of occupation most likely had something to do with their middling status. In the later seventeenth century, contemporaries deemed only certain trades acceptable for genteel (or nonlaboring) women. Singlewomen of this status who needed to maintain themselves took to the shopkeeping, millinery, and linen drapery trades. These occupations involved selling rather than making textiles and clothing accessories. A linen draper would have sold a variety of cloth (not just linen), as well as ribbons, laces, tapes, and other accessories. The development of these new trades revolutionized the options available to a never-married woman needing to support herself in early modern Britain.

The Zaines sisters lived in a period of increasing opportunities for urban singlewomen. England's provincial towns underwent an "urban Renaissance" in the late seventeenth and early eighteenth centuries.[7] At this time, local economies picked up after years of war and uncertainty, trade increased due to a growing demand from the genteel visitors who began to patronize the provincial towns near their country estates, and the influx of new visitors led to a boom in commercial and municipal building. By the early 1700s Southampton was one of the provincial towns benefiting from such a renaissance. The local gentry began to come to the town for their shopping and entertainment needs. In response, Southampton's High Street became the site of various new shops and inns catering to visitors with money. These economic changes transformed the way that Southampton and other provincial towns looked at working singlewomen.

Through much of the early modern period Southampton had been actively hostile toward never-married women who worked on their own or started their own businesses. This was because early modern people thought of the family as the basic economic unit, rather than the individual. The goal was to further family businesses, run by a father, with the help of the mother, children, servants, and perhaps apprentices and journeymen. In doing so, local officers were assisting families to thrive and survive. The only women that officials assisted in running a business were widows, who were deputies of their deceased husbands, and as such were allowed to continue their family trades. Singlewomen, however, were not deemed worthy of assistance because they presumably had no families to support. Rather, they were expected to work in another person's household or assist their family members with their businesses. But when urban economies began to improve, and shopkeepers and tradespeople were in demand, attitudes changed. It is no coincidence that the first significant numbers of single tradeswomen appeared in Southampton in the early 1690s, just as the local economy was taking off.

Among these very first female traders was Jane Zaines. In 1694 Jane appeared before the town's Court Leet (which dealt primarily with misdemeanors and public nuisances). Jane was fined sixpence for incorrect measuring—it appears her yardstick was too short. A yardstick was used for measuring cloth, something a linen draper would have done on a regular basis. With a short yardstick Jane Zaines might have been cheating her customers out of their fair share of cloth. For the next seven years Jane, then Jane and Alice, and finally just Alice paid a Stall and Art fee. This was an annual fee that allowed a person to trade in Southampton. While men and widows paid a nominal Stall and Art fee of 2 pence each year, the Zaines sisters paid the considerably larger amount of 5 shillings. Their fee was thirty times higher than the average one. Jane and Alice obviously experienced the continued leeriness that Southampton's Corporation exhibited toward independent single tradeswomen. Jane and Alice were not unique; almost all singlewomen had to pay a higher Stall and Art fee for the privilege of trading in the town.

The last time Jane Zaines appeared in Southampton's Stall and Art records was in 1698. It is likely she died sometime after this because no further records make mention of her. Alice continued paying a fee to trade on her own until 1701 when the documents record her name and her death. On the next line after her name, the Stall and Art records list her niece's name, Elizabeth Wheeler, and the amount of her Stall and Art fine. With the stroke of a pen, the Zaines's linen drapery business passed down to another single, female member of the family. But Elizabeth Wheeler paid dearly to inherit her aunts' trade. Instead of the 5 shillings Stall and Art fee paid by her aunts, Wheeler was charged £5, or twenty times as much. Perhaps Southampton viewed this as an informal inheritance tax, but it was not a common custom.

Elizabeth Wheeler's story is indicative of the type of economic disadvantages and obstacles that singlewomen who needed to support themselves had to face. The town officers did not stop at a large entry or inheritance fee. In July of 1702 Elizabeth Wheeler was also brought before the town's Quarter Sessions court for practicing the trade of a linen draper without having served a seven-year apprenticeship. Elizabeth's male kin were cutlers, so they could not have trained her as a linen draper. Instead, like many women, she received informal training from her female relatives. Since 1692 Elizabeth had been living with her spinster aunts, Jane and Alice Zaines. Her aunts would have engaged in practical training, having her wait on customers in their shop. But they also would have taught their niece what to buy from wholesalers, how to outfit the shop with goods, and perhaps how to present her wares in the new bow windows that were being installed in the High Street shops. Elizabeth Wheeler also would have had to be literate and numerate and be able to keep accounts. Unfortunately, the Zaines sisters had not formalized the training of their niece with an indenture or a contract, so she had no proof of her abilities. This was the problem for many young, single women trying to earn a living at this time. Most kin did not formally apprentice young women; instead they trained them in a trade and assumed they would marry and assist their husbands. If the men died, then as widows they had the right to trade, but singlewomen who had no husbands did not. They were at a town's mercy.

Elizabeth Wheeler had two things on her side though; she was a confident woman and her aunts had left her with both the goods and the shop to establish herself in her trade. When the sergeant called her to appear before the court he reported that he "went to the shop where the said Elizabeth was and told her she must appear immediately and Elizabeth told him that she would do her owne business first."[8] Although she was convicted of trading without an apprenticeship, Elizabeth covered the £2 fine, in addition to the £5 Stall and Art fee she had already paid. It seems that the money satisfied the Southampton officers because the following year Elizabeth Wheeler only had to pay the nominal 2 pence Stall and Art fee and more importantly, she continued her trade.

WOMEN'S SOCIAL RELATIONSHIPS

Elizabeth Wheeler may well have benefited from her ties to a prosperous and established extended family in Southampton. What this reveals is the importance of kinship in the early modern period. Family members were expected to support one another materially and emotionally, and this was especially true when it came to the up-and-coming younger generation. Elizabeth would not have gone on to become a linen draper and would not have been able to survive without marrying if it were not for her relatives. Her aunts, Jane and Alice Zaines, chose her from among their numerous nieces and nephews as their heir. As such she inherited the household goods of her aunts, £50 in shop goods, and their shop. Elizabeth Wheeler also received help from her kin at another time of need. When Southampton's courts were hounding her for trading without an apprenticeship, it was her uncle Robert Zaines and her brother John Wheeler who each pledged £20 (a considerable sum for a trades-man) that she would appear before the Court of Quarter Sessions and would be of good behavior. These men put their money and their reputations on the line for their kinswoman.

The importance of kinship ties to women who never married is something that Alice Zaines also illustrates. Women without husbands and children forged their primary relationships with siblings, nieces and nephews, and other kin. Female relatives were especially important to singlewomen, who were "woman identified" in their wills. We do not know if Jane made a will, and if she did, it did not survive, but Alice's will is extant. This 1701 docu-ment is a blueprint for the type of social relationships a singlewoman might have had at the end of her life. The most prominent people in the will were her siblings and their children and spouses. These same kin were also the primary recipients of her estate.

Alice Zaines mentioned three siblings in her will. Siblings were the kin with whom never-married women had the closest ties. Although parents were also significant, it was a brother or sister who shared a singlewoman's life-span and life experiences. The material and emotional reciprocity between siblings was perhaps more important in the early modern period than today. Alice bequeathed £20, a gown, a black crape coat, and a gray coat to her sister Elizabeth Wheeler. It was common for women to leave such personal items to their female kin. To her brother, Thomas Rowse, she bequeathed £12 in shop debts (that is, money that had yet to be recovered from creditors). To her brother Robert Zaines, Alice bequeathed the most responsibility, for she made him the executor of her will, but she also gave him £50, the largest amount she left to a sibling.

Alice Zaines also remembered the spouses of her siblings. Although her sister Sarah Sharp had predeceased her, the first person Alice mentioned in her will was Sarah's husband Richard Sharp. It seems that Alice had loaned him the significant sum of £150, which she was now considering part of the estate that she wished to bequeath in her will. Showing she felt no ill will toward her brother-in-law, Alice left his second wife (the one he married after her sister died) a cup worth 20 shillings as a token of her regard. Alice also bequeathed to her brother Robert Zaines's wife four broad pieces of gold, "one of which I wear about my neck."[9] Such a gift was not only of material worth, it was also a sign of intimacy between Alice and her sister-in-law.

Alice Zaines's nieces and nephews received the bulk of her estate. This was a way not only to assist the children of her siblings, but also to honor her siblings indirectly. Alice bequeathed the large sum of £150 to her deceased sister's three sons. As mentioned above, this money was already in the hands of their father (Alice's brother-in-law Richard Sharp) in the form of a loan. Alice's intention was that Sharp should pass the money on to his sons instead of back to her since she would be deceased. But this loan was not a gift to a kinsman. Alice made it clear that she was charging Richard Sharp interest at the rate of 5 percent and that once she died, he should continue to pay £7 a year to her executor (her brother Robert Zaines) until he gave the £150 legacy to his sons. The bequests to her sister Elizabeth Wheeler's children were less complicated. To Robert and John Wheeler she left £15 apiece, which she intended them to share with their children since they were grown and married. And she left clothes to both Robert and John's wives. To their sister Elizabeth Wheeler, the singlewoman mentioned above, Alice bequeathed much more than to her Wheeler nephews. Elizabeth received her aunt's best silk crape gown, all her aunt's household goods, and £50 in shop goods (something she needed to carry on her aunt's trade).

As spinsters, the Zaines sisters had no direct descendents, so like many singlewomen in early modern Britain, they chose to assist the children of their siblings. They also picked out one niece and made her their particular heir. In the early modern period, a never-married woman frequently chose as her heir a person to whom she was related not only biologically but also spiritually. Singlewomen were frequently called upon to be godmothers to nieces and nephews, and this could lead to a special bond across the generations. It is not clear if Elizabeth Wheeler was Alice or Jane Zaines's godchild, but she was the only niece or nephew who resided with them, learned their trade, and ultimately inherited the largest portion of their estate.

Alice Zaines remembered friends as well as kin in her will. For instance, Sarah Bourne received a bed, dinnerware, and a coat. Others received tokens with which to remember Alice. William Bolar received half a guinea (about 10 and a half shillings). Ann, the wife of Daniel Farmer, was given the same along with a small gold ring. And Mary Cleft received a small piece of gold valued at 5 shillings. Widow Tibby also got 5 shillings in ready money. Besides William Bolar, an important figure in the Nonconformist community, all of the nonkin that Alice mentioned were women. It was the same when it came to the witnesses to her will. All three were female—Anne Gregg, Ann Mitchell, and Margaret Tull—and literate, since they signed their names. Like many other singlewomen in the early modern era, Alice was "woman identified," meaning that the majority of her primary relationships were with other women.

Alice Zaines's will disproves one of the stereotypes about singlewomen that emerged in seventeenth-century Britain and lasts even to this day. Before the late 1600s, the word "spinster" was a neutral, legal term used to describe a woman who had never or not yet married. It was not associated with old age; the court records of the time referred to women as young as 16 or 18 as spinsters. But as the number of men and women who never married rose over the seventeenth century, the popular stereotype of the "spinster" or "old maid" (as she also came to be known) began to emerge. One of the first authors to create the negative and satirical depiction of never-married women was Richard Allestree. In *The Ladies Calling* he reserved unparalleled contempt for what he termed "superannuated virgins." He stated that an "old maid is now thought such a curse as no poetic fury can exceed, looked on as the most calamitous creature in nature."[10] Over time writers developed this stereotype further. These women were characterized as ugly, unattractive, and old. And they were assumed to be isolated, lonely, useless individuals, as opposed to wives and mothers who were kept busy and fulfilled by their families.

But when we examine the lives of actual singlewomen, such as Jane and Alice Zaines, we find that the cultural stereotype does not stand up to reality. Alice was by no means lonely or isolated. She named twenty-three people in her will in addition to two other beloved sisters who had predeceased her. She also had an heir in the person of her niece Elizabeth Wheeler. Alice did not have biological children, but she certainly had a descendent to carry on her trade. Alice's will also illustrates that she was not a useless or functionless "old maid." She had led an active life, established a business, and amassed an estate worth over £300. Alice then used her money to assist her kin. Her sister Sarah Sharp's three sons received £150, enough to set each of them up in a trade. Her Wheeler nephews and niece received over £80. It is unlikely that these beneficiaries thought of their aunt as a useless spinster; instead they benefited from the active assistance of this important family member.

RELIGIOUS NONCONFORMITY

Never-married women not only found solace in their relationships with kin, but they also attained it in their religious communities. For many singlewomen, religion was an important part of their lives. This is not surprising in some respects, since early modern people were much less secular than people today. Nevertheless, religion seems to have served a special purpose for women who never married. Some women may have stayed single for religious reasons. Although they could not be nuns after the English Reformation of the 1530s, some of them did still dedicate themselves to lives of piety and charity. The Zaines sisters do not seem to have gone in this direction, but they were like other singlewomen who searched for a religious community that provided a greater and more autonomous role for women. The Zaines family was Huguenot, and as such Queen Elizabeth had granted them the right to worship in their own Calvinist churches instead of attending the Church of England. In Southampton, a "French church" was established early on. Here female members of the extended Zaines family served as godparents and engaged in other actions that illustrated their membership in the Huguenot community.

After the Restoration of Charles II in 1660 another religious option appeared in the town. During the Civil Wars and Interregnum a number of Puritan ministers had preached in Southampton's churches, but with the return of the king and the Church of England, these Puritans found themselves ejected from their pulpits. Two of them founded Independent churches, one of which came to be known as the Above Bar Independent Chapel. Situated in All Saints parish, but outside the city walls, the member lists of the Above Bar church reveal the popularity of the church with the singlewomen of Southampton. Many of these female Nonconformists (as Non-Anglicans came to be termed between the Restoration and the Act of (Religious) Toleration in 1689) were English, but a good number were also of Huguenot heritage. Jane and Alice Zaines's niece and heir Elizabeth Wheeler worshipped here, and their widowed sister Elizabeth might have as well. Anne Gregg, one of the three female witnesses to Alice Zaines's will, also appears in the membership lists of the Above Bar Independent Chapel. Were independent singlewomen more attracted to an Independent church, one where they had more of a say in church governance, discipline, and charity than in the state church that was dominated by Anglican men? There is a striking correlation between marital and religious autonomy among the singlewomen of Southampton.

Jane and Alice Zaines seem to have died around the age of fifty. This was not an uncommon lifespan for the time, although a good number of Southampton singlewomen lived on into their late sixties and seventies. What is more interesting is how close together the sisters died, at most three years apart. Single sisters who lived and worked together, who may have thought of each other as life partners, frequently died within a short time span of each other. Or at least wished to do so. The affection single sisters had for one another is well illustrated by the words of a famous never-married woman who lived in Southampton in the late eighteenth century. The author Jane Austen wrote about the death of her sister Cassandra, saying: "I have lost a treasure, such a sister, such a friend as never can have been surpassed. She was the sun of my life, the gilder of every pleasure, the soother of every sorrow, I had not a thought concealed from her, and it is as if I had lost a part of myself."[11] For a never-married woman, losing a single sister may have been like losing a spouse or a child; it was a primary relationship in her life. But when Alice Zaines made her will she could look back on a half-century of successes, both personal and professional, and know that her legacy would live on in the form of her niece and heir Elizabeth Wheeler, who also never married.

We can conclude by asking the question that is of interest to us in the present day. Did the Zaines sisters choose to never marry? Or was singleness thrust on them despite their wishes? It is impossible for us to know if Jane and Alice Zaines were spinsters because they actively chose to remain single. Nevertheless, we do know that they succeeded in living prosperous lives despite not having husbands to support them. One of the benefits of marriage was economic security, but the Zaines sisters achieved this for themselves without the help of a spouse. We could also ask if Jane and Alice influenced the marital status of their niece and heir Elizabeth Wheeler, who never married. Was singleness something that was passed down between generations in the Zaines family? It is clear that Jane and Alice provided their niece Elizabeth with a positive model of how singleness could result in a relatively prosperous and fulfilled life. For some women in early modern Britain, whether singleness was a choice or not, it was a viable alternative to marriage, and one that was much more common than we once thought.

SUGGESTED READINGS

The best survey of women's history for this period is Sara Mendelson and Patricia Crawford, *Women in Early Modern England, 1550–1720* (New York, 1998). The growing scholarship on singlewomen in early modern Britain consists of my own *Never Married: Singlewomen in Early Modern England* (Oxford, forthcoming); Judith M. Bennett and Amy M. Froide, ed., *Single-women in the European Past, 1250–1800* (Philadelphia, 1999); Bridget Hill, *Women Alone: Spinsters in England, 1660–1850* (New Haven, 2001); Olwen Hufton, "Women Without Men: Widows and Spinsters in Britain and France in the Eighteenth Century," *Journal of Family History,* 9/4 (1984), 355–76; Pamela Sharpe, "Literally Spinsters: A New Interpretation of Local Economy and Demography in Colyton in the Seventeenth and Eighteenth Centuries,"

Economic History Review, 44/1 (1991), 46–65; and "Dealing with Love: The Ambiguous Independence of the Singlewoman in Early Modern England," *Gender & History* 11/ 2 (July 1999), 202–32. On the numbers of single-women in early modern Britain, see my "Hidden Women, Rediscovering the Singlewomen of Early Modern England," *Local Population Studies,* 68 (Spring 2002), 26–41. For research on women's work in urban areas, see the essays in Hannah Barker and Elaine Chalus, eds., *Gender in Eighteenth-Century England: Roles, Representations and Responsibilities* (New York, 1997); Peter Earle, "The Female Labour Market in London in the Late Seventeenth and Early Eighteenth Centuries," *Economic History Review,* 2nd ser., 42/3 (1989), 328–53; Margaret R. Hunt, *The Middling Sort: Commerce, Gender and the Family in England, 1680–1780* (Berkeley, CA, 1996); Mary Prior, "Women and the Urban Economy, Oxford 1500–1800," in Mary Prior, ed., *Women in English Society 1500–1800* (London, 1985), 93–117; and Elizabeth Sanderson, *Women and Work in Eighteenth-Century Edinburgh* (New York, 1996). For general overviews of urban history in the early period, see Peter Clark and Paul Slack, eds., *Crisis and Order in English Towns, 1500–1700: Essays in Urban History* (London, 1972); and Peter Borsay, *The English Urban Renaissance: Culture and Society in the Provincial Town 1660–1770* (Oxford, 1989). And for women in Nonconformist religions see Patricia Crawford, *Women and Religion in England, 1500–1720* (New York, 1993); Richard Greaves, "Foundation Builders: The Role of Women in Early English Nonconformity," in R. Greaves, ed., *Triumph over Silence: Women in Protestant History* (Westport, Conn., 1985); and Anne Laurence, "A Priesthood of She-Believers: Women and Congregations in Mid-Seventeenth-Century England," *Studies in Church History* 27 (1990), 345–63.

NOTES

1. For other localities where singlewomen made up a third or more of adult women, see Amy M. Froide, "Hidden Women: Rediscovering the Singlewomen of Early Modern England," *Local Population Studies* 68 (Spring 2002): 26–41.

2. By the later sixteenth century the common legal terms for a woman who had never married (but might yet marry) were "spinster" or "singlewoman." The latter usually was spelled as a compound word. I follow this early modern convention.

3. This article is based on the following records which are held in the Southampton Record Office: Assessment Books, SC 14/2/43, 58, 86, 97; Poll Taxes SC 14/2/37a–b, 50b; Court Leet Records SC 6/1/70, 73, 74, 75; Scavage Books SC 5/17/35, Quarter Session Rolls SC 9/1/63; Corporation Journal Books SC 2/1/9; Deposited Records D/Z 403/ 22, Above Bar Independent Chapel Registers, (1726–27).

4. E. A. Wrigley and Roger Schofield, *The Population History of England, 1541–1871: A Reconstruction* (London: Edward Arnold, 1981), 255.

5. Amy M. Froide, "Old Maids: The Lifecycle of Singlewomen in Early Modern England," in *Women and Ageing in British Society since 1500*, ed. L. A. Botelho and Pat Thane (New York: Pearson Education, 2001).

6. Jenny Uglow, *Hogarth* (New York: Farrar, Straus and Giroux, 1997), 23, 152–53.

7. Peter Borsay, *The English Urban Renaissance: Culture and Society in the Provincial Town, 1660–1770* (Oxford: Clarendon Press, 1989).

8. Southampton Record Office, Sessions Rolls, SC 9/1/63 (July 3, 1702).

9. Hampshire Record Office, Will, 1701 A107.

10. Richard Allestree, *The Ladies Calling, in Two Parts* (Oxford: At the Theater in Oxford, 1673), pt II, 3–4.

11. Jane Austen's letters quoted in Terry Castle, "Sister-Sister," *London Review of Books* 17:5 (August 3, 1995): 3–6.

Chapter Three

Charles Townshend and Eighteenth-century British Politics

Andrew C. Thompson

When describing Charles, Second Viscount Townshend, the Earl of Chesterfield noted that business was "his only passion." Indeed, he was an "able man of business," by which he meant a man well versed in public affairs. Townshend was not interested in power because of the riches he could gain from it. "He did not add one acre to his estate . . . though he had been in considerable and lucrative employments near thirty years." Rather, he wanted to reshape his world according to his plans and ideas. According to Chesterfield, "he only loved power for the sake of power."[1]

Charles Townshend was born in 1674 and died on his Norfolk estates in 1738. His grandson and namesake, Charles Townshend the Chancellor of the Exchequer, may now be better remembered for his contributions to the loss of the American colonies. Yet the career of the elder Townshend was marked by the attainment of political office at the highest level. Townshend also lived through and was involved in a series of important transitions in both the character and structure of the British state. As such, a study of his career offers the opportunity to examine the changing nature of politics in Britain in the early eighteenth century.

ROUNDHEADS AND CAVALIERS
TO WHIGS AND TORIES

Townshend's father, Horatio, had been created Baron Townshend of Lynn Regis in 1661. Horatio had worked tirelessly to gather support for Charles II in Norfolk prior to the Restoration of Charles to the throne in 1660. The title was a reward for his efforts. He was also appointed Lord Lieutenant of Norfolk in 1661. His office meant he had an important mediating role between the central and local government. The Lord Lieutenancy was also in the gift of the Crown, so it was another means by which the king could exercise influence in the localities. The county formed the chief stage for Horatio Townshend's political activities. It was here that he took the lead in organizing the county's militia when England found herself at war with the Dutch in the 1660s and 1670s.[2]

Despite his good royalist credentials, Horatio Townshend had difficulty procuring further royal favors, and in 1676 he was replaced as Lord Lieutenant. The nature of politics was changing. An additional layer had been added to the older division between Cavalier and Roundhead—those who had supported the king and those who had supported Parliament in the conflicts of the 1640s and 1650s.

Disquiet had been growing in the political nation for a number of reasons in the 1670s. The king, Charles II, lacked a legitimate heir. In these circumstances it seemed likely that Charles would be succeeded by his brother James, Duke of York. James's religious beliefs had already provoked suspicion. It was suspected that he had Roman Catholic sympathies. Charles's wife and his mother were known to be Catholic. Some began to draw the conclusion that the court was dominated by Catholics.

This concern was not provoked merely by worries about personal religious conviction. Catholicism was associated with a particular style of government, encapsulated in the frequently repeated slogan "popery and arbitrary government." This combination appeared to threaten the liberties of the freeborn Englishman. The hard line taken against Dissenters (non-Anglican Protestants) and ministerial foreign policy in the 1670s did little to calm these fears. In 1672 Louis XIV of France invaded the United Provinces (Holland). Charles II had made an alliance with Louis and the English found themselves fighting against Dutch Protestants and in alliance with French Catholics. This state of affairs increasingly worried Parliament, and England had withdrawn from the conflict by 1674.[3]

This did not, however, provide a neat solution to the succession issue. The opposition to the perceived corruption of the court has sometimes been termed the "country" position in the 1670s, although much of its influence was in and around Westminster. Those opposed to the Crown had two main aims: they wanted to reverse what they thought was a drift towards absolutist government, associated with Louis's France, and they wanted to ensure that this achievement was not undermined by preventing James, whose politics were tainted by his religion, from succeeding Charles. Between 1679 and

1681 bills to exclude James from the succession were debated in Parliament. They failed, but it was from this period that there emerged the outlines of the political divisions still important in Charles Townshend's time.

The major split was between those who opposed the exclusion of the Duke of York from the throne and those who advocated it. The latter became known as the whigs and the former as the tories. While the whigs claimed that English liberties and the Protestant religion would be destroyed if James became king, the tories emphasised the rights of the Crown, the illegitimacy of Parliament's interfering in the succession, and the extent to which the Church of England was protected by acts of Parliament and so could withstand any pressure from a Catholic monarch. The tories felt that it was vital to preserve both the state and the Church of England in the form in which they had been secured after the Restoration of Charles II to the throne.[4]

When Charles II died in 1685, he was succeeded by his brother. James's policies confirmed some of the whigs' worst fears. He released Catholics from prison. He made moves to establish toleration for them. He appointed Catholic officers in the army and also attempted to increase the size of the army. This gave both the whigs and the tories pause for thought. When James's second wife gave birth to a son on June 10, 1688, matters came to a head. James now had an heir. This meant that there was now the prospect of a long line of Catholic monarchs and that the changes that James had introduced would not be quietly removed at the start of the next reign. This fear prompted some of the leading members of the political nation to issue an invitation to William of Orange, the Stadtholder of the United Provinces. William invaded, landing on November 5, 1688. James panicked and then fled into exile.[5]

TOWNSHEND'S EARLY CAREER

This was the political world into which Charles Townshend was born. His father had been made a viscount in 1682, and it was this title that Charles inherited when his father died in 1687. In line with his royalist sympathies, Charles's father had tended to side with tories when party divisions emerged as the crucial determinant of political allegiance. In 1687, however, the opportunities offered by this political world were still far in the future for Charles. He was still a boy and had yet to complete his education.[6]

Charles Townshend's education followed a pattern common to many of his generation and social class. He went to school at Eton College and from there proceeded to Eton's sister foundation, King's College, Cambridge. Townshend matriculated at King's in 1691. There is no evidence that he finished a degree but this was not uncommon for those of aristocratic backgrounds—degrees were important only for those wishing to pursue careers in the church, law, or medicine.[7] Townshend then spent some of the time between 1694 and 1698 travelling in Europe on what was known as "the Grand Tour."[8] This provided young aristocrats with the opportunity of discovering something of the beauty and diversity of Europe's cultural heritage. The young noble was usually accompanied by an older tutor or traveling companion who could instruct his young charge on what to see and do. While each tour would be slightly different, it was usual to spend some time in Paris and to visit classical sites in Italy. Others spent time in Germany and the United Provinces. As well as appreciating the sublime beauty of architecture and the visual arts, such trips also offered the chance to indulge in the more earthly pleasures of the table and the bottle and to meet one's social equals from other countries.

THE IMPACT OF THE "GLORIOUS REVOLUTION"

However, this was all preparation for the more serious matters of local and national government. Townshend took up his seat in the House of Lords in 1697, although he does not appear to have spoken in a debate until 1701. Initially he followed his father's politics and sided with the tories.[9] The 1690s were a decade of considerable change and political commotion. William of Orange used his new throne to cement a military alliance between England and his native Holland. This union was the cornerstone of the coalition he assembled to combat the ambitions of Louis XIV, and England was engaged in war with France from 1688 to 1697. Charles II and James II had tended to support Louis XIV. William ensured that British foreign policy was reoriented towards opposition to France, and this remained a reasonably constant feature of British policy for most of the eighteenth century.

The effects of the war were diverse and far-reaching. Armed conflict was a costly business, and William found it necessary to call upon Parliament more frequently to provide him with money to fund arms and men. It was this that helped to turn Parliament from an event, as it had been for much of the seventeenth century, into an institution. However, parliamentary grants of taxation proved insufficient to fund the cost of the conflict. In 1694 the Bank of England was established by a number of private individuals to provide a means to fund the ever-increasing national debt. Taken together, it is fair to claim that the "Glorious Revolution" of 1688 was both followed and secured by two further revolutions in the 1690s: in finance and foreign policy.[10]

OPPOSITION TO THE
WILLIAMITE SETTLEMENT

These "revolutions" did not go uncontested. Various strands of opposition to them can be identified. One form of opposition refused to acknowledge the legitimacy of William's claim to the throne. William demanded that the clergy swear a new oath of allegiance to him. Those who refused to do so, known as non-Jurors, were forced to leave the Church of England. Non-Jurors believed kings received their legitimacy directly from God, and humans could not interfere in this relationship to remove them. They emphasised the importance of obedience to the divinely ordained "powers that be." Consequently, many non-Jurors remained loyal to the exiled James II.[11]

More generally, those who supported the claims of James II were known as Jacobites (from the Latin version of James's name), and the Jacobite threat continued to trouble successive governments until at least 1745. Not all Jacobites were Catholic, but support for the exiled Stuarts was more extensive in areas with large Catholic populations, such as Ireland and the Scottish highlands. Regardless of religious conviction, the Jacobites were useful pawns for those European powers who happened to find themselves opposed to Britain because of their potential for causing trouble within the British Isles. Thus, the exiled Jacobite court came to rely increasingly on support, both financial and physical, from foreign powers to press their claims. Conversely, British diplomats came to link British support to assurances of refusal to aid the exiled Stuarts. Until 1717 the Stuart court enjoyed hospitality from France at St. Germain and in Lorraine. After 1717 the French withdrew their support, as the result of an alliance with the British, and the Stuarts retreated to Rome.

SUCCESSION AND THE
PROBLEMS OF STATECRAFT

The existence of the Stuart court in exile was given additional importance because William III lacked heirs. The worry was not immediate because William's sister-in-law, Anne, James II's daughter from his first marriage, could succeed William. However, as the 1690s progressed and Anne's children died before attaining adulthood, the question as to who might succeed her became more pressing. In 1701 the Act of Settlement was passed that permanently excluded from the line of succession all Catholics and all those married to Catholics. The act confirmed the prohibition of Catholic succession, which had first appeared in the Bill of Rights in 1689. The nearest Protestant claimant to the throne was now Sophia, Electress of Hanover, whose grandfather had been James I.[12]

The succession in England was not the only succession issue worrying William. Charles II of Spain was also without heirs and who ruled Spain was of critical importance to the European state system. When he had made peace with Louis XIV in 1697, William had tried to forestall this problem through a partition treaty. Louis and William agreed that a compromise candidate could succeed to the Spanish throne. However, before this plan could be put into operation, the compromise candidate died. This left two main claimants: one of Louis XIV's grandsons and the second son of the Holy Roman Emperor. The two major ruling houses of Europe, the Bourbons of France and the Habsburgs of Austria, seemed set on a collision course because neither could accept the Iberian peninsula falling into the hands of the other.[13]

William remained keen to contain the power of France. However, the nine years of war after 1688 had not made him universally popular in England. He had been put under severe pressure after 1697 from those concerned about his unwillingness to reduce the size of the standing army. The fear remained from the days of the Stuarts that the standing army was an instrument of royal and arbitrary government and that its existence tended to subvert liberty. William had considerable difficulty in convincing the political nation of the threat posed by Louis XIV. Despite this, when he died in 1702, the Act of Settlement had been passed, and it appeared that Parliament would support further attempts to curb Louis XIV's power.

When Charles II of Spain died in 1701, Louis XIV's attempts to support the claims of his grandson Philip to the Spanish throne were opposed by what became known as the "Grand Alliance." This alliance consisted of Austria, Holland, England, and a number of German princes, among them the Elector of Hanover. The relationship between Austria, Holland, and England was crucial to the success of the alliance, and Charles Townshend's role in securing that relationship will be considered below.

TOWNSHEND AND THE ACT OF UNION

First, however, it is necessary to say something about the first major political event in which Townshend was personally involved. In 1706 Townshend was named as one of the commissioners to negotiate the proposed union of Scotland and England.[14] The reasons for the proposed union were again closely related to the questions of legitimate succession that have already been given a prominent place in describing the nature of politics in the period. When William had come over from Holland in 1688, the Scottish Parliament in

Edinburgh had deposed James VII (as he was in Scotland) and replaced him as sovereign with William and his wife Mary. William had agreed to reform Scottish church government so that the Church of Scotland ceased to be overseen by bishops, as in England, but returned to a system where supreme authority resided in church councils and synods (the Presbyterian form of church government). Despite this concession, the Scots had not passed their own Act of Settlement. This meant that there was a risk that the personal union of the crowns of Scotland and England that had existed since the accession of James VI of Scotland to the English throne in 1603 might be dissolved. In any circumstances, this situation would have posed difficulties for the government in London. Given the prevailing conditions at the turn of the eighteenth century, it was vital that a solution was found to this problem. The risks of Scottish Jacobites and their French allies using the succession issue to provoke trouble for the English, while the English were at the center of an alliance system designed to contain France, were too great. Hence the English ministry's solution to the problem was to propose a political union with Scotland. Townshend was one of those sent to negotiate the nuts and bolts of this deal. In exchange for access to English markets both at home and overseas in her expanding collection of colonies, the Scots would have to give up their Parliament and Privy Council. The Church of Scotland and the Scottish legal system would be kept separate from their English counterparts (a situation which continues even now), but political independence for the Scots would be lost. This was the deal to which the Scots agreed, in part because they had been chastened by their own failures in attempts to take advantage of colonial markets. Townshend's precise role in these negotiations, which came to fruition with the Act of Union of 1707, is less important than the fact that the negotiations provided him with the opportunity to be noticed by those in power. He was appointed a Privy Councillor in 1707, and two years later was sent as ambassador and plenipotentiary to Holland.[15]

TOWNSHEND AS DIPLOMAT

The mission to Holland was Townshend's most important to date. He had become Lord Lieutenant of Norfolk in 1701 and now seemed to be firmly rooted in the whig camp, but his diplomatic appointment was recognition that he was now cutting a figure in national, as well as local, politics. Townshend's task in Holland was a delicate one. Cracks were appearing in the Grand Alliance. The Dutch were concerned about the future security of their borders with France. The British were keen to secure Dutch recognition of the succession arrangements outlined in the Act of Settlement. Townshend negotiated what became known as the "Barrier Treaty." In exchange for a guarantee of the succession arrangements in Britain, the Dutch received assurances that there would be a number of barrier fortresses in the southern Netherlands, which could be garrisoned by Dutch troops and which would provide a first line of defense against future French invasion.[16]

The negotiations had been protracted, but Townshend thought that he had managed to achieve a reasonable deal. Unfortunately, he was undermined by domestic political events. Partisan conflict between whigs and tories had been intense in England since 1688, so much so that some historians refer to the period as witnessing the "rage of party." The frequency of elections—every three years—meant that there was an atmosphere of near constant election-eering.[17] A number of elements contributed to the party struggle. The removal of a king in 1688 and his replacement with another had been a traumatic event. Whigs and tories were divided as to whether this was a singular, exceptional event or whether the people had the right to remove any monarch in similar circumstances.

There was also disagreement as to the wisdom of continued involvement in continental warfare. One of the results of William's accession had been that legislation had been passed which legalized non-Anglican Protestant worship, provided that meetinghouses were registered with local authorities. Many tories, it will be recalled, looked back to the restoration of 1660 and linked the continuing existence of the state to the preservation of the Angli-can church. With the relaxation of the laws against Protestant Dissenters, the fear was that there would be a return to the dangerous situation of the 1640s and the 1650s when religious sectaries had destroyed the state and executed a king in 1649. Tories made little secret of their dislike of Protestant Dissent-ers and attempted to further restrict their rights through legislation. In 1709 Henry Sacheverell preached a sermon that attacked Dissenters and the whig ministry. The ministry impeached him for attacking revolution principles. The trial was a public relations disaster. Mobs, fearing that the Church of England was in danger, destroyed Dissenting meetinghouses in London and elsewhere.[18] In the general election of 1710, the tories made significant gains.

The change in the political balance meant that Townshend, and his treaty, was no longer so popular. The tories had made much of their desire for peace and the profligacy of the whigs in pursuing a strategy of conflict. Townshend was recalled. His treaty was considered by Parliament, and he was accused of conceding too much to the Dutch. In 1713 he was dismissed as Lord Lieu-tenant of Norfolk—one of the few ways Anne could reassure Norfolk tories.[19]

A NEW DYNASTY

Yet Townshend's career was about to be revitalized, and again the politics of succession were to play an important role. The Act of Settlement had left

Electress Sophia of Hanover as Anne's heir to the British throne. Sophia died weeks before Anne in June 1714. Anne herself died in August 1714. This left the heir to the British throne as Sophia's eldest son, George, the Elector of Hanover. The new king had to travel from Hanover to London to claim his throne. Various letters and petitions reached George en route. Many were keen to press their claims for promotion with the new monarch. One of the first appointments announced was that of Townshend as one of the two secretaries of state.[20]

What had Townshend done to achieve this honor? His negotiation of the Barrier Treaty must have been significant. He was trusted by the Dutch. Moreover, he had been punished and fallen out of favor with the tory administration of Anne's last years. This might not seem much of a commendation, but the tories' actions in the last years of Anne's reign had considerably irritated George. Tired of war, the tories had pressed forward with the negotiations with the French that had led to the Treaty of Utrecht. They had abandoned the old whig slogan of "no peace without Spain," in part because the death of the Holy Roman Emperor in 1711 had left the Habsburg claimant to Spain as Holy Roman Emperor as well. This outcome was now less desirable than having a Bourbon on the Spanish throne because, although the kings of Spain and France would be close relations, they would not be the same person. The consequences for the European balance of power of the rulers of Austria and Spain being embodied in one individual were too dire to think about. It recalled the sixteenth-century example of Charles V, who had ruled Spain, the Netherlands, Germany, and Austria, who was the paradigmatic case of the evils of multiple monarchy. However, all this bothered George less than the fact that he felt that the British had betrayed their allies, the Dutch and the Hanoverians among them, by signing the Treaty of Utrecht. By this logic those who were the enemies of George's enemies, the Tories, were likely to be his friends. Townshend found himself back in favor.

THE TRIUMPH OF THE WHIGS

George I's choice of ministers left little doubt that he favored the whigs and disliked the tories. This view was reinforced by events in 1715. Although George's popularity with his new subjects has tended to be underestimated by historians, it is clear that there were certain sections of the population who were prepared to oppose his rule actively. James II's exiled son James, known in Jacobite circles as James III, led an invasion. The invasion was unsuccessful, but it proved a very useful propaganda weapon for the whigs. They claimed that many tories had welcomed the invasion and were secret supporters of the Jacobite cause. This provided George with further evidence of the dubious loyalty of the tories and further strengthened his reliance on the whigs to form his ministry. The proportion of tories who were actually Jacobite has been the subject of intense historiographical debate. Unfortunately, the nature of the evidence, such as lists of potential supporters produced for the exiled Jacobite court, means that it is unlikely that a satisfactory conclusion can ever be reached on the matter. What is beyond doubt, though, is that it was in the interests of the whigs to depict their tory opponents as treacherous and unreliable to cement their own hold on power. The whigs made further efforts to reinforce their political position after the rebellion by passing a bill that increased the length of time between parliamentary elections from three to seven years.[21]

TOWNSHEND AND FOREIGN POLICY

While Townshend was involved both in the measures to defeat the Jacobite rebellion and in the efforts to consolidate the whig regime domestically, his primary field of operations was that of foreign policy. There were two secretaries of state who shared responsibility for foreign affairs: the secretary of state for the Northern Department and for the Southern Department (the unified position of foreign secretary was not created until 1782). The secretary of state signed the official instructions sent to British diplomats abroad. These instructions were drafted by under-secretaries in the Northern and Southern departments, but their final form was determined by consultation between the secretary of state and the monarch.

This description of the process of policy formation indicates that British monarchs in the eighteenth century were more than mere figureheads. Admittedly, parliamentary influence had increased in certain areas and power over taxation gave Parliament additional leverage, but when it came to formulation of policy, royal influence could be, and frequently was, decisive. This is important to remember because the eighteenth-century state did not perform the various and complex tasks which we associate with the state today. Control of foreign policy was one of the few areas where the eighteenth-century state had a degree of authority comparable with that enjoyed by sovereign states now. This serves as a warning against assuming too readily that modernization of state structures and decline in monarchical forms of government are necessarily linked.

Townshend's initial experience as secretary of state clearly indicates the problems that could befall those who disagreed with the king in foreign policy terms. George I remained Elector of Hanover after 1714. His German homeland was still high in his affections, and he tried to visit it as frequently as possible during the summer months when Parliament was not in session. His reasons for visiting Hanover were not related merely to sentimental preference for the land of his birth. In Hanover it was possible for George to meet other important European diplomats and consult with his allies in person. It gave him a freedom to conduct his own diplomacy, and he was not as exposed to inquisitive journalists as he was in London. One of the secretaries of state accompanied George on his foreign travels, while the other was left to manage things in London. In 1716 Townshend remained in London, and George was accompanied to Hanover by his colleague James Stanhope.[22]

During this period George was involved in a complicated series of negotiations to secure the peace of both southern and northern Europe. One aspect of this was an alliance with France. Although Britain and France had been at war only a few years previously, the death of Louis XIV meant that France was now governed by a regent so was keen to secure its international position through alliances. It was this weakened position that enabled George to extract concessions which both recognized the legitimacy of the Protestant succession in Britain and ensured that the exiled Jacobite court had to leave France. Townshend was given the task of making the final arrangements from London. George, in Hanover, felt that Townshend was not acting vigorously enough on this matter. More importantly, though, it became clear that Townshend did not support the policy that George wanted to pursue in the Baltic because Townshend felt that it was in Hanoverian, but not British, interests. The conflict in the Baltic, known as the Great Northern War, was between Sweden, on the one hand, and Russia, Denmark, Saxony-Poland, and Hanover, on the other. George wished to use the British Navy to help those opposed to Sweden in the Baltic. Townshend did not object to this in principle, but he did suggest in October 1716 that the campaign was not perhaps being conducted in the best way. George objected to the suggestion that some of the gains Hanover had made should be sacrificed to make peace, and Townshend was dismissed.[23]

TOWNSHEND AND WALPOLE

Between 1717 and 1720 Townshend and his political ally Robert Walpole went into opposition and sided with the Prince of Wales in his disputes with his father, George I.[24] A reconciliation between George and his son and a financial scandal that rocked the existing ministry gave Townshend and Walpole the opportunity to rejoin the ministry in 1720.[25] Townshend returned as secretary of state for the north, and he remained the key ministerial figure in foreign policy until his resignation in May 1730. He appears to have learned from his earlier mistakes. He was careful to ensure that when the king traveled to Hanover in the summer months, it was Townshend and not his fellow secretary who accompanied the king. His proximity to the king ensured that he could monitor the advice that the king was receiving from others and attempt to direct the king more effectively.[26]

Townshend had also learned the importance of not upsetting the king on issues which related to his Hanoverian possessions. His policies in the 1720s reflected this and showed an increased awareness of the need to consider the likely impact of a particular move on Hanover. Townshend had realized the importance of royal confidence for maintaining high office and that this also necessitated an awareness of the king's likes and dislikes.[27] This awareness meant that both Townshend and Robert Walpole were retained by George II when he succeeded his father in 1727, despite talk that they would be dismissed. Indeed, according to the Earl of Chesterfield, looking after electoral concerns was "the only way by which a British minister could hold either favor or power during the Reigns of King George the First and Second."[28]

Robert Walpole had been a close political ally of Townshend for many years. They had been near neighbors growing up together in Norfolk. Walpole had followed Townshend to both Eton and King's, and Townshend's patronage had helped to launch Walpole's parliamentary career under Anne. Of the two, Walpole is now better remembered. It is often claimed that Walpole was Britain's first "Prime Minister." Certainly, Walpole remained at the highest level in British politics from 1721 to 1742. He also managed to emerge from Townshend's shadow during the 1720s. Indeed, the traditional explanation of Townshend's fall from grace in 1730 is that he lost out in a policy dispute with Walpole and was forced to resign. Chesterfield commented that "Lord Townshend was not of a temper to act a second part, after having acted a first, as he did during the reign of King George the First" so perhaps Townshend was jealous of Walpole's increased influence.[29]

Walpole was an accomplished performer in the House of Commons, while Townshend was regarded by contemporaries as a more pedestrian orator. Chesterfield described him as a "most ungraceful and confused speaker in the House of Lords, inelegant in his language, perplexed in his arguments but always near the stress of the question."[30] This characterization is almost certainly too harsh on Townshend's abilities and achievements but, in the absence of a modern scholarly biography, this view must remain mere conjecture for the moment.

CONCLUSION

Townshend's career illustrates a number of important characteristics of British politics in the period. Townshend lived through a period of intense political polarization between the whigs and the tories. This conflict ran deep. At its heart was a series of interconnected issues about the location of authority within the constitution and the likely impact on both church and state of the succession of a Catholic to the throne. In one sense, Townshend's whole career can be seen as a prolonged attempt to secure the Protestant succession in England and ensure that this was recognized abroad. This can be seen both in his efforts in Scotland and Holland and then in the negotiations he conducted as secretary of state to remove foreign support for the Jacobites. Questions of succession dominated the European politics of the period. Three of the wars fought in the first half of the eighteenth century took their names from succession disputes: the war of the Spanish Succession (1701–1713), the Polish Succession (1733–1735), and the Austrian Succession (1740–1748).

Townshend's father based his political life around the politics of the county. When he died in 1687, England was a minor player on the European stage. Charles Townshend, by contrast, was involved in county politics but also performed on both the national and international stages. Yet Charles never lost his affection for his native Norfolk. He did not become a smooth, sophisticated urban political animal. As Chesterfield remarked, "His manners were coarse, rustic, and seemingly brutal, but his nature was by no means so; for he was a kind husband to both his wives, a most indulgent father to all his children, and a benevolent master to his servants, sure tests of a real good nature, for no man can long together simulate or dissimulate at home."[31] When he became secretary of state in 1714, England had united with Scotland and Britain was regarded as crucial to what happened in European politics. Military success and the institutional features that had made this possible, such as the creation of the Bank of England, had been crucial to this transformation. Townshend, as secretary of state, was able to negotiate from a novel position of strength. His successors rapidly became accustomed to this.

SUGGESTED READINGS

All the direct quotations are taken from Philip Dormer Stanhope, Fourth Earl of Chesterfield's "Character of Lord Townshend," which can be found in manuscript form in Stowe MSS 308, folio 14 in the British Library, London. There is no modern scholarly biography of Townshend. Details on aspects of his career and that of his father can be found in James M. Rosenheim, *The Townshends of Raynham: Nobility in Transition in Restoration and Early Hanoverian England* (Middletown, CT, 1989). There is also much of value in

Ragnhild Hatton, *George I* (1978 Reprint, New Haven, 2001). The details of Townshend's eventual resignation are reassessed in Jeremy Black, "Fresh Light on the Fall of Townshend," *Historical Journal* 29 (1986): 41–64. The classic study of Robert Walpole's career remains J. H. Plumb, *Sir Robert Walpole*, 2 vols. (London, 1956–1960).

Tim Harris's *Politics under the Later Stuarts: Party Conflict in a Divided Society, 1660–1715* (London, 1993) is an excellent introduction to the nature of political discussion and the issues which divided whig from tory. The impact and importance of the changes brought about by the warfare of the 1690s are considered in John Brewer, *The Sinews of Power* (London, 1989). The collection of essays in Geoffrey Holmes, ed., *Britain after the Glorious Revolution* (London, 1969) remain useful, especially Graham Gibbs's contribution on foreign policy.

There has been a considerable increase in interest in Jacobitism in recent years. For a reasonably balanced overview see Paul K. Monod, *Jacobitism and the English People* (Cambridge, UK, 1989).

The importance of the Act of Union to British identity is explored in Linda Colley's seminal study *Britons* (New Haven, 1992).

NOTES

1. British Library, London, UK, Stowe MSS 308, fo. 14r (hereafter cited as BL, Stowe MSS 308).

2. James M. Rosenheim, *The Townshends of Raynham: Nobility in Transition in Restoration and Early Hanoverian England* (Middletown, CT: Wesleyan University Press, 1989), 6–7.

3. Tim Harris, *Politics under the Later Stuarts: Party Conflict in a Divided Society, 1660–1715* (London: Longman, 1993), 52–54.

4. Harris, *Politics*, 61–66.

5. Harris, *Politics*, 128–29.

6. Rosenheim, *Townshends*, 7.

7. Susanna Wade Martins, *"Turnip" Townshend: Statesman and Farmer* (North Walsham: Poppyland, 1990), 28.

8. Martins, *"Turnip" Townshend*, 25.

9. Rosenheim, *Townshends*, 192–93.

10. See John Brewer, *The Sinews of War* (London, 1989) for the financial side and G. C. Gibbs, "The Revolution in Foreign Policy," in *Britain after the Glorious Revolution*, ed. Geoffrey Holmes (London: Macmillan, 1969), 59–79 for foreign policy.

11. Harris, *Politics,* 208–16.

12. Ragnhild Hatton, *George I: Elector and King* (London: Thames and Hudson, 1978), 70–77.

13. Hatton, *George I,* 84–86.

14. Martins, *"Turnip"Townshend,* 36.

15. Rosenheim, *Townshends*, 211–13.
16. Rosenheim, *Townshends*, 214.
17. Harris, *Politics*, 188–89.
18. Harris, *Politics*, 180–82.
19. Rosenheim, *Townshends*, 221.
20. Hatton, *George I*, 124–25.
21. Harris, 226–28.
22. Hatton, *George I*, 158–59.
23. Hatton, *George I*, 180–92.
24. Hatton, *George I*, 212–13.
25. Rosenheim, *Townshends*, 232–33.
26. Hatton, *George I*, 213.
27. Rosenheim, *Townshends*, 234.
28. BL, Stowe MSS 308, fo. 14r.
29. BL, Stowe MSS 308, fo. 14v.
30. BL, Stowe MSS 308, fo. 14r.
31. BL, Stowe MSS 308, fo. 14r.

Chapter Four

Evangelical Religion

Grayson Carter

The English literary tradition has bequeathed to posterity many colorful portraits of the "long" eighteenth century (1688–1832) and its rich and colorful religious life. One conspicuous progenitor is Jane Austen, both the daughter and sister of a clergyman, who used exquisite irony to expose the foibles of the English church and its clergy.[1] In *Pride and Prejudice*, the inscrutable Mr. Collins and his elderly patroness, the Lady Catherine de Bourgh, vividly illustrate the potential for abuse inherent in the ecclesiastical patronage system. In *Emma*, the amiable and obliging Mr. Elton, a vicar in search of a wife, demonstrates how the character of a clergyman may be no more consistent than that of a doctor or lawyer. Finally, in *Mansfield Park*, the gentle Edmund Bertram, yet another Austen character in the hunt for a spouse, rushes to the defense of the church and its clergy against the rationalistic attacks of the Age of Enlightenment, personified by the beautiful and wealthy Mary Crawford. Memorable among these literary portraits are clergy drawn from the ranks of the church's evangelical wing. In *Jane Eyre*, Charlotte Brontë (another clerical daughter) based the character of Mr. Brocklehurst, the grim treasurer of Lowood School, on a local evangelical clergyman, William Carus Wilson. Some years later, in *Barchester Towers*, Anthony Trollope created one of the most extraordinary clerical figures in all of English literature, the Rev. Obadiah Slope, whose unstable and ambitious nature was, to many critics of evangelicalism, a stereotype of clerical "enthusiasm." Similar caricatures can be found as far back as the early evangelistic campaigns of John Wesley and George Whitefield during the 1730s and 1740s.

Despite opposition from both inside and outside the church, evangelical religion played an important role in British life during this period, shaping the spiritual views and practices of many in England, Wales, Scotland, and even Ireland.[2] This influence was gained primarily through the efforts of both lay and clerical evangelicals, including a number of important public figures who left an enduring legacy of activism and spirituality within British society. These evangelicals challenged outdated and unjust laws and social conventions and served as leaders of a number of reform campaigns, including abolition. Their moral and spiritual impact extended to the realms of politics, economics, literature, education, social welfare, and, especially, family life. As Britain expanded her colonial holdings in the nineteenth century, evangelicalism was exported throughout its vast empire. This essay will explore the origins of evangelical religion in the "long" eighteenth century, its leaders, and its achievements.

HISTORICAL BACKGROUND

For the past century and a half, there has been extensive debate among historians over the religious nature of eighteenth-century England. Victorian churchmen, attached to the idea of social and religious progress, unselfconsciously dismissed those of the previous age as "inferior spirits."[3] In 1860, for example, the well-known Oxford critic Mark Pattison, referring to the eighteenth century, concluded "the genuine Anglican omits that period from the history of the church altogether."[4] Though advancing a more balanced assessment of the Georgian church, the Victorian historians Abbey and Overton nevertheless lapsed into a similar spirit of pessimism. While admitting that there were healthy signs at both the beginning and the end of the eighteenth century, during the intervening period "the Church partook of the general sordidness of the age; it was an age of great material prosperity, but of moral and spiritual poverty, such as hardly finds a parallel in our history."[5] Nor had this sense of historical gloom diminished much by the first decade of the twentieth century, when a new account characterized the eighteenth century as an age "of lethargy instead of activity, of worldliness instead of spirituality, of self-seeking instead of self-denial, of grossness instead of refinement."[6] Hampered by clerical pluralism (clergy holding more than one appointment at a time) and nonresidence (clergy living away from their parishes), by a corrupt patronage system, and by its dependence on a large body of poorly trained and impoverished curates, the eighteenth-century church failed to provoke either the admiration or the sympathy of those who succeeded them. Nor did the various Nonconformist or Dissenting bodies (e.g., Baptists, Congregationalists, Presbyterians, and Quakers) prove any more attractive.

This bleak picture remained widely accepted among historians until the publication of Norman Sykes's influential revisionist study in 1934, *Church and State in England in the Eighteenth Century*.[7] Sykes's assessment of the Georgian church was one of qualified approval.[8] He pointed out that many new sources, both printed and manuscript, had recently become available and that, when examined without reference to the anachronistic standards of the nineteenth century, these justified a more sympathetic and impartial assessment of the nature of the Hanoverian church.[9] Nor has Sykes been alone in upholding a more optimistic revisionist interpretation of the period. Employing a diversity of methodological approaches, a number of recent historical studies have concurred with Sykes that, during the eighteenth century, the English church was far healthier—its clergy far more effective—than previous accounts have assumed.[10]

EVANGELICAL CONVERSIONS

Wherever the truth lies in this complex debate, it appears that some who were alive at the time found at least some aspects of eighteenth-century English spirituality lacking in substance. Perhaps most famous of these was John Wesley, the founder of Methodism.[11] Wesley was raised in a religiously devout home. His father was a devoted Anglican rector, and his mother was a pious and conscientious believer. Even after his ordination in the Church of England, after assisting his father in his parish, and after serving as a missionary to the Indians in Georgia, Wesley remained spiritually unsettled. In particular, he was worried about obtaining life after death and worried that he was not good enough to merit God's love. After his return from Georgia, Wesley fell in with a group of German Moravians now living in England. In May 1738, while attending a mixed Anglican-Moravian meeting on Aldersgate Street in London,[12] his heart was (in a famous expression beloved by Methodists) "strangely warmed."[13]

What does Wesley mean by this? And what was its significance, for him and for others similarly converted? He had, after all, been a Christian his entire life; was he now more of a Christian? Though the appropriateness of the term can be debated, it is clear at least that Wesley's "conversion" engendered profound changes in his life. It enabled him fully to accept the Protestant doctrine of salvation by faith alone, not just for others but also for himself, and it provided him with a powerful assurance of God's love and of eternal life. He then became more at ease with himself and more confident in preaching the Gospel. Set against the cool, rationalistic atmosphere of eighteenth-century England, Wesley's spiritual journey was somewhat unusual, though it was not unique. Unlike many of his contemporaries, he had passed beyond a mere knowledge of God (or a mere rational assent to divine truths) to an intimate and abiding experience of God. In short, Wesley had come to know God personally. The results, though not instantaneous, were profound. And he was not alone: throughout the eighteenth century, many others would be drawn to evangelical faith through the simple appeal of heartfelt religion.

As has often been observed, Wesley's conversion was similar to that experienced by the Puritans in seventeenth-century England and America. It also bore a striking resemblance to the conversion experience of many contemporary evangelicals, including that of his brother, Charles, who later became a famous hymn writer, and that of George Whitefield, who went on to become the first mass revivalist in England and America.[14] In Wales, a number of powerful conversions began even earlier than in England.[15] Griffith Jones, who as a child had received a "heavenly call" to spread God's word, became the first of many influential Welsh evangelicals.[16] His conversion was followed by that of Howell Harris and Daniel Rowland, who became early pioneers of the Methodist movement in Wales.[17] A number of evangelical conversions also occurred in Scotland and Ireland during the 1740s, in part the result of the repeated preaching tours made in those parts of the British Isles by Wesley and Whitefield.

In England, things were much the same. In 1748, the life of an obscure slave trader by the name of John Newton was transformed by a powerful encounter with divine grace. After abandoning the slave trade, and after ordination in the Church of England, Newton exercised an important ministry as curate of Olney in Buckinghamshire, where he befriended the famous poet and hymn writer William Cowper. After his appointment as rector of the important parish of St. Mary Woolnoth in the City of London in 1779, he became one of the most influential and famous evangelical clergymen of his generation. Though for complex reasons he was slow to join the abolitionist campaign, in 1788 Newton appeared before a committee of the Privy Council that had been convened by the prime minister to investigate the nature of the slave trade, where he denounced the practice in no uncertain terms. In the same year, he also published a tract that revealed to the public—*from the inside*—a number of shocking details of the slave trade and of slavery itself.[18] Despite his ascendancy in the church and society, Newton never forgot the shame of his former life and what God had done in redeeming even him, the "African blasphemer" (as he often referred to himself), from a life of gratuitous sin.[19] Out of gratitude, he immortalized his conversion experience in the words of what would become one of the world's most beloved hymns, *Amazing Grace*:

> Amazing Grace! (how sweet the sound)
> That sav'd a wretch like me!
> I once was lost, but now am found,
> Was blind, but now I see.
>
> 'Twas grace that taught my heart to fear,
> And Grace my fears reliev'd;
> How precious did that grace appear,
> The hour I first believ'd!
>
> Thro' many dangers, toils and snares,
> I have already come;
> 'Tis grace has brought me safe thus far,
> And grace will lead me home.[20]

Though the nature and extent of this conversion experience varied within the evangelical revival (as it had become), it was familiar to virtually all eighteenth-century evangelicals. Equally familiar was the belief that salvation could not be earned by merit or by performing a series of "good works," but only by Christ's sacrifice on the cross. Evangelicals also held the Bible in high regard and believed that it alone was authoritative in revealing God's plan of salvation for the world. Moreover, they believed the Christian life should be characterized by activism—caring for the poor; visiting the sick, the needy, and those in prison; and opposing vice and immorality.[21] John Wesley expressed this final point powerfully, yet succinctly, in his well-known rule: "Do all the good you can, by all the means you can, in all the ways you can, in all the places you can, at all the times you can, to all the people you can, as long as ever you can."[22]

It was through the conversion of such individuals in Wales, England, Scotland, and Ireland—including John and Charles Wesley, Whitefield, Jones, Harris, Rowland, Newton, and a host of others—that the evangelical revival was set in motion. Though many of these early evangelicals were associated with the Methodist movement (which remained within the Church of England until after Wesley's death in 1791), others were Baptists, Congregationalists, or members of the Established Church in Wales, Scotland, Ireland, or England. Indeed, the *raison d'être* of early Methodism was the spiritual transformation of the Church of England from within. Committed to a ministry of evangelism and activism after its separation from the Church of England,

Methodism became one of the largest and most dynamic of the various Protestant denominations, especially in America.

EVANGELICALISM AND SOCIETY

By the time of Wesley's death, evangelical religion had gained considerable
momentum, though not respectability. Why? In part, this lack of recognition
was due to the widespread perception that its leaders were disrespectful of
ecclesiastical authority. While the evangelical clergy welcomed invitations to
preach in parish churches, when excluded from the local pulpit they took to
preaching in the open air and to moving about from one parish to another—
activities that were not only illegal at the time but were thought of by some
as potentially subversive and therefore dangerous. In part, it was also because
evangelical religion had gained a reputation for advancing extreme doctrines,
such as the militant—and Calvinistic—Puritanism of the seventeenth century, which was blamed for cutting off the head of King Charles I, for pros-
cribing the Anglican Prayer Book, for sweeping away episcopacy, and for a
number of other revolutionary acts. The fact that few if any evangelicals held
such radical notions did little to satisfy their critics. Another factor was that,
around 1793, with the French Revolution descending still further into anarchy
during the notorious "Reign of Terror," a strong conservative reaction set in
across the English Channel. As a consequence, anything that appeared subversive or disrespectful of authority was stridently opposed, and evangelicalism, with its clerical "irregularity" and its perceived resemblance to the
militant Puritanism of the previous century, was often viewed with suspicion,
or worse. A final factor was that evangelical religion had failed to capture
the sympathies of the higher classes of society; during the second half of the
eighteenth century, evangelicalism remained primarily a movement of middle
to lower middle-class adherents. This was about to change, however, with
important consequences for evangelicalism, and for the religious and social
life of the nation as a whole.

   Though both Wesley and Whitefield benefited from the patronage of a
number of wealthy and influential evangelicals, their ministry was often
directed at those on the edge of society. Both ministered to the coal miners
at Kingswood, near Bristol, and Wesley devoted considerable time and
energy to working among the Cornish tin miners—one of the poorest and
most deprived groups in all of Britain. Though politically conservative and a
Tory, Wesley held an unusually high view of the spiritual capacity of the poor
and uneducated—hence his sanctioning of plebian lay preachers, local
preachers, and the like—a practice that many clerical evangelicals thought

dangerous. His ideas of charity were also very radical for the time: he was contemptuous of the socially prominent, sometimes expressing himself in language that could appear quite violent; he even thought that the rich were generally far less religious than the poor.[23] In both his sermons and his writings, Wesley proclaimed that in Christ all people—rich and poor, men and women, slave and free—were equal, a potentially radical ideology during an age of strict hierarchical authority and rigid class distinctions. Many (though not all) evangelicals joined Wesley in challenging such social conventions and in welcoming men and women from all walks of life—a factor that was often reflected in the backgrounds of the evangelical leaders and converts, who were drawn increasingly from a wide variety of social classes.

Toward the end of the eighteenth century, however, the sociology of evangelicalism began to change, albeit unintentionally. This was primarily a result of the movement's ability to attract members of the upper classes, and even the aristocracy, to its ranks, and the tireless effort of these new converts to promote evangelical religion among their wealthy friends and relatives. Perhaps most influential in this effort was Selina Hastings, the Countess of Huntingdon, who was converted to "serious religion" in 1739.[24] For a time, especially while her unconverted husband remained alive, she labored quietly to advance the "doctrines of grace" among her friends and acquaintances. Around 1769, however, after his death, she began holding religious gatherings in her London drawing room, where a number of members of fashionable society were converted. She also used her considerable wealth and influence to support the evangelistic efforts of the Wesleys, Whitefield, and a number of other "gospel clergy," and drew upon her connection with Fredrick, the Prince of Wales and heir to the throne, to shield "Gospel" preachers from criticism and to advance their career prospects (especially Whitefield's) in the Church of England. Moreover, she built chapels in fashionable towns, such as Brighton, Bath, and Tunbridge Wells, where a succession of leading evangelical clergy preached to wealthy and cultivated congregations. One of her early converts was Lady Gertrude Hotham, sister of the notorious Fourth Earl of Chesterfield, who supported numerous evangelical causes and opened her houses in Bath and London for evangelistic preaching. Still another was William Legge, the Second Earl of Dartmouth. Lord Dartmouth held a number of influential positions in government and, as a favorite of George III, moved freely among the upper classes. After his conversion, he assisted Newton in securing ordination in the Church of England, and he became an important patron of a number of leading evangelical clergy and causes.

Another influential figure in this effort was Hannah More.[25] Though raised in modest circumstances, her talent and natural intelligence ensured her rapid elevation in society. During the early 1780s, she became a successful playwright and member of London's fashionable literary society. Later in the same decade, while in the midst of an extended evangelical conversion, she came to admire both Newton and the well-known biblical commentator Thomas Scott. Around the same time, she also became active in the evangelical circle at Teston in Kent, where the early abolitionist campaign was launched. In 1785, having matured in her faith and tired of fashionable society, she relocated to her native West Country, where she labored diligently to establish charity schools in the impoverished villages of the Mendip Hills. So successful was she in this endeavor (over twenty thousand poor children were educated at her schools) that her methods were soon being exported to other regions of England. She also established a number of Sunday schools in poor areas and women's friendly societies, which provided a measure of financial security for poor women through cooperative effort. During the French Revolution, she wrote a series of pamphlets in an attempt to prevent the spread of radical ideology to Britain.[26] During the debate over the future of the daughter of the Prince of Wales and his estranged wife, Caroline of Brunswick, More urged that the princess (and, by implication, all women) be granted access to formal education—a notion that was as remarkable at the time as it was controversial.[27] Not inconsequentially, More had been denied access to formal education as a child. She also published works of fiction,[28] which sold in great quantities,[29] and moral improvement,[30] where she attempted to walk a fine line between her belief in traditional social values and her desire to help advance a more democratic and egalitarian society—a moderate political and social stance that was endorsed by many of her contemporaries in the evangelical movement.

As one of the most significant lay leaders of the evangelical movement, More's influence was extensive. In particular, her efforts to enact moral improvement cast a long shadow over the nature of traditional family life in Victorian Britain. Moreover, as an important proto-feminist, she illustrated, through her writings and through the example of her own life, how women, though denied access to power by social convention, were able to exercise power in a number of creative (that is, indirect) ways. In short, she epitomized many of the values and opinions of the evangelical clergy and laity who set the revival in motion during the eighteenth century, and she helped pave the way for the next generation who would follow in their footsteps.

EVANGELICALISM AND REFORM

During the late eighteenth and early nineteenth centuries, the leadership of the revival shifted to a group of lay evangelicals known as the Clapham

Sect.[31] Though neither a sect nor exclusive to Clapham Common (a small village south of London, where a number of "the Saints," as they were originally called, maintained substantial villas), the Clapham Sect nevertheless left an important legacy that impacted many aspects of British life during the late eighteenth and early nineteenth centuries. Its membership included wealthy merchants and philanthropists, influential politicians, and powerful government officials. Hannah More was a frequent visitor to Clapham (and the only woman to become an honorary member of the "Sect" in her own right), as was Charles Simeon, the influential vicar of Holy Trinity Church, Cambridge, who had developed a remarkably influential ministry among undergraduates at the university.

Of the Clapham Sect's many achievements, the most celebrated is its contribution to the abolition of the slave trade in 1807 and of slavery itself throughout the British Empire in 1833. Though many groups and individuals contributed to its eventual success, most notably Quakers, Methodists, and a number of political and social radicals, it was the dedication, political skill, and financial resources of Claphamites, especially its leading member William Wilberforce, that sustained the abolition campaign through countless setbacks and defeats.

Though he had been troubled by the practice of slavery for many years, Wilberforce did not assume the leadership of the abolition campaign until the late 1780s.[32] This came about through the encouragement of a number of leading evangelicals, including Sir Charles and Lady Middleton of Teston in Kent; Thomas Clarkson, one of the most influential advocates of the abolition cause in Britain; and John Wesley. Just four days before his death in 1791, Wesley penned a famous letter to Wilberforce urging him to press on with the campaign:

> Unless the divine power has raised you up to be an Athanasius *contra mundum* [Athanasius against the world], I see not how you can go through your glorious enterprise, in opposing that execrable villainy, which is the scandal of religion, of England, and of human nature. Unless God has raised you up for this very thing, you will be worn out by the opposition of men and devils. But if God be for you, who can be against you? Are all of them together stronger than God? O be not weary in well doing! Go on, in the name of God and in the power of His might, till even American slavery (the vilest that ever saw the sun) shall vanish away before it.[33]

It is easy today to underestimate the astonishing magnitude of their accomplishment. The opponents of abolition argued that the economy of Britain and its overseas colonies would be ruined if enacted. Others claimed that freed slaves would rise up and murder their masters. Still others alleged that Wilberforce and his supporters were religious subversives bent on destroying traditional English society. Moreover, the campaign dragged on for almost fifty years and consumed the lives and financial resources of many of its leading proponents. Its ultimate success, however, swept away a most villainous evil and established the Saints' legacy as humanitarian reformers of the first order.

The Saints were also active in a number of other causes. They were instrumental in founding and sustaining the freed-slave colony of Sierra Leone in West Africa. They labored tirelessly on behalf of the establishment of Christian missions in India, the Far East, and elsewhere. They promoted (in and out of Parliament) humanitarian and educational causes in Africa and at home. They gave generously (and often sacrificially) of their personal fortunes in support of poor relief and other benevolent causes. And they actively supported the great voluntary agencies, such as the British and Foreign Bible Society, the Religious Tract Society, and the Church Missionary Society, through which many (both at home and abroad) were attracted to "vital religion," and through which many unjust and inequitable aspects of modern British society were reformed.[34]

Despite their many accomplishments, history has not always been kind to the Claphamites. Radical historians and social reformers have criticized their emphasis on religious conversion and the reform of the individual (especially the elimination of vice and immorality), while allegedly turning a blind eye to a number of underlying social conditions, such as poverty and unemployment. To be fair, however, while the Claphamites are widely recognized for their efforts to encourage religious conversion and personal responsibility, they also campaigned extensively (though often without attracting much publicity) for the reform of a number of social ills.

By the end of the long eighteenth century, the members of the Clapham Sect were quickly passing from the scene. There were relatively few evangelicals now active in Parliament or occupying influential positions in government or commerce, and, with few exceptions, those who were so engaged often lacked the political, social, or spiritual *gravitas* of their predecessors.

The situation in the church and the ancient universities was somewhat different. After struggling for years to gain a foothold in the Church of England and at Oxford and Cambridge, evangelicals had by now worked their way into a number of important ecclesiastical livings up and down the country and into numerous college fellowships. Though many had come to exercise important and influential parochial ministries, the "Gospel clergy" continued to face widespread discrimination from clerical colleagues from both the high church and broad (or liberal) traditions. Clerical evangelicals faced perhaps their greatest challenge in the outbreak of the Oxford Movement in 1833, which aimed to reclaim the Catholic (as opposed to the Protestant) nature of the Church of England.[35] Despite being handicapped by these various difficulties, evangelicals eventually began to rise to senior positions in the church, including Henry Ryder who became bishop of Gloucester in 1815,[36] and John Byrd Sumner who, after serving as bishop of Chester from 1828, was appointed the first evangelical archbishop of Canterbury in 1848.[37]

In the wider English society, things were different still. The successors of the Clapham Sect lived at a time of rapid and fundamental social change, arising primarily from the continued effects of industrialization. Many Whigs and those from the so-called "lower orders" clamored for political reform, resulting in the "constitutional revolution of 1828–1832." The many beneficiaries of Britain's sustained commercial and industrial growth, brought about principally by industrialization and the expansion of its overseas empire, contributed to an unprecedented expansion of the middle classes and to the relocation of a large segment of the population from rural villages to the rapidly expanding urban centers. The remarkable growth of both Protestant Dissent and Roman Catholicism (the latter fed primarily by Irish immigration) led many in England to agitate for the removal of the exclusive privileges of the Established Church. Finally, chartists and political liberals, inspired by the examples of the American and French Revolutions, protested against the traditional hierarchical forms of social and political life and even against the continued existence of the monarchy.

Each of these various issues challenged in different ways the spiritual aspirations of the evangelical movement, producing considerable pressure (and even unrest) within its ranks. As a result, during the late 1820s and early 1830s, the "Gospel movement" began to fragment into a number of diverse, but not altogether distinct, parties and even denominations.[38] Examples of millennial and apocalyptic speculation, ultra-Calvinistic doctrines, and even extreme forms of Pentecostalism, could now be found among the adherents of evangelical religion, leading many traditional evangelicals to lose confidence in the ability of the "Gospel movement" to bring about the spiritual renewal of the English church and the nation as a whole.

Though evangelical religion was less prominent after the 1830s, it still remained a potent spiritual force. Its hard-won acceptance in the church and society during the previous century and the belief of its adherents in the leading of divine providence, helped to insulate the movement from the prolonged attacks of its numerous critics, as well as from the various religious, political, and social upheavals that featured so prominently in Britain during the nineteenth century.

CONCLUSION

Having secured its place within the wider culture, evangelicalism went on to leave an indelible mark on the religious landscape of Britain. Its emphasis on the need for spiritual renewal helped transform the inner life of countless men, women, and children; it strengthened the institutional life of the Church of England; and it exerted considerable influence upon the various Nonconformist denominations throughout Britain. It made significant contributions to the campaigns to enact humanitarian reform, especially its inspired leadership of the abolitionist movement, as well as its championing of a vast number of voluntary societies. Its moral and devotional teaching, with its emphasis on the necessity of personal transformation and responsibility and on the importance of domestic prayer and biblical study, deeply influenced the nature of Victorian family life.[39] And finally, its evangelistic energy and missionary zeal contributed greatly to the worldwide expansion of Christianity during the Age of Empire.

SUGGESTED READINGS

The Evangelical Revival has been extensively studied on a number of divergent levels. The best general survey of the movement is David Bebbington's *Evangelicalism in Modern Britain* (London, 1989). Other broad surveys worth examining include Charles Smyth, *Simeon and Church Order* (Cambridge, 1940); L. E. Elliott-Binns, *The Early Evangelicals: A Religious and Social Study* (London, 1953); J. D. Walsh, "The Yorkshire Evangelicals in the Eighteenth Century; With Especial Reference to Methodism," PhD thesis (Cambridge, 1956); A. Skevington Wood, *The Inextinguishable Blaze: Spiritual Renewal and Advance in the Eighteenth Century* (Exeter, 1960); Ford K. Brown, *Fathers of the Victorians* (Cambridge, 1961); Haddon Wilmer, "Evangelicalism, 1785–1835," Hulsean Prize Essay (Cambridge University Library, 1962); J. D. Walsh, "Origins of the Evangelical Revival," in *Essays in Modern English Church History*, ed. by G. V. Bennett and J. D. Walsh (London, 1966); Ian Bradley, *The Call to Seriousness: The Evangelical Impact on the Victorians* (London, 1976); Donald M. Lewis, *Lighten Their Darkness: The Evangelical Mission to Working-Class London, 1828–1860* (New York, 1986); and Bruce Hindmarsh, *John Newton and the English Evangelical Tradition* (Oxford, 1996). A number of studies examining the progress of the Revival within Anglicanism include J. D. Walsh, "The Anglican Evangelicals in the Eighteenth Century," in *Aspects de l'Anglicanisme*, ed. by M. Simon (Paris, 1974); Michael Hennell, *Sons of the Prophets: Evan-*

gelical Leaders in the Victorian Church (London, 1979); Kenneth Hylson-Smith, *Evangelicals in the Church of England, 1734–1984* (Edinburgh, 1988); Christopher J. Cocksworth, *Evangelical Eucharistic Thought in the Church of England* (Cambridge, 1993); Grayson Carter, *Anglican Evangelicals: Protestant Secessions from the Via Media, c. 1800–1850* (Oxford, 2001); Martin Wellings, *Evangelicals Embattled: Responses of Evangelicals in the Church of England to Ritualism, Darwinism and Theological Liberalism, 1890–1930* (Carlisle, 2003); James C. Whisenant, *A Fragile Unity: Anti-Ritualism and the Division of Anglican Evangelicalism in the Nineteenth Century* (Carlisle, 2003); and Nigel Scotland, *Evangelical Anglicans in a Revolutionary Age, 1789–1901* (Carlisle, 2004). The theology of the Revival is examined in David Hempton, "Evangelicalism and Eschatology," in *The Journal of Ecclesiastical History* 31.2 (1979), 179–93; Peter Toon, *Evangelical Theology, 1833–1856* (London, 1979); and Cocksworth (cited above). The impact of the Revival on society and culture is examined in K. Heasman, *Evangelicals in Action: An Appraisal of their Social Work in the Victorian Era* (London, 1962); Paul Sangster, *Pity my Simplicity: The Evangelical Revival and the Education of Children, 1738–1800* (London, 1963); Doreen Rosman, *Evangelicals and Culture* (London, 1984); Boyd Hilton, *The Age of Atonement: The Influence of Evangelicalism on Social and Economic Thought, 1785–1865* (Oxford, 1988); John Wolffe, ed., *Evangelical Faith and Public Zeal: Evangelicals and Society in Britain, 1780–1980* (London, 1995); Christopher Tolley, *Domestic Biography: The Legacy of Evangelicalism in Four Nineteenth-Century Families* (Oxford, 1997); and Richard R. Follett, *Evangelicalism, Penal Theory and the Politics of Criminal Law Reform in England, 1808–30* (London, 2001). Evangelicalism and literature is considered in Elizabeth Jay, *The Religion of the Heart: Anglican Evangelicalism and the Nineteenth Century Novel* (Oxford, 1979). The impact of the Revival beyond the confines of Britain is examined in George A. Rawlyk and Mark A. Noll, eds., *Amazing Grace: Evangelicalism in Australia, Britain, Canada, and the United States* (Grand Rapids, MI, 1993); and Mark A. Noll, David W. Bebbington, and George A. Rawlyk, eds., *Evangelicalism* (Oxford, 1994). There is as yet no adequate survey of women and evangelicalism, though the following works have begun to address this omission: E. M. Forster, *Marianne Thornton, 1797–1887: A Domestic Biography* (London, 1956); John Wolffe, *Evangelicals, Women and Community in Nineteenth-Century Britain* (Milton Keynes, 1994); Jocelyn Murray, "Gender Attitudes and the Contribution of Women to Evangelicalism and Ministry in the Nineteenth Century," in John Wolffe, ed., *Evangelical Faith and Public Zeal: Evangelicals and Society in Britain, 1780–1980* (London, 1995); and Ann Stott, *Hannah More. The First Victorian* (Oxford, 2003).

NOTES

1. Irene Collins, *Jane Austen and the Clergy* (London: Hambledon Press, 1994).

2. J. D. Walsh, "Origins of the Evangelical Revival," in *Essays in Modern English Church History in Memory of Norman Sykes*, ed. Gareth V. Bennett and John D. Walsh, 141–48 (New York: Oxford University Press, 1966); Kenneth Hylson-Smith, *Evangelicals in the Church of England, 1734–1984* (Edinburgh: T & T Clark, 1988); D. W. Bebbington, *Evangelicalism in Modern Britain* (London: Unwin Hyman, 1989).

3. See Yngve Brilioth, *The Anglican Revival* (London: Longmans, Green and Co., 1933), 8.

4. M. Pattison, "Tendencies of Religious Thought in England, 1688–1750," in *Essays*, ed. H. Nettleship, 2 vols. (Oxford: Clarendon Press, 1889), II: 43.

5. C. J. Abbey and J. H. Overton, *The English Church in the Eighteenth Century*, 2 vols. (London: Longmans, Green and Co., 1878), II, 4.

6. J. H. Overton and F. Relton, *The English Church from the Accession of George I to the End of the Eighteenth Century* (Oxford, 1889), 1.

7. Norman Sykes, *Church and State in England in the Eighteenth Century* (Cambridge: University Press, 1934).

8. John Walsh, Colin Haydon, and Stephen Taylor, eds., *The Church of England c.1689–c.1833* (Cambridge: Cambridge University Press, 1993), 2.

9. Sykes, *Church and State in England*, 6–7.

10. See especially Walsh, Haydon, and Taylor, eds., *Church of England*; J. C. D. Clark, *English Society, 1688–1832* (Cambridge: Cambridge University Press, 1985).

11. Albert C. Outler, ed., *John Wesley* (New York: Oxford University Press, 1964); Stanley Ayling, *John Wesley* (London: Collins, 1979); Henry Rack, *Reasonable Enthusiast* (London: Epworth, 1989).

12. Rack, *Reasonable Enthusiast*, 141.

13. John Wesley, *The Journal of the Rev. John Wesley, A.M.*, 5th ed., (London, n.d.), I: 103.

14. Harry S. Stout, *The Divine Dramatist: George Whitefield and the Rise of Modern Evangelicalism* (Grand Rapids, MI: W. B. Eerdmans, 1991), xiii.

15. Derec Llwyd Morgan, *The Great Awakening in Wales* (London: Epworth Press, 1988).

16. R. T. Jenkins, *Gruffydd Jones Llanddowror* (Caerdydd, Wales: Gwasg Prifysgol Cymru, 1930).

17. G. F. Nuttall, *Howell Harris* (Cardiff, 1965); Eifion Evans, *Daniel Rowland* (Edinburgh: Banner of Truth Trust, 1985).

18. John Newton, *Thoughts upon the African Slave Trade* (London: Printed for J. Buckland and J. Johnson, 1788).

19. Bruce Hindmarsh, *John Newton and the English Evangelical Tradition* (Oxford: Clarendon Press, 1996), 57.

20. Hindmarsh, *John Newton*, 276.

21. Bebbington, *Evangelicalism in Modern Britain*, 3.

22. John Wesley, *Rule of Conduct* (London, 1774).

23. See J. D. Walsh, "John Wesley and the Community of Goods," in *Studies in Church History*, Subsidia 7, *Protestant Evangelicalism: Britain, Ireland, Germany and America, c.1750–c.1950*, ed. Keith Robbins, 25–50 (Oxford: Blackwell, 1990).

24. A. C. H. Seymour, *The Life and Times of Selina, Countess of Huntingdon* (London: W. E. Painter, 1839–1840); Alan Harding, *The Countess of Huntingdon's Connexion—A Sect in Action in Eighteenth-Century England* (Oxford: Oxford University Press, 2003).

25. M. G. Jones, *Hannah More* (Cambridge: Cambridge University Press, 1952); Anne Stott, *Hannah More: The First Victorian* (Oxford: Oxford University Press, 2003).

26. Hannah More, *Cheap Repository Tracts* (London, 1797–1798).

27. Hannah More, *Hints Towards Forming the Character of a Young Princess* (London, 1805).

28. Hannah More, *Coelebs in Search of a Wife* (London: T. Cadell and W. Davies, 1808).

29. More was the most financially successful woman writer of her generation, eclipsing in fame and fortune even her now-celebrated contemporary, Jane Austen.

30. Hannah More, *Practical Piety* (London: T. Cadell and W. Davies, 1811).

31. James Stephen, "The Clapham Sect," in *Essays in Ecclesiastical Biography* (London: Longman, Brown, Green and Longmans, 1849).

32. Robin Furneaux, *William Wilberforce* (London: Hamilton, 1974), 71–2.

33. John Wesley, Letter to William Wilberforce, February 24, 1791, in *The Letters of the Rev. John Wesley, A. M.*, 8 vols., ed. by John Telford, VIII: 265 (London, 1931).

34. Ford K. Brown, *Fathers of the Victorians* (Cambridge: Cambridge University Press, 1961); John Walsh, "Religious Societies: Methodist and Evangelical, 1738–1800," in *Studies in Church History*, 23, *Voluntary Religion*, ed. W. J. Sheils and Diana Wood, 279–302 (Oxford: Blackwell,1986).

35. Peter Nockles, *The Oxford Movement in Context* (Cambridge: Cambridge University Press, 1994); Martin Wellings, *Evangelicals Embattled* (Carlisle: Paternoster Press, 2003).

36. G. C. B. Davies, *The First Evangelical Bishop* (London: Tyndale Press, 1957).

37. Nigel Scotland, *The Life and Work of John Bird Sumner* (Leominster: Gracewing, 1995).

38. Grayson Carter, *Anglican Evangelicals. Protestant Successions from the Via Media, c.1800–1850* (Oxford: Oxford University Press, 2001), 256.

39. Doreen Rosman, *Evangelicals and Culture* (London: Croom Helm, 1984), 97–118.

Chapter Five

Captain Rock, Captain Swing: "Primitive" Rebels and Radical Politics in England and Ireland, 1790–1845

Michael Huggins

This essay will consider the similarities between popular rebellions in England and Ireland and their relationships to radical politics in both countries. It will demonstrate that Irish and English popular protest used remarkably similar tactics and motifs drawn from the stock of popular culture, albeit with important local inflections. It is also, as a consequence, possible to reconsider some frequently made assumptions about the relationship of popular protest to radical movements in both islands. It is apparent that the leaders of political radicalism—educated and often wealthy—had different agendas from lower class rebels and that popular support was at best contingent and often passive.

What is the provenance of the strange names that appear in the title of this essay? "Captain Rock" was a nonexistent, mythic leader of Irish rebels whose name frequently appeared at the foot of threatening notices issued when landlords, employers, and retailers diverged from customary notions of their duties, which were to lease, hire, or sell at rates that were considered just. Clandestine groups known as "combinations" met at night to swear oaths and intimidate people who appeared amenable to paying higher rents, to taking land from which others had been evicted, to paying higher prices, or to accepting lower wages. These nocturnal combinations sent threatening letters and posted threatening notices to impose their sense of what was fair in economic relations. The dire consequences of being identified made it essential that anonymity was preserved, hence the adoption of such romantic names as Captain Rock. The Rockite disturbances affected the south of Ireland during the 1820s, but similar movements rose and fell across Ireland throughout the period under consideration. In 1830 machine-breaking riots spread across southern England under the leadership of a similarly mythic "Captain Swing," accompanied again by threatening letters and arson. There were similarities between such covert protest actions on the two islands.

Historians have frequently identified the Irish "primitive rebels" as proto-nationalists, resisting the brutal authority of absentee English landlords and employers, prefiguring the popular appeal of Irish nationalism later in the nineteenth century. The trajectory of English popular protest has been characterized as moving from crude local protests into organized political radicalism and ultimately the founding of a political party to represent labor. Captain Swing was thus an expression of the death throes of primitive rebellion. Both these assessments rather neglect the conflicts between the aims of the elite leaderships of Irish nationalism and English radicalism on one hand and popular rebels on the other.

The struggles of the laboring poor in both Ireland and England in this period may be viewed as part of the defense of a customary sense of economic justice and rights. Economic relationships had been viewed in such terms since time out of mind, and the withdrawal of landlords, employers, and retailers from such need-based relationships signaled the embracing of a utilitarian approach to those relationships in which the language of duty and right was supplanted by a language of contract and price. Indeed, some of these relationships had been formalized since Tudor times in paternalist legislation that regulated bread prices, food distribution, and apprenticeships (important to skilled workers in defending their trades against the use of cheaper, unskilled labor).

The expression "primitive rebels" is borrowed consciously here from Hobsbawm's work on the apparently archaic methods of resistance used by the rural poor in Europe before the age of industry. However, to characterize the struggles of the poor as primitive is seriously to underestimate their ability to make choices about how to pursue their struggles for what they considered just. It also compounds the error of viewing the history of popular movements in this period as one of unilinear progress from local protest to political organization. These rebels were aware of the worlds of "high" politics, of the democratic possibilities opened up by the French and American revolutions, and of the events of their own day. Their apparently conservative language and tactics were flexible and readily adapted for use in new situations. They were, indeed, much too extreme for the leaders of radicalism. The pronouncements of, for example, the Luddites (machine-breakers active in central England between 1811 and 1816) and Molly Maguire (another mythic leader of a movement that swept across the Irish midlands in the mid-1840s—and whose name reemerged in the Pennsylvania coalfields twenty-five years later) contained the nucleus of later democratic programs clothed in a language of precedent and conservatism.

POPULAR PROTEST: INDUSTRIAL, AGRARIAN, AND MARKETPLACE

First, it will be useful to examine the motifs and tactics of popular protest in the period, particularly through the language of threatening letters and notices. In the years following the French revolution and in the context of rapid economic transformation through industrialization, enclosure, and agricultural consolidation (frequently justified by the less-than-impartial term "improvement"), both Ireland and Britain were much troubled by popular protest. These protests, however, did not occur in a vacuum and formally were shaped by the inheritance of earlier methods of expressing grievances. However, they were also strongly influenced by the new world order that appeared to be offered by the revolutions in America and France. The ideas of the Enlightenment had challenged monarchic absolutism and transformed elite politics.

In turn their influence was reflected in the notices that appeared in Ireland and England from the mid-eighteenth century. Such notices would frequently urge a return to customary dealing in economic relations. However, custom could also be invoked to legitimize new demands in connection with a concrete contemporary situation. The tactics of the rebels who wrote the notices also included nocturnal outdoor meetings to swear each other (and new members of the group) to loyalty, nighttime visits to intimidate people who had broken the law of custom (through arson and occasionally assassination), and maiming or killing transgressors' livestock. E. P. Thompson pointed out that without the evidence of these threatening letters and notices, it would be possible to consider that England in the late eighteenth and early nineteenth centuries was a "land of moderate consensus, within which the lower orders showed their gratitude towards a humane paternalism by a due measure of deference."[1]

THE INDUSTRIAL CONTEXT

Thompson discriminated between three different contexts in which the voice of the poor was raised against their masters through the medium of threatening letters, which tended to take the form of handbills and notices after the turn of the nineteenth century. These contexts were the industrial (including wages and opposition to technological change), the agrarian, and the market-place. Popular protest may initially be considered under these categories, rather than in chronological order, as it is thus easier to establish the formal similarities between the tactics of English and Irish rebels. However, the poor tended not to see these contexts separately, and their political programs could invoke a series of general economic prescriptions.

This was an age of unprecedented industrial struggle as rapidly capitalizing industries attempted to introduce new machinery during a period of wartime boom. In Wiltshire, England, the skilled shearmen (woolen cloth finishers) had long resisted the introduction of gig mills and shearing frames with some success. The shearmen of Wiltshire also used other "primitive" tactics, such as the threatening letters sent to clothiers who had installed gig mills, and assembled in their hundreds at night with blackened faces to destroy machinery.[2]

A connection between the violence of the Wiltshire shearmen and the Lud-dite outbreaks ten years later can readily be made. The derivation of tactics from the stock of popular cultural motifs is noticeable, and the connections between English and Irish forms apparent. Captain Ludd was the mythic leader of resistance to unwelcome economic change in Nottinghamshire, Lancashire, and Yorkshire in midland and northern England during 1811. Nobody ever knew who Ned Ludd was. Nevertheless, he readily dictated notices threatening dire consequences to those who disobeyed him. One Not-tinghamshire threat accused lacemaker Charles Lacy of making £15,000 "by making fraudulent Cotton Point Nett" of low quality material and ruining the livelihoods of seven hundred men. Lacy was ordered "to disburse the said sum, in equal shares among the Workmen." Whether Lacy did or not is not the issue here. The point is to note the ways in which the workers attempted to regulate economic activity by a formally conservative means, threatening notices, but which had their own contemporary rationale.[3]

Wages were also the subject of protest. A typical notice posted in 1795 on a church door in County Devon, England, demanded of the "gentlemen of this parish . . . no more than Nature Doth Crave . . . which is for Every man to have one shilling and sixpence per Day."[4] In 1800, a notice fixed to a sign-post in Oxfordshire, England, warned the gentlemen of Bicester "if they dont rise Poor Mens pay as they can live better we will rise and Fight for our Lives better fight and be killed nor be starved an inch at a time."[5]

The threatening notice and secret combination also attempted to regulate workplace economics in Ireland during the early nineteenth century. Threat-ening notices were used frequently to prescribe certain rates of pay. This example from County Galway is typical, although the declared rate could differ: "Notice that any person or persons found working on the new road without 10 pence per day will be dealt with according to law, Galway dated ———."

There is evidence that combinations were attempting to organize on a regional basis to enforce wage rates. While claims that the notices were issued by an "Independent Committee" may have been theatrical devices to assume authority, they were widespread enough in the westerly province of Connacht in 1837 to give some credibility to the suggestion of county or regional organization. The assumption of authority is also evident in the writer's invocation of law, although his conception of law was that it should regulate the free contract of employer and laborer equitably and customarily. On other occasions, men who took jobs from which others had been sacked were threatened, and action was taken against employers who paid by piece rate, rather than daily rate. Notices prescribing minimum rates of pay continued to be posted in the 1830s and 1840s.[6]

THE AGRARIAN CONTEXT

Agrarian conflict was a second context in which threatening notices, secret combinations, and the collective discipline of the poor were used to enforce customary notions of economic duty. In England, the enclosure of land that had been used customarily as part of the household economy by the poor was resisted. As far back as 1767 a threat that "wee will put to death all that have united their Farms" was issued in Shropshire, England. In 1799 one landowner in Hertfordshire, England, received a letter from people claiming to be "the Combind in the defence of the rights of the parrish . . . which you unlawfully are about to Disinherit us of." The writers sought to ensure everyone had rights "to turn on the Commonds in proportion to what they hold."[7] However, enclosure was not the only subject of popular resentment and combination. A letter sent to a landlord just across the Welsh border in 1843 warned, "Your rent is as high as ever therefore if you will not consider in time and at your next Rent day make a considerable allowance to your Tenantry I do hereby warn you to mind yourself." This letter was sent during the "Rebecca" agitation, led by yet another mythic redresser of wrongs. It is notable that the invocation of a female leader occurred on both sides of the Irish Sea. The female figurehead may have popular associations of looking after children, of relationships based on need and care rather than on the cold contractual deal of landlord and tenant. The notion that land's primary use was to provide subsistence rather than for exploitation in the drive for "improvement" was embedded in popular belief.[8]

Irish agrarian movements also organized against landlords. It should be noted that this did not necessarily mean the owner of the land but possibly a substantial tenant farmer who had sub-let portions of land on his farm. Irish land tenure was a layered pyramid. Thus Catholic Irish subtenants, cottiers, and laborers were most often paying their rents to Catholic farmers, rather than absent English landlords. These rebels might object to evictions, increased rents, consolidation of holdings, or conversion of arable land to grazing (this was perceived to remove land from its proper function, the growing of the staple potato crop, thus endangering the subsistence of the poor). When the combinations met at night they frequently paid visits to men to make them swear oaths: for example, to give up work as herdsmen on land that had been converted from arable to grazing land. Animals were usually raised for export, reflecting the growing integration of even fairly remote parts of Ireland into a capitalized marketing and distribution nexus.

Typical examples of agrarian actions included the delivery on a night in March 1820 of threatening letters to farmers and agents in Killinvoy, County Roscommon, by a party of more than one hundred men. Their letters demanded that conacre (potato garden) rents be reduced. Arson and violence could be the consequences if the oath was not kept. Suspicion for arson attacks routinely fell upon people who had recently been evicted. The pattern continued until the great famine of the late 1840s. Property distrained in lieu of unpaid rent was seized and removed by combinations. Occupants were visited at night and made to swear to give up land they had taken following a previous occupier's eviction. It is apparent that the possession of land was seen as a customary rather than a contractual right. The Irish rural poor cherished the idea that there was a supralegal right to the means of subsistence that was more important than trifling matters like the nonpayment of rent. Indeed, the threatening notices and oath swearing often took a quasi-legal form that conveyed a sense of a moral law that took precedence over the contractual obligation to pay rent. Such nocturnal mobilizations were endemic in Ireland and England during the period. The Irish and English national archives contain many thousands of reports from concerned magistrates, landowners, and police officers to the Home Office (England) or Dublin Castle (Ireland), the office of the chief secretary and Irish civil administration.[9]

THE MARKETPLACE CONTEXT

The third context identified by Thompson was the marketplace in which food riots occurred. It was in this context alone that women were as active (and sometimes more active) than men. Such events were often characterized by the setting of a "just price," one seen as fair by consumers, and the money raised later handed to the retailer. One historian has concluded that this was perhaps the most commonly adopted tactic in the northwest of England around the turn of the nineteenth century. It might follow the object of the protesters' odium being warned by a threatening letter or notice. This shows that the actions were not mere rebellions of the belly, in which the poor simply plundered what they could when they briefly found themselves able to, perhaps before the forces of law arrived. They were instead based on widely held notions of just economic practice in which food was not merely a commodity. Riots could also be against the export of grain from a locality as happened in Cheshire and Cumberland in the north of England during the 1790s.[10]

It is commonly believed that Ireland did not experience food rioting. This is not true. In 1807 a yeomanry major reported that secret combinations were "swearing the people who have potatoes and other articles for sale not to demand (or take) above a certain price." Regulation of food prices was reported to be the object of secret combinations again in 1811 and 1812. Threatening notices were posted against people who sold provisions at markets. A notice posted near Ballaghadereen, and then in County Mayo, warned, "Any person that charges a penny more than half a crown here for potatoes and two shillings a stone for meal . . . shall be made an example to the whole country."[11] Another notice proclaimed:

> This is a general notice to all those pitiful rascals that has . . . potatoes or meal to sell dare demand or receive no more than three shillings per hundred and two shillings per stone for meal . . . I dont mean harm to King and Country but shivering to prevent starvation . . . God Save the King.[12]

In February 1817, a crowd took meal and potatoes from stores at Athlone market, County Westmeath, and set prices for the sale of the goods.[13]

In May 1837, a notice was posted on a retailer's door, ordering him to return to the buyers six pence per hundredweight of the money he had charged for potatoes. "Captain Rock" said he should have charged one shilling and six pence, not two shillings.[14] In June 1839 three men were attacked and made to swear that they would demand no more than sixteen shillings per hundredweight for meal and two shillings and six pence for potatoes. Where they had sold potatoes at a higher price they were to refund the difference. Such price-fixing took place during the spring and early summer when the previous year's potato crop was exhausted and people needed to buy potatoes until the summer's harvest from their own conacre plots. Food rioters also prevented produce being taken away from the locality in which it was grown and marketed.[15]

THE POLITICS OF POPULAR PROTEST

Thus it can be seen that both Ireland and England were afflicted by formally very similar acts and discourses of popular protest during the late eighteenth and early nineteenth centuries within the three categories identified by Thompson. However, such grievances were often part of a broader sense of justice and customary rights. Wages, prices, rents, and other economic factors were part of the subsistence calculations of the poor, whether in town or country, laboring in a mechanized workplace or in a field. They can be seen as part of an ambient customary sense of rights and duties between employers, landlords, and retailers on one hand and workers, tenants, and consumers on the other. The worker was usually also both a tenant and a consumer, and thereby possessed an integrated "worldview." Consider this threatening notice posted in County Roscommon:

> March 11th 1812. God bless the king. Gentlemen and farmers of the parish . . . We will not allow any priest but 11 shillings and 4 pence half pence for publick marridge and 1/ for anointing and 11/7 for baptism. No man or woman shall lay offerance only one Crown for Mass and we will not allow any Proctor on any account. Let the parish minister come forth and set his Thydes as usually in the year 1782 any man that asks more than £6 an acre for dunged ground woe be to that man any man that gives more shall share of the same fate any whose lease is up no man shall bid for it till three years after date we were waiting in this parish this many years back Woe be to any man that take this down for 21 days. No more at present but we desire that ye Land Holders and priest and minister of the parish . . . to take warning by this we will not allow any publican but 4/ Noggin for spirits, 6 for punch and 4 for brandy. So fare well for a short time. James Farrell, Captn.[16]

This notice betrays a number of aspects of lower-class grievances. First, the medium itself is noteworthy. The posting of a threatening notice may appear a primitive method for expressing grievances, but in the circumstances of illegality and the possibility of transportation if discovered, the anonymous threat made in the name of a mythic soldier begins to make sense. Similarly, the disposition of these rebels to meet at night with blackened faces, often disguised as women, appears less archaic and more like a sensible precaution. Furthermore, cross-dressing connects with the inversionary aspects of carnival so deeply embedded in popular culture during the period in which, for a finite celebratory period, the "lords of misrule" might overturn the established order of things. Secret combinations in both England and Ireland frequently wore white shirts or hats for group identification or solidarity.

Second, the notice asserts loyalty to the Crown. This might be a theatrical flourish designed to mislead or to afford some protection against the most serious charges, if discovered. It might also express a genuine loyalty. Whatever the thinking, it cannot be construed as nationalist. The notion of a just monarch who was ill-served by his court and would rectify the situation if he knew about it was a common motif in European popular culture during the period, and this pledge of loyalty may express such a hope. It is noticeable also that the writer of the notice spends as much time prescribing maximum fees payable to Catholic clergy as to the tithes payable to the Church of Ireland minister. If the lower-class writer of the notice was a nationalist, he or she might be expected to be a comrade of the Catholic clergy rather than an adversary. It was during this period, after the secular Enlightenment hopes of the defeated 1798 rebellion had been dashed, that modern Irish nationalism was taking its confessional, clerical, Catholic form. That rebellion had seen the emergence of secular republicanism led by radical Protestants who had been motivated by the ideas of universal human rights and liberty that had inspired revolutionaries in America and France. After the rebellion's defeat, religious identities were swiftly to become entrenched in high Irish politics. Indeed, the Catholic clergy became the organizing foot soldiers of O'Connell's campaigns for "Catholic emancipation" (1829) and the repeal of the union between Ireland and Britain (1840s).

Third, the writer of the notice asserts customary levels for tithes (as they were thirty years earlier), names maximum rents for conacre, and prescribes retail prices for alcoholic drinks. The notice looks backward to a time when prices (retail, rents, religious exactions) were reasonable and just. The paying of tithes is not rejected, only the amount demanded. The writer does not accept the right of a proctor to collect tithes on behalf of a minister (levying his own charge in addition). Thus the prescriptions of Captain Farrell use custom as the legitimation of present demands.

It is noteworthy that tithes caused opposition among the rural poor in England as well as Ireland. Such opposition in Ireland has frequently been explained as evidence of nationalist opposition to a "foreign" religion and its clergy, yet although some protesters called for the abolition of tithes, more frequently it was the amount levied that caused resistance. There is more often nothing to distinguish resentment over tithes in Ireland from similar sentiments expressed by English protesters. In December 1830, as the Captain Swing machine-breaking movement swept across southern England, a vicar in Maresfield, Sussex, was warned:

Sir,
   We have inquired into your tithes, and we have determined to set fire to you in your bed if you do not lower them. You receive from Fletching £500 a year, and give your curate only £100 a year, and you starve your labourers that works for you, you old canibal.[17]

Many threats took the form of "general complaints" that identified farmers, millers, shopkeepers, and employers as the enemy.

Alan Booth has suggested that food rioting in northwest England became increasingly entwined with other protests by 1801, with demands that encompassed immediate economic ends and more general political aims. This "worldview" found concrete expression in the postrevolutionary appropriation of emblems, such as the cap or tree of liberty, and the emergence of "organic intellectuals" who organized popular protest and rebellion locally, integrating local demands in a general political vision. A group of men was arrested at the Britannia Inn, Manchester, in March 1801, their leader acknowledging under examination that they had been discussing the continuation of the war with France, the high price of food, and wage levels. In the same month the overseer of the poor in Wigan, England, was warned in a threatening letter that "when we erect the Tree of Liberty then you like all others will wish you had acted otherwise." Booth concludes, "Henceforth the food riot became an integrated part of a wider conception of working class protest."[18]

In the early 1800s, English protesters were making simple political propaganda like "we by all mean disstroay the King and Parlement" or "put down like torrent all Kings, Regeants, Tyreants . . . and to Beuray famine and distress in the same grave."[19] Others protested their loyalty to the Crown. Whether rhetorical stratagem or honest sentiment, the point about professions of love or loathing for the king is that they represent a level of generalization. Common to most protest was a discourse of oppression in the midst of plenty, with political causes. A notice in Essex, England, in 1800 complained that "we will not bear it no longer for we live in a Land a planty and if you do not chuse for to lower things so eveary wone may live . . . we will kill and burn eveary thing we come at spesely the great Landholders." In the same year soldiers sent a letter to a lieutenant general warning that "we are Determin'd one and all, not to see our Families and the People at Large Starve In a Plentiful Country, through a Tyrant and a Dam'd Infernal Imposing Lords & Commons, a Republic must Ensue."[20]

In Ireland such general political sentiments took similar forms, grafting Painite and "half-digested French principles" on to customary consciousness.[21] A notice posted in County Leitrim in 1830 proclaimed:

General Notice to the people of Ireland to be firmly united together without any distinction whatsoever in either church or creed but true and Loyal to each other oppressing Land Lords and Clergy tythes and taxes all overbearing men of Ireland be ready when called on and throw off the yoke which we are long under God Save the King.[22]

Misery in the midst of plenty was again a motif. A Molly Maguire notice exhorted her children "not to starve in the midst of plenty" (note once more the appropriation of the feminine to denote succor).[23] Another was almost lyrical: "See before your eyes all the fine lands of that parish—to see the produce sent off every year without . . . getting a mouthful . . . or even a days work . . . I'll let them know that might is not always right."[24] These general sentiments were given more concrete form through the period under question by the appropriation of language and emblems from beyond Ireland. During the 1790s, this included the example of France and the emblem of the tree of liberty. After the "Peterloo massacre" of 1819, when the yeomanry in Manchester, England, slaughtered at least eleven people at the culminating meeting in Henry Hunt's parliamentary reform campaign, an "address to Irishmen" was posted in Clonmel, County Tipperary. It spoke of the "murdered patriots of Manchester."[25] Three hundred copies of a handbill talking of Peterloo and Hunt's triumphant procession were seized from a man at a fair in Thurles, also in County Tipperary.[26] A printed copy of Hunt's address on the eve of Peterloo had been widely distributed in Ireland.[27] Importantly, the address to Irishmen made no distinction between Irish and English patriots (the meaning of the word was routinely contested, radicals and conservatives each claiming they were the true patriots).

What is most interesting here is the consciousness among the lower-class Irish that they and the lower-class English were fighting the same enemy. The patriotism of this Irish protest was devoid of its later nationalist inflection. The parliamentary reform agitation of the early 1830s found a way into Irish plebeian discourse, through the foundation of "trades political unions," such as that at Carigallen, County Leitrim, which espoused the reform cause and sought to "promote the interest and better the condition of the industrious and working classes."[28] By the early 1840s, Chartism was developing in Ireland. Lower-class rebellion increasingly took the form of daylight mass meetings, organized to turn over grazing land in order to grow potatoes for food and to demand the lowering of conacre rents. These meetings attracted thousands. Michael Burke, of Cloonygormican, County Roscommon, led one such campaign, naming himself captain. Captain Rock was now incarnate. After he was imprisoned, he made an impassioned appeal for clemency in which he launched a general attack on landlordism and reminded the government that the poor were always "at the point of the swoord at time England was in need," that is they were expected to serve in wartime.[29] Threatening notices now began to appear in print, suggesting an increased measure of organization.

POPULAR PROTEST AND
RADICAL REFORMERS

In England, mass radical movements such as that led by the demagogue Henry Hunt gathered momentum following the end of the Napoleonic wars in 1815. However, there was a significant gap between the discourses of radicalism and the concerns of the poor, glimpsed through threatening notices and the actions of secret combinations. Radical leaders did not seek any fundamental economic reorganization. They identified England's troubles with a corrupt, unreformed, and unrepresentative Parliament, not with fundamental inequities in land and capital ownership. Thus Hunt gave his support to radicals' plans for mass open-air meetings in 1816 only "after he had satisfied himself that he was not being drawn into a revolutionary plan to abolish private property in land."[30] The distressed masses would enroll in a campaign of petitioning for relief to be achieved somehow through the reform of Parliament. The cap of liberty was deployed as a symbol of the movement because of its general radical connotations (constitutional yet republican, that at once meant all and meant nothing). The poor were thus persuaded in thousands to attend a series of mass meetings in 1816 and again in 1819 to increase the pressure for political reform on the basis of an inchoate expectation that their practical demands would be met. The sense of carnival (appropriating and inverting dominant motifs) and the symbolism deployed made connections with popular culture that cemented the loyalty of the masses to the radical cause.

Radicals campaigning for the parliamentary reform that was to culminate in the act of 1832 were opposed to the lower-class collective protests of Captain Swing. Eric Hobsbawm and George Rudé noted that "a great deal of the Radical agitation, far from condoning or being sympathetic to 'Swing's' activities, was actively opposed to them." Indeed, one radical pamphleteer from Northamptonshire urged the Swing rioters to "give up all these petty outrages against property . . . and unite all for a Glorious Revolution," by which he meant parliamentary reform.[31] For the participants in Swing, on the other hand, the Radicals had misled them by insisting that the problem lay with an unreformed Parliament. By disallowing these "primitive rebels" any independent politics of their own, the tensions and contradictions in radicalism and the early labor movement have been obscured. Hobsbawm and Rudé too readily dismissed Swing as the death throes of a primitive organizational form, the rioters' complaints being "the usual baggage of the pre-political poor."[32] Threatening letters and notices continued to appear until the 1840s in England, albeit with less frequency, as the radical press increasingly became the voice of opposition.

From Hunt's time forward, radical politics provided a structure of emblems, rituals, and ideas that was able intermittently to channel lower-class demands into its campaigns for parliamentary reform and representation. Chartism was the culmination of this phase of radical activity in England, its campaigns from 1838 attracting mass support. However, it is questionable whether in this period English radicalism ever resolved the contradictions and tensions between itself and the amorphous political demands of the poor. The grievances of the poor may have been subsumed organizationally (though that did not prevent major outbreaks like the "Rebecca riots") during the Chartist agitation for parliamentary reform. However, the conflict between factions within the Chartist movement, one advocating "physical force" (necessarily a revolution) and the other "moral force" (parliamentary and peaceful mass pressure) partly reflected these tensions. The development and transmutations of this tension can be traced through the threatening notices, secret combinations, and acts of rebellion that characterized lower class grievances against landlords, employers, and retailers, which occurred quite independently of radical political mobilization. The apparent formal conservatism of these should not mislead.

It is quite possible to view in similar terms Daniel O'Connell's campaigns in Ireland during the 1820s for the extension of the right to become Members of Parliament to Catholics and in the 1840s for the repeal of the political union between Britain and Ireland. Recent scholarship has questioned the extent to which O'Connellism was a movement with a genuine mass following, despite its reputation as such. Séan Connolly has argued that the figures for subscriptions of the poor to O'Connell's campaign for "Catholic emancipation" must be treated with great caution and that it remains doubtful how far down the social scale either that campaign or the later one for repeal of the union between Britain and Ireland actually penetrated.[33] Writing of O'Connell's Repeal campaign in the 1830s and 1840s and addressing directly the tension between O'Connellism and popular protest, Maura Cronin has suggested, "The frequency of more spontaneous types of crowd activity throughout the two decades under review show the consensus of O'Connellite meetings to have been largely illusory or temporary."[34] Popular protest, vehemently opposed by O'Connell, continued throughout twenty years of campaigning by this, the father of modern Irish nationalism. Here the tension between political radicalism and popular rebellion was most apparent.

In Ireland such "primitive" forms persisted until the dénouement of the great famine in the late 1840s. This suggests that O'Connellism was, if anything, less successful in subsuming Irish popular protest than English radicalism was in incorporating the aspirations of the poor in that country. The "General Notice to the people of Ireland" quoted above makes plain its nonsectarian aims, whereas O'Connell made no pretense of recruiting Protestants to his campaign, which needed a unifying mechanism. The organizing of theatrical processions before the speeches, replete with unifying Catholic symbols and the incorporation of stock phrases from the Irish language served to create an illusory bond between O'Connell and his audience. The bond was illusory because after the meetings were over and O'Connell had warned his audience to desist from combination, they went home and continued to combine. Catholic priests were the organizers and stewards of the crowds turning up at O'Connell's mass meetings, offering a sectarian solidarity to transcend the bitter divisions between farmers and laborers that were exposed by the activities of combinations, yet these priests were often themselves the object of the combinations' odium. O'Connell was perhaps most adept at rhetorically tying the concrete and profoundly radical demands of the poor to his own schemes for middle-class Catholic inclusion in the political nation.

Much as the English Radicals' demands were abstract and quite irrelevant for the mass audience, so were O'Connell's calls for "emancipation" and repeal of the union. This did not go unnoticed. Before the granting of "emancipation" in 1829, O'Connell acknowledged that this would remove only the "double aspect" of the oppression of the poor.[35] Following "emancipation," a leader of a combination known as the Whitefeet in the province of Leinster, southeast Ireland, responded thus to questions about his actions:

> The law does nothing for us, we must save ourselves. We are in possession of a little bit of land which is necessary to our and our families' survival. They chase us from it, to whom do you wish we should address ourselves? We ask for work at 8 pence a day, we are refused—to whom do you want us to address ourselves? Emancipation has done nothing for us. Mr O'Connell and the rich Catholics go to parliament. We are starving to death just the same.[36]

The Chartists organized in Ireland in the fall of 1841, bringing the campaign for further and more far-reaching parliamentary reform across the Irish Sea. Many of these men were migrant seasonal laborers, returning from harvest work. A government spy reported that at a Dublin meeting that fall, the secretary of the Dublin branch, Peter Brophy, read a letter from a man living in

Bradford "recommending Physical Force for the Charter, and denouncing Mr O'Connell and his Humbug Repeal Association."[37]

The poor have mistakenly been characterized as homogeneously nationalist in Ireland, and the protests of the English lower orders as uncomplicatedly subsumed into radicalism and thence laborism. These assessments are both inaccurate. While popular protest took apparently conservative forms in England and Ireland, such protests were not prepolitical, unless the proper activity of politics is defined narrowly as parliamentary debate and elections.

The relationship between popular mobilizations and radical politics was complex. Peaceful and gradualist parliamentary reform campaigns and trade union organizations did not simply replace the brutal directness of "primitive" protest once economic and political change had reached a certain maturity under the impact of industrialization and reform. Such unilinear explanations of popular protest fail to account satisfactorily for the symbiosis of that relationship, which involved tension and conflict over the contested meanings of symbols and rituals. Popular protesters did not surrender the meaning of carnival and symbols to the radical movement but instead engaged during the late eighteenth and early nineteenth centuries in campaigns of their own, using a long-established stock of cultural motifs and emblems. However, while radicals used a stock of popular motifs to connect with their mass audiences, the masses also appropriated the texts and symbols of political radicalism and adapted them for their own use. Thus popular protest from the 1790s to the mid-nineteenth century had its own agendas. For much of this time radicals opposed them.

The weaknesses of radical political movements in Ireland and England in the late eighteenth and early nineteenth centuries can partly be explained by the unresolved tensions between the concrete aspirations of the lower orders and the programs of radical leaders. Thus support for radical campaigns could quickly evaporate when they did not deliver meaningful changes for their supporters. Demagogues like Hunt and O'Connell succeeded in building mass support only to the extent to which they were able to use motifs and ritual meanings that connected with the aspirations of the lower orders or conferred a sense of collective cohesion on assemblies for which reform or repeal were otherwise abstractions. Much of the time their success was indeed temporary and illusory.

SUGGESTED READINGS

For a short introduction to popular protest and social conflict in the late eighteenth and early nineteenth centuries in England, read J. Archer, *Social*

Unrest and Popular Protest in England, 1780–1840 (Cambridge, 2000). The same ground (and more) is covered more thoroughly in J. Stevenson, *Popular Disturbances in England, 1700–1832* (London, second edition, 1992). The growth of radicalism in England is covered in J. Belchem, *Popular Radicalism in Nineteenth-Century Britain* (Basingstoke, 1996). For an overview of the cultural contexts in which popular protest developed during the early modern period with much relevant material, especially on carnival and "misrule," read P. Burke, *Popular Culture in Early Modern Europe* (Aldershot, revised edition, 1994), especially chapters 6 and 7.

For the importance of custom as a legitimation of protest see the seminal article by E. P. Thompson, "The Moral Economy of the English Crowd in the Eighteenth Century," *Past and Present* 50 (1971), 76–136. The article is reproduced along with Thompson's "second thoughts," in E. P. Thompson, *Customs in Common* (London, 1993). The article is concerned most of all with late eighteenth-century food riots, and this theme is developed further in A. Booth, "Food Riots in the North-West of England, 1790–1801," *Past and Present* 77 (1977), 84 –107. The work of Eric Hobsbawm and George Rudé was significant in establishing the legitimacy of "history from below." They may be criticized for taking a teleological view of the modernization of conflict and protest, but E. J. Hobsbawm, *Primitive Rebels* (London, 1969); E. J. Hobsbawm and G. Rudé, *Captain Swing*, (London, 1985); and G. Rudé, *The Crowd in History* (London and New York, 1964) remain vitally important and meritorious studies.

E. P. Thompson, *The Making of the English Working Class* (London, 1963), is justly famous. Industrial strife during the period is considered in A. J. Randall, "The Shearmen and the Wiltshire Outrages of 1802: Trade Unionism and Industrial Violence," *Social History* 7 (1982), 283–304. Two important articles by Thompson further pursue the subject of eighteenth- and early nineteenth-century protest: E. P. Thompson, "The Crime of Anonymity," in ed. D. Hay et al., *Albion's Fatal Tree: Crime and Society in Eighteenth Century England,* (New York, 1975), 255–308; and E. P. Thompson, "Eighteenth Century English Society: Class Struggle without Class?" *Social History* 3 (1978), 133–165. The view that enclosure met little resistance is challenged in J. Neeson, *Commoners: Common Right, Enclosure and Social Change in England, 1700–1820* (Cambridge, 1993). For criticism of the "history from below" approach, read M. Harrison, *Crowds and History* (Cambridge, 1988), which argues that the approach taken by the above historians fails to account for the ubiquity of consenting crowds rather than protesters.

The single most comprehensive work on prefamine popular protest in Ireland is M. R. Beames, *Peasants and Power* (Brighton, 1983). See also M. Huggins, *The Secret Ireland* (Dublin, forthcoming 2006). Séan Connolly effectively challenges long-cherished views of the relationship between Catholics and their church in pre-famine Ireland in S. J. Connolly, *Priests and People in Pre-Famine Ireland, 1780–1845* (Dublin, 1982). This book quickly became a classic and has recently been reissued. A very important essay on another of nationalist Ireland's shibboleths is M. Cronin, "'Of One Mind'?: O'Connellite Crowds in the 1830s and 1840s," ed. P. Jupp and E. Magennis, *Crowds in Ireland, c. 1720–1920*, (Basingstoke, 2000), 139–172. The American historian Jim Donnelly blazed the trail in modern studies of Irish secret combinations and popular protest in J. S. Donnelly Jr., "The Whiteboy Movement, 1761–1765," *Irish Historical Studies* xxi, no. 81 (March 1978), 20–54.

NOTES

1. E. P. Thompson, "The Crime of Anonymity," in *Albion's Fatal Tree: Crime and Society in Eighteenth Century England,* ed. D. Hay et al., 255–308, quoted at 304 (London: Allen Lane, 1975).

2. A. Randall, "The Shearmen and the Wiltshire Outrages of 1802: Trade Unionism and Industrial Violence," *Social History* 7 (1982), 283–304.

3. Thompson, "Crime," 321.

4. Thompson, "Crime," 312, 331; Outrage Reports, National Archives of Ireland, Dublin, (hereafter OR) 25/1837/37, Chief Constable Robert Curtis to Inspector George Warburton, March 21, 1837.

5. Thompson, "Crime," 331.

6. OR 25/1837/37, Chief Constable Robert Curtis to Inspector George Warburton, March 21, 1837.

7. Thompson, "Crime," 313.

8. Thompson, "Crime," 317.

9. State of the Country Papers Series 1, National Archives of Ireland, Dublin, (hereafter SOCP1) 2176/30, Major John Wills to William Gregory, chief secretary for Ireland, April 3, 1820.

10. A. Booth, "Food Riots in the North-West of England, 1790–1801," *Past and Present* 77 (1977), 84–107.

11. State of the Country Papers Series 2, National Archives of Ireland, Dublin, 158/4233, Brigade Major Ninian Crawford to Sir Arthur Wellesley, chief secretary for Ireland, July 1, 1807.

12. SOCP1 1408/24, notices enclosed by Charles Costello to Dublin Castle, March 30, 1812.

13. SOCP1 1838/19, abstracts of reports from general offices and brigade majors of yeomanry, February 1817.

14. OR 25/1837/62, Curtis to W. Miller, deputy inspector general of police, May 26, 1837.

15. OR 25/1839/4577, Chief Constable James Reed to inspector general of police, June 23, 1839.

16. SOCP1, 1408/39, enclosed with letter from Lt. Gen. G.V. Hart, Athlone, to Sir Charles Saxton, March 23, 1812.

17. Thompson, "Crime," 315.

18. Booth, "Food Riots," 107.

19. Thompson, "Crime," 331, 324.

20. Thompson, "Crime," 331, 333.

21. J. Smyth, *The Men of No Property: Irish Radicals and Popular Politics in the Late Eighteenth Century* (Basingstoke: Macmillan, 1992), 3.

22. Chief Secretary's Office Registered Papers, National Archives of Ireland, Dublin, (hereafter CSORP) 1830/W103, copy of notice posted at Mohill marketplace, County Leitrim, November 14, 1830.

23. *Roscommon and Leitrim Gazette*, July 8, 1845.

24. OR 25/1845/5001, copy of notice, March 11, 1845.

25. S. R. Gibbons, *Rockites and Whitefeet, Irish Peasant Secret Societies*, (PhD diss., University of Southampton, 1983), 204.

26. S. H. Palmer, *Police and Protest in England and Ireland, 1780–1850* (Cambridge: Cambridge University Press, 1988), 218.

27. D. Macraild, *Irish Migrants in Modern Britain, 1750–1922* (New York: St. Martin's Press, 1999), 131.

28. CSORP 1832/1247, enclosed with letter from Warburton to Sir William Gosset, undersecretary for Ireland, July 23, 1832.

29. OR 25/1845/11481, memorial of Michael Burke to Lord Lieutenant, March 22, 1845.

30. J. Belchem, *Popular Radicalism in Nineteenth-Century Britain* (Basingstoke: Macmillan, 1996), 40–41, 46–47.

31. E. J. Hobsbawm and G. Rudé, *Captain Swing* (London: Lawrence and Wishart, 1969 ed.), 219.

32. Hobsbawm and Rudé, *Captain Swing*, 65.

33. S. J. Connolly, "Mass Politics and Sectarian Conflict, 1823–1830," in *A New History of Ireland, vol. 5*, ed. W. E. Vaughan, 74–107 (Oxford: Clarendon Press, 1989); S. J. Connolly, *Priests and People in Pre-Famine Ireland* (Dublin: Gill and Macmillan, 1982), 30.

34. M. Cronin, " 'Of One Mind'?: O'Connellite Crowds in the 1830s and 1840s," in *Crowds in Ireland, c. 1720–1920*, ed. P. Jupp and E. Magennis, 139–172, quoted at 167 (Basingstoke: Macmillan, 2000).

35. Select Committee of the House of Lords to inquire into the state of Ireland with reference to disturbances. Reports, minutes of evidence, index. 1825 (129) viii.1.127, evidence of Daniel O'Connell.

36. E. Larkin, trans. and ed., *Alexis de Tocqueville's Journey in Ireland* (Dublin: Wolfhound, 1990 ed.), 92.

37. Public Record Office of Great Britain, Kew, Colonial Office (CO) papers 904/8, "PM" to Police Inspector James O'Connor, June 9, 1841.

Chapter Six

The Oxford Movement in Wales: A Catholic Revival in a Protestant Land

Frances Knight

In May 1899, Charles F. Reeks, the vicar of Monmouth, an ancient town just inside the Welsh border, received a petition signed by forty-five parishioners objecting to the Catholic nature of eight different liturgical practices that were observed in his church. These included "undue elevation" of the bread and wine at communion, the use of wafer bread, the lighting of candles when not required to give light, the introduction of a second holy table in the church, and the wearing of unauthorized eucharistic vestments. The Reverend Reeks took the unusual step of sending a printed questionnaire to each of the complainants to ascertain how much they really knew about what went on in his church and to find out whether he still had the confidence of any of them.[1] It turned out that most of the respondents did have confidence in him, although one submitted a rather cryptic reply: "If as a Church of England minister—yes. If as a sacerdotal priest—no." Three months later in August, the vicar of St. Mary's Cardiff, a town-center church some twenty-five miles to the southwest of Monmouth, was also the recipient of a long letter about liturgical practices. It was from his churchwardens, written on behalf of the churchgoers. But unlike their coreligionists in Monmouth, the Cardiff worshippers were full of praise for the "beautiful and symbolical adjuncts to Divine worship" that had been introduced by their vicar. They were particularly distressed that the bishop of Llandaff, in whose diocese they were located, had called for a ban on the use of incense, which they described as "one of those innocent and scriptural accessories to divine worship."[2] But not everyone in Cardiff felt the same way. Indeed, it is a feature of British life in the late-nineteenth century that anti-Catholic sentiment could be visceral, semiliterate, and pungently articulated. It was well summed up in the words of an anonymous correspondent who wrote to the Bishop of Llandaff, "What is being practiced in Cardiff especially at St. Mary's is what the Bishop should put a stop to as its *illegal* not according to the Prayer Book . . . we can easily make it a *topic* at the next general Election *which will be done* . . . there is not the shadow of a doubt but it will end in a *great row,* I should be very sorry to see it you know its the *Protestantism* of this *land we* want to *preserve* if that is not done down we go . . ."[3] Whether intentionally or not, the author of this letter was conjuring up the powerful image of a tidal wave of (Roman) Catholicism gathering strength to sweep across the English Channel and engulf Protestant Britain. The presence of incense and altar lights in an Anglican church in Cardiff was thought in some way to be contributing to this possibility.

What was it about the Catholic revival that provoked such strong responses, both positive and negative, in ordinary churchgoers? This chapter explores the way in which the Oxford Movement, from which the Catholic revival within the Anglican Church originated and which became one of the most influential strands in nineteenth-century British Christianity, made an impact in Wales. In doing so, it is hoped that it will introduce the reader both to one of the major themes within Victorian Anglicanism and to the history of one particular part of the United Kingdom, that small Celtic nation located to the West of England and across the sea from Ireland. For a variety of reasons, Wales was not a promising location for what was primarily a revival of a Catholic form of religion; its religious traditions were strongly Protestant and Calvinist. Conquered by the English in the eleventh century, Wales had been ruled from England ever since and had maintained a distrust of English culture and intellectual movements, which were always seen as in danger of swamping the indigenous Welshness of Wales. It was an isolated, sparsely populated place, predominantly upland with a long coastline and difficult internal communications. Rather smaller than Massachusetts, Wales had a population in 1851 of 1,163,000. The Welsh language, a Celtic tongue derived from the original speech of the British and quite different from English, was widely spoken. (It is still used by 20 percent of the Welsh population today).

HIGH CHURCHMANSHIP IN THE
CHURCH OF ENGLAND

In the sixteenth century, the Church of England became the official religion in England and Wales "by law established." It was a curious amalgam of late medieval Catholicism and new Lutheran and Calvinist ideas, which had been brought across from the continent. The Church remained Catholic in structure but became Protestant in theology. In order to succeed as a national Church to which the majority of the population would in time be prepared to give allegiance, it was necessary for the Church of England to be as inclusive as possible, and from the beginning it claimed to be both Catholic and Reformed. This also meant that from the beginning, it contained within it high-church and low-church traditions. The high-church adherents were anxious to emphasise the Catholic strands within the *Ecclesia Anglicana* and the continuity with the past. They stressed the importance of the sacraments, the episcopate, and the divine basis of the relationship between Church and State. The low-church adherents were more committed to the new Protestant, Calvinist ideas, stressing the importance of the word and of the individual interpretation of scripture. In time, it became clear that these highly divergent strands could not be held together within one church. In 1662, many who were most sympathetic to Protestantism left the Church of England, thus inaugurating what was to become a lively tradition of Nonconformity. After 1688, some of the high churchmen, known as the non-Jurors, were also deprived of their livings as a result of their refusal to take an oath of allegiance to the Protestant monarchs, William and Mary, on the grounds that to do so would invalidate the oaths they had earlier made to the Catholic Stuarts and would undermine the high-church principle of the monarchy's divine right to hereditary succession.

Nevertheless, even after the departure of the Nonconformists and the non-Jurors, distinctive traditions of high and low churchmanship still remained within the eighteenth-century Church of England. High churchmanship flourished, associated with men like Francis Atterbury and Daniel Waterland. It was a group of high churchmen who succeeded in obtaining the episcopal consecration of Samuel Seabury as first bishop of the Protestant Episcopal Church in America in 1784. In the late eighteenth and early nineteenth century, the high-church perspective was characterized by the belief that the Church of England was the pure and uncorrupted branch of the Catholic Church, having been purified of corruption at the Reformation. (The other, corrupt branches were seen as the Roman and the Orthodox Churches.) Seeing themselves as part of a long continuity in Christendom, high churchmen were interested in the writings of the early Fathers. They were intolerant of "schismatic" Protestant Dissenters, and they believed that it was imperative that the close relationship between Church and State be maintained with full privileges only extended to those who were members of the Church of England. They were intolerant of any who had abandoned episcopacy or appeared to give insufficient emphasis to the sacraments. The Bible was regarded as important, but it was believed that it needed to be interpreted in the light of the "Anglican standards," the Book of Common Prayer (the book which provided the liturgy for all services), the catechism, and the creeds.[4]

THE BIRTH OF THE OXFORD MOVEMENT

By the 1830s, high churchmen were in a powerful position. Several recent prime ministers either were or had been high churchmen and because of the Church-State link, they were able to appoint other like-minded men to senior church posts as bishops and deans. The influence of high churchmen was felt at all levels within the Church, in the universities, and through the charitable societies that they promoted in order to encourage such causes as the elementary education for the poor and church building. It was against this background of high-church ascendancy that a new high-church movement, known as the Oxford Movement, began to develop quite suddenly in 1833. Why did the Oxford Movement happen? The essential ingredients were the coming together of a small group of individuals who combined forceful personalities with formidable intellects and who also cared deeply about religion and about the Church of England. They happened to be Oxford dons (academics) at the same period, and most of them ended up in Oriel College, which was regarded as the most intellectual place in Oxford. They were young (except for John Keble), but they already had the self-assurance that comes from being in the heart of an ancient seat of learning, a university which was in the 1830s still very much a bastion of the Church of England.

At the center of the Movement was John Henry Newman, often regarded as the greatest religious thinker that Britain has ever produced—an ex-Evangelical who was to have an extraordinary spiritual journey that would result in his becoming a Roman Catholic cardinal. Also involved from the beginning was John Keble, the Oxford Professor of Poetry; William Palmer, an Irishman in Oxford; and Richard Hurrell Froude, Newman's contemporary and particularly close friend, known for his vehement hostility to the Reformation. It was a bitter blow to Newman when Froude died in 1836 at the age of thirty-four. Within a few months the Movement had been joined by Edward Bouverie Pusey, the professor of Hebrew, a man plagued by religious scruples and terrible headaches and with a reputation for being stern and unbending. He was later to found the first sisterhoods (convents) for Anglican women. The Oxford Movement had support from other individuals, but these were the central players. Because they were clever and opinionated and relatively leisured and relatively affluent, they were able to make their mark on the Church of England.

The trigger for the Oxford Movement had come in 1833 when the Whig government in the newly reformed House of Commons (for the first time it contained non-Anglicans) passed the Irish Church Temporalities Act. In order to understand the significance of this, it is important to understand something about Oxford, about Parliament, and about Ireland. Oxford was an intensely conservative bastion of Anglicanism, and many in Oxford were alarmed by the recent changes that had taken place in the relationship between Church and State, believing that they seriously weakened the Church's position. With the recent admission to Parliament of Nonconformists and Roman Catholics in 1828 and 1829, Parliament could no longer be seen as the lay synod of the Church (as it had originally been intended to be) legislating for the Church with its best interests at heart. Ireland had a majority Catholic population, and only about 10 percent of its people were Anglican. This amounted to about 850,000 Anglicans. Yet for this relatively small number, there were twenty-two bishops. The Irish Church Temporalities Act was concerned with amalgamating some of these bishoprics to make the Irish Church function more efficiently; the government planned to do away with ten of the bishoprics. For the Oxford churchmen, however, the Act amounted to the newly constituted un-Anglican Parliament claiming the authority to alter the ministry and government of the Church, and it was the thin end of the wedge. They believed that what was contemplated in Ireland at one moment could be contemplated in England the next.

On July 14, 1833, Keble preached a sermon to a packed congregation at the university church in Oxford. His sermon attacked the government for its "sacrilegious" conduct in Ireland. The sermon was printed with the title of "National Apostasy" and was circulated within Oxford. The Assize sermon, as it is known, has traditionally been regarded as the beginning of the Oxford Movement because Newman referred to it as the turning point that marked the start of something new in the spiritual autobiography that he wrote in 1864, the *Apologia pro vita sua*. After a meeting in Hadleigh, Suffolk, during the summer vacation of 1833, splits began to appear between the traditional high churchmen and the young men of Oxford. The old high churchmen were against breaking away from the State. They did not believe that the Church could survive without being established and without its endowments; they thought the clergy would starve if they had to rely on the voluntary contributions of parishioners. The new "Oxford" opinion, represented in Hadleigh by Richard Hurrell Froude, was to regard the union of Church and State as evil, and he argued that the Church needed to become a more popular institution, prompting greater affection from ordinary people.

Back in Oxford, Newman, Froude, and Palmer began to plan their new movement. First, they decided to proclaim that the authority of the priesthood derived from apostolic succession. Secondly, that it was sinful for persons or bodies who were not members of the Church to interfere with it. Thirdly, they wanted to try to make the Church more popular, and fourthly, to contemplate the possibility of disestablishment (severing the link between Church and State) though not to press for it straight away.[5] They agreed to publicize their principles by means of little tracts, which could be circulated widely to the clergy in the hope of gaining their support. It was because they issued tracts that the Oxford men became known as Tractarians. (Later on, their successors would be known as Ritualists or Anglo-Catholics.) The early tracts were written by Newman and started off as short, pithy little pamphlets which tackled single issues. Tract 1 urged the clergy to recognize that their authority did not depend upon their birth, education, wealth, or connections but upon the apostolical commission which they had received at their ordination. Apostolic succession, in particular, became one of the hallmarks of Newman's theology. He hoped to shock people with the realization that with the recent constitutional changes, non-Anglican members of the Whig government could now control the nomination of bishops in the apostolic line.

TRACTARIAN THEOLOGY

Although the spark which lit the fire of the Oxford Movement was a political crisis, the subsequent history of the Movement was not characterized by involvement in politics. Tractarianism was a religious movement; a movement of the heart more than of the head, which aspired to rediscover "the beauty of holiness." It was in part thrown up by the Romantic movement as a reaction against the perceived rationalism of an earlier generation. For the Tractarians, religious truth was an awesome thing to be approached with wonder and fear, not with the axe of the critical intellect. They saw themselves as reacting against what had been a prominent eighteenth-century understanding of Christianity, articulated particularly by William Paley, in which faith was seen as assent to an argument after weighing the probable evidences. The Tractarians did not believe that faith should be treated like some kind of logical wager. They wanted to return to the New Testament understanding of faith as the gift of God.

If the Tractarians disliked rationalist approaches to religion, they also had little time for the methods employed by the low church (usually known as the Evangelicals). In particular, they shrank from evangelistic methods which involved (or so they supposed) flaunting the deepest truths of Christianity before crowds of the unbelieving, in the hope of securing conversions. It seemed to them irreverent to hold up the cross before crowds who would be inclined to mock. In 1836, Isaac Williams, the only Welshman to be directly involved with the first phase of the Oxford Movement, wrote Tract 80 "on reserve in communicating religious knowledge," in which he outlined the Tractarian approach to teaching the faith. He drew on the methods that had been used in the early church, in which the catechumens (those preparing for baptism) were gradually instructed in the faith. To critics, however, the whole notion of "reserve" seemed to smack of a devious, "Jesuitical" concealing of the truth and—not unnaturally—it caused people to wonder what exactly these religious teachings were that had to be withheld from all but the initiated.

The Tractarians also believed in the value of the "tradition." When Keble read Newman's sermons and found new ideas in them, he urged him not to be original. Instead, he urged him to preserve the traditions that he had received from the Church. A proper emphasis on the Church's past would help to revive a belief in the authority of the Church. It was also a reaction against the Protestant doctrine that "the Bible, and the Bible alone is the religion of Protestants," an axiom which had been first articulated in the seventeenth century. The Tractarians held the Bible in high esteem, but they disliked the idea of every individual extracting from the Bible whatever his or her individual reason found there without regard to the corporate judgement of the Christian community. To Keble, Newman, and Froude, it seemed imperative to teach the authority of the corporate judgment of the Church, and to do this it was therefore necessary to understand correctly the Christian tradition. It followed that they were very interested in teaching about Christian history, particularly the history of the early Church.

The Movement's Achilles heel came in relation to its attitude to the Reformation. On this subject, its protagonists displayed a mixture of naïveté and ignorance that ill-befitted them as religious intellectuals. Frequently repeated comments about the evil consequences of the policies pursued by the English Reformers could only inflame the feelings of the majority Church of England members, both clerical and lay, who had been taught since the cradle to honor the Reformation and revere the names of the leading Protestant Reformers— Cranmer, Latimer, and Ridley. Contemporary churchmen were baffled that the Oxford men not only repudiated the Reformation, but that they appeared to see nothing wrong with late medieval Catholic doctrine and practice. Newman seems to have been guilty of making generalizations about the Reformation without having read Luther and Calvin for himself. If the Oxford Movement had been rather more circumspect on this contentious topic, they would have been far less controversial and more widely supported. The fact that its later phases more or less coincided with Pope Pius IX's decision to restore Catholic bishops in England and Wales in 1850, an act which caused a great deal of anxiety to many British Protestants, meant that Protestant churchmen were particularly fearful of a movement that appeared to have the potential to subvert the Church of England from the inside and to lead it in a Romeward direction.

THE OXFORD MOVEMENT IN WALES

It took at least several decades for the ideas of the Oxford Movement to be accepted at parish level in England, and the Movement fell on much more stony ground in Wales. There were a number of reasons why this should be. For one reason, the majority religious tradition in mid-nineteenth-century Wales was Protestant Nonconformity. Indeed, the Religious Census of 1851 revealed that whereas in England roughly equal numbers of churchgoers were attending the services of the Church of England and those of Nonconformity, in Wales the proportion supporting the established Church (known rather bizarrely as the Church of England in Wales) was much less—about 20 percent, compared with the 80 percent who supported Nonconformity. For the Nonconformist majority, there was a general distrust of the established church. It was seen, rather unfairly, as an oppressive, alien institution that paid little regard to the distinctive cultural and linguistic traditions of Wales. While it was true that until about 1870, most of the senior posts in the Church did tend to go to Englishmen, most of the parish clergy tended to be Welsh. Tractarian clergy in Wales certainly tended to be Welshmen—often, as we shall see, with a strongly Welsh outlook. On the whole, however, Welsh Anglicanism was solidly low church, reflecting the fact that almost all religion in Wales at this date was strongly Protestant. The old high-church network, which was so strong in England (and also in the Episcopal Church in Scotland), had made very little impact in Wales, and so there was not a preexisting high-church tradition into which the ideas of the Oxford Movement could be absorbed.

Nevertheless, there was some gradual assimilation of Oxford Movement thought into some parishes, particularly in North Wales. One important person who made this possible was Christopher Bethel, bishop of Bangor from 1830 to 1859. He approved of Tractarian teaching, and unlike many of his fellow bishops, he was willing to ordain and appoint men with clear Tractarian sympathies.[6] Another significant influence was Welshmen who had studied at Oxford. In the mid-nineteenth century, the Welsh clergy tended to be trained in one of three places. Some were ordained after following a divinity course at a local grammar school. This was the cheapest form of training, but it was increasingly frowned upon by bishops who were anxious to recruit an all-graduate ministry. Others studied at St. David's College Lampeter, founded in 1822 specifically to train clergy for the Welsh Church. The third group read for degrees at the universities of Oxford or Cambridge, and particularly Jesus College Oxford, which was the Welsh college at Oxford University. Many of the students at Jesus were enabled to study there as a result of a system of closed scholarships, which assisted poor boys from Welsh grammar schools to move on to Oxford. Thus the Jesus College men were not necessarily more affluent than their brethren who studied for ordination in Wales, although their sojourn in England did mean that they were exposed (even if to a limited extent) to a broader range of cultural influences. Jesus College itself was certainly not a hotbed of Tractarianism, but its students could not but be aware of, and sometimes influenced by, the developments elsewhere in the university.

Some of the men who had studied at Jesus College (or at some of the other Oxford colleges) became influenced by Tractarianism, but the Tractarianism that they espoused was significantly different from Tractarianism in its English expression. These Welsh high churchmen did not look to the ancient authority of the early Fathers, as their English counterparts did, but to that of the early British Church, the Church founded in Wales in the fifth century by St. David, which had remained entirely free from English or Roman interference for many centuries. They made much of the "golden age" of the Celtic saints of Wales, and of the authentic and unbroken strand of Catholic Christianity in which they saw themselves as standing. It followed that they were sternly anti-Roman, believing in the pure and uncorrupted nature of the Celtic Church before the arrival of Augustine, who was sent from Rome to Canterbury by Pope Gregory in 597. Whereas some of the English Tractarians eventually converted to Rome, including some of the most notable figures such as Newman, W. G. Ward, and H. E. Manning, conversions amongst Welsh Tractarians were almost unknown. The Welsh Tractarians also had a much more positive evaluation of the Reformation than had Newman and Froude. They continued to follow the Protestant line that it had swept away the corruptions of the late medieval Church, an institution which they believed had defaced the purity of the ancient Celtic Church. The Reformation had also bestowed on the Welsh people such blessings as the Welsh Bible, which had been translated by William Morgan and published in 1588, and had been instrumental in the survival of the Welsh language.

Another interesting characteristic of the Welsh Tractarians was their intense nationalism, exhibited in their support for and participation in such cultural institutions as the National Eisteddfod (a type of competitive arts festival of ancient Welsh origin) and in societies such as the Cambrian Archaeological Association. *Eisteddfodau* provided a natural platform for Tractarian poets, and some clergy who were attracted to Tractarianism may also have been attracted by the rituals, processions, and vestments that were used on these occasions. Morris Williams, a clergyman and Jesus College graduate whose bardic name was "Nicander," won a prize at the Aberffraw Royal Eisteddfod of 1849 with a poem which drew attention to the holy days and seasons of the church's year. It seems to have been in a similar vein to Keble's famous volume of poetry *The Christian Year*. Nicander used the Aberystwyth Eisteddfod of 1865 to present a poem that claimed that St. Paul had preached in Welsh, alluding to the ancient tradition that Christianity was first introduced to Wales by St. Paul himself.[7] Such odd views could, however, have the effect of alienating those who held them from some of the less eccentric Tractarian clergy. Other Jesus College clerics were instrumental in reviving the National Eisteddfod and the *Gorsedd* (a meeting of bards and druids), a development that took place at the Llangollen Eisteddfod of 1858. Another Tractarian clergyman from Jesus College, Canon J. D. Jenkins of Aberdare, took a keen interest in the South Wales Choral Union. His particular contribution to their success in choral competitions in London was to coach them in the words of Latin works, at a time when singing in Latin would have been seen as a controversially "Catholic" practice.[8]

WELSH TRACTARIAN CHURCHES

When Tractarians had the money to do so, they were usually enthusiastic to reorder their church buildings along specifically Tractarian lines, or better still, to build new places of worship that reflected their ecclesiological principles. Not surprisingly, such churches came only slowly to Wales. The first Tractarian church in Wales was built at Llangorwen, near Aberystwyth, in 1841. It was financed largely by the Williams family, the relatives of the Oxford Tractarian Isaac Williams, mentioned earlier as the author of Tract 80 "on reserve in communicating religious knowledge." The church itself is fairly small, which is appropriate for its rural location, and it is largely unchanged, still representing the Tractarian ideal more than one hundred and sixty years after it was first opened. It is built in the Early English style, with lancet-type windows and a spacious chancel, which is raised one step above the nave and separated by a low screen. Three steps, symbolizing the Trinity, lead up to what was the first stone altar to be set up in Wales since the Reformation. The central panel of the arcaded reredos has a stone cross set in it, which would have been regarded as a very high-church innovation at the time of its construction. As a concession to traditional Welsh church building styles, however, the Creed, the Lord's Prayer, and the Ten Commandments appear in Welsh on side panels. The interior itself is quite simple, and the most eye-catching fixtures are four bronze candelabras supposedly given by Newman and a brass eagle (on which to rest the Bible), which is allegedly the gift of Keble.[9]

Llangorwen church was not the only Ritualist church to be built by a family with Tractarian sympathies. St. Paul's Church in Sketty near Swansea, which opened in 1850, was another very early building erected by the Vivian family in memory of Jessie Vivian, the young wife of Henry Hussey Vivian, who was the first Lord Swansea. Henry Hussey Vivian had come into contact with the new form of high churchmanship while a student at Trinity College Cambridge in the early 1840s. At Cambridge he had met the members of the newly formed Ecclesiological Society, known as the Camden Society at this early stage of its existence. They were Benjamin Webb and John Mason Neale, men who were to have a profound influence on the transposition of Tractarian ideals into bricks and mortar. It followed that when Vivian found himself in a position to build a new church just a few years later, he sought the advice and approval of the ecclesiologists and appointed an architect, Henry Woodyer, who had been a friend and pupil of the celebrated Tractarian architect William Butterfield. Within a few years, however, Vivian began to experience a profound change in his religious views. He became skeptical about Tractarianism and began to move in a distinctly Evangelical direction. When Prime Minister Benjamin Disraeli introduced the Public Worship Regulation Bill in 1874, which aimed to curb Ritualist excesses, Henry Hussey Vivian gave the bill his full support. The legislation attempted to stop the spread of Ritualism by giving parishioners the power to prosecute the clergy for ritualistic practices. Meanwhile, the worship at St. Paul's Sketty moved in a progressively more low-church direction.[10]

Another influential Welsh Tractarian who experienced a change in his religious views was the third marquis of Bute, whose family were major landowners in South Wales.[11] He became a Roman Catholic in 1868 when he came of age and succeeded to the title. Thirteen parishes in the diocese of Llandaff were in the patronage of the Bute family, but as a Catholic the third marquis was legally prevented from exercising his rights as patron. Rather than allowing his rights to lapse, however, the marquis shrewdly appointed a group of his Anglican high-church friends to act on his behalf. Naturally, they appointed very high churchmen to the Bute parishes, and thus Anglo-Catholicism entered the Cardiff area by this means.[12] St. Mary's in Cardiff, mentioned at the outset of this chapter because of its use of incense, was one of the Bute parishes, as was Aberdare.

These parishes were, in reality, a few Catholic drops in a Protestant ocean. By 1874, only three Welsh churches used vestments, three had daily communion, twenty-three had communion on holy days, and thirty-two had communion every Sunday.[13] This is in the context of there being nearly one thousand parishes in Wales. Communion every Sunday was regarded as the hallmark of advanced high churchmanship at this date. Ritualism established itself more easily in the city of Cardiff, in some of the large industrial parishes in the South Wales valleys, and in the English-speaking parts of Pembrokeshire, rather than in the Welsh-speaking rural areas. The strength of Ritualism in the fashionable seaside resort of Tenby, in southwest Wales, also parallels the Ritualist strongholds on parts of the English south coast. The overall picture, however, was of an odd religious phenomenon that was spread thinly, and limited to parishes that were often isolated from others espousing similar views.

It may be concluded that the influence of the Oxford Movement in nineteenth-century Wales was strictly limited, and its progress was slow and patchy. The four Welsh dioceses, when compared with their English counterparts, were among those least influenced by Tractarianism, and when it made a mark at all, its impact tended to be modest rather than overt. Anglo-Catholic clergy and laymen were heavily criticized by their coreligionists if they supported the campaign to disestablish the Welsh Church, an objective that was finally achieved in 1920. This campaign was largely led by Nonconformist Liberals and was vehemently opposed by most Anglicans, who saw it as tantamount to the dismantling of their religion. For Anglo-Catholics, however, particularly those who were inspired by Welsh nationalism, disestablishment offered the great opportunity for the Welsh Church to break free from the shackles of Canterbury and from the political interference of measures like the Public Worship Regulation Act.[14] After disestablishment, the Church in Wales did indeed move in a much more Anglo-Catholic direction, particularly under the leadership of Charles Green, who was Archbishop of Wales from 1934 to 1944. Green had spent much of his ministry in Aberdare, one of the Anglo-Catholic parishes under the patronage of the Bute trustees. Green's concept of the role of the bishop was so high that it has been recently described as "monarchical authoritarianism."[15] The advancement of other influential Anglo-Catholic priests such as Timothy Rees and Glyn Simon had the effect of making the interwar Church in Wales a strongly high-church institution. Thus from very small and unpromising beginnings, the legacy of the Oxford Movement helped to reshape Welsh Christianity in decisive ways in the twentieth century.

SUGGESTED READINGS

A great deal has been written about the history of the Oxford Movement, much of it from a rather partisan perspective by those who saw themselves as the Movement's theological heirs. A detailed narrative of events, and one on which this essay has drawn, is that provided by Owen Chadwick, *The Victorian Church* Part I, third edition (London, 1971). This standard account remains very much still worth reading, particularly for those who want to capture the flavor of the unfolding events. The best place to start for those who want an up-to-date overview of the topic is with one of the newer short introductions, either Michael Chandler, *An Introduction to the Oxford Movement* (London, 2003) or George Herring, *What was the Oxford Movement?* (London, 2002). The best modern scholarly account of the Movement, which sets it in its proper context of a much older movement within high churchmanship is Peter B. Nockles, *The Oxford Movement in Context: Anglican High Churchmanship, 1760–1857* (Cambridge, 1994). Indispensable for understanding the impact of the Oxford Movement in the broader culture of nineteenth-century British religion are John Shelton Reed, *Glorious Battle: The Cultural Politics of Victorian Anglo-Catholicism* (London, 1998) and Nigel Yates, *Anglican Ritualism in Victorian Britain, 1830–1910* (Oxford, 1999). The essays in the volume edited by Paul Vaiss, *From Oxford to the People: Reconsidering Newman and the Oxford Movement* (Leominster, 1996) contain some items of interest but nothing specifically on Wales. For an account of anti-Catholicism in nineteenth-century Britain, see E. R. Norman, *Anti-Catholicism in Victorian England* (London, 1968) and John Wolffe, *The Protestant Crusade in Great Britain, 1829–1860* (Oxford, 1991).

The impact of the Oxford Movement in Wales remains a relatively little explored topic. The only significant contributions are an unpublished PhD thesis by D. P. Freeman, "The Influence of the Oxford Movement on Welsh Anglicanism and Welsh Nonconformity in the 1840s and 1850s" (PhD diss., University of Wales Swansea, 1999) and Nigel Yates, "The Progress of Ecclesiology and Ritualism in Wales, 1840–1875" *Archaeologia Cambrensis* Volume CXLIX (2000) 59–88. An older work by Owain Jones, *Isaac Williams and his Circle* (London, 1971), provides what is still the only major work on Wales's most famous Tractarian, and Frances Knight's "Welsh Nationalism and Anglo-Catholicism: The Politics and Religion of J. Arthur Price (1861–1942)" in *Religion and National Identity: Wales and Scotland, c.1700–2000,* ed. Robert Pope (Cardiff, 2001) provides some insight into a Welsh Anglo-Catholic layman in the later period. A good general history of the Welsh Church in the nineteenth century has still not been published, but for those whose interests extend as far as the twentieth century, Densil Morgan's *The Span of the Cross: Christian Religion and Society in Wales, 1914–2000* (Cardiff, 2000) is recommended.

NOTES

1. National Library of Wales (NLW) LL/Misc/237–242. Alleged ritual irregularities at St. Mary's Monmouth.

2. NLW LL/Misc/458–462. The use of incense and processional lights at St. Mary's Cardiff.

3. NLW LL/Misc/459. Letter from 'a Churchman not ritual' (sic) to the Bishop of Llandaff, May 23, 1899.

4. Peter B. Nockles, *The Oxford Movement in Context: Anglican High Churchmanship, 1760–1857* (Cambridge: Cambridge University Press, 1994), 25–32.

5. Owen Chadwick, *The Victorian Church* Part I, third edition (London: Adam and Charles Black, 1971), 71.

6. Nigel Yates, "The Progress of Ecclesiology and Ritualism in Wales, 1840–1875," *Archaeologia Cambrensis*, Vol CXLIX (2000), 59–88.

7. D. P. Freeman, "The Influence of the Oxford Movement on Welsh Anglicanism and Welsh Nonconformity in the 1840s and 1850s," (PhD diss., University of Wales Swansea, 1999), 303.

8. Christopher B. Turner, "Ritualism, Railwaymen and the Poor: The Ministry of Canon J. D. Jenkins, Vicar of Aberdare, 1870–1876," in *Politics and Society in Wales, 1840–1922: Essays in Honour of Ieuan Gwynedd Jones,* ed. Geraint H. Jenkins and J. Beverley Smith, 71 (Cardiff: University of Wales Press, 1988).

9. O. W. Jones, *Isaac Williams and His Circle* (London: S.P.C.K., 1971), 96–7.

10. F. G. Cowley, *A History of St. Paul's Church Sketty, Swansea* (Swansea: Vicar and Churchwardens of St. Paul's Church, 2001), 1–25.

11. John Davies, *Cardiff and the Marquesses of Bute* (Cardiff: University of Wales Press, 1981).

12. Roger L. Brown, "The Bute Church Patronage in Glamorgan: A legal note on *pro hac vice* patronage," *Journal of Welsh Religious History* 5, (1992): 92–98.

13. Nigel Yates, *Anglican Ritualism in Victorian Britain, 1830–1910* (Oxford: Oxford University Press, 1999) 115.

14. Frances Knight, "Welsh Nationalism and Anglo-Catholicism: The Politics and Religion of J. Arthur Price (1861–1942)," in *Religion and National Identity: Wales and Scotland, c. 1700–2000,* ed. Robert Pope (Cardiff: University of Wales Press, 2001), 103–122.

15. D. Densil Morgan, *The Span of the Cross: Christian Religion and Society in Wales, 1914–2000* (Cardiff: University of Wales Press, 2000), 83.

Chapter Seven

Albert and the Great Exhibition of 1851: Creating the Ceremonial of Industry

John R. Davis

By any standard, the opening ceremony of the Great Exhibition was one of the most impressive events in human history. Thirty thousand people in all their finery, some of the most prominent figures of the age, and the finest and most opulent produce of the world, were all gathered under one roof, the "Crystal Palace" in Hyde Park, London. It had a deep impact on those who experienced it. It still represents a landmark for British historians and for historians of the nineteenth century. In stretching old traditions to cover a new occasion and setting, however, the Great Exhibition also provides a clear example of the way in which ceremony evolves over time and often combines elements of the old with those of the new. An in-depth investigation of the opening ceremony reveals, however, that the creation of new ceremony involved a great deal of tension, conscious deliberation and manipulation, as well as some luck. It also reveals the key role played by Prince Albert, Queen Victoria's husband.

Prince Albert had come to Britain from Germany in 1840. His position before 1851 had been weak, both because of his foreignness and his anomalous status as male consort to the reigning Queen, but then he assumed a leading position in the Exhibition. Despite this position, however, he was essentially just one voice among many involved in creating a new national agreement based upon the harmonization of old interests and ancient traditions with the new forces of modernization. Though playing a key role in developing the ceremony for the opening of the Exhibition, he would be forced to compromise with many others as well as accept the force of circumstance and chance.

From the 1780s onwards, Great Britain was transformed by industrialization. Particularly after the end of the Napoleonic Wars in 1815, which had hindered international trade and kept government expenditure and taxes high for over two decades, the British economy became a modern one. In an extremely short space of time, the country's society and political system were forced into the modern age. This caused all sorts of problems as old interests—the landed aristocracy and premodern groups, such as the artisans and small-scale farmers—were rudely shoved aside and forced to make way for the new entrepreneurs and the growing middle class.

The changes taking place in Britain were radical and, insofar as no precedent existed for such far-reaching transformation, unique. The ruling elites were forced to compromise with modernization if they were to survive at all. But there was no model for them to follow. No country, before Britain, had ever industrialized. It was Britain that was leading the way into the modern age. It was also to Britain that other countries were looking as they, too, began to grapple with modernity.

It is within this context that the ceremonies connected with the Great Exhibition can be understood. The Great Exhibition allowed the ruling elite—Prince Albert, the monarchy, the aristocracy, and the politicians—to collaborate with entrepreneurs and show themselves in sympathy with the interests of industry and the middle classes. There were, after all, things they could all agree on, such as the importance of art and design, the necessity of educating the new middle classes, and even the principles of ownership and market economics.

THE CAMPAIGN FOR GOOD TASTE

To understand the opening ceremony of the Exhibition and interpretations of it, the Exhibition's background must be explained. The Exhibition was conceived at the Society of Arts to promote science and art among industrialists. The Society wished to raise its own profile by helping improve the standards of British industrial produce. Foreign—particularly European—produce was seen as aesthetically and technically better than Britain's cheap, mass-produced goods. The appreciation of good taste by consumers was perceived as having political and social, as well as economic, advantages. It strengthened public respect for the aristocracy (the most significant owner of art) and came to the assistance of artists and designers, who had lost both the support of aristocratic patrons and their privileged position in artisan workshops as factory production increased.

Prince Albert, the president of the Society, sympathized with the modernizing aims of the Society of Arts, industrialists, and artists. As an aristocrat, however, he also wished to preserve social order. He therefore loaned royal artifacts to trial exhibitions at the Adelphi buildings in the late 1840s. However, Albert had his own motives for supporting the Exhibition and mediating government help. He was aware of his own unpopularity in Britain as a German (in the wake of the reviled Hanoverians) and as a weak male consort in a patriarchal society. He also worried about the public's alienation from the monarch, particularly among the new industrial middle classes. Albert's support for the Exhibition therefore had wider political, economic, and social foundations, as well as more personal ones.

Politicians were similarly concerned. Since the abolition of the Corn Laws in 1846, the country remained deeply divided. Free trade had succeeded at a pinch, but powerful landed interests had been alienated, and there was mutual distrust between the aristocracy and the masses. Albert, Sir Robert Peel, who had brought in free trade, and the government of Lord John Russell all supported the Great Exhibition. They hoped it might bind the country together.

Revolution in Europe in 1848 made this all the more urgent. Too few histories of the Great Exhibition appreciate its context in the face of economic, social, and political turbulence abroad. Albert hoped his vision of a monarchy united with new, industrial classes would appeal in Britain as well as in continental countries.

REACHING AGREEMENT: CREATING A CEREMONY OF EXHIBITIONS

The Great Exhibition needed to appeal to the masses for educational and political reasons. However, there were also financial ones. With Albert organizing things it was important to maintain financial honesty, prevent any connection of Victoria with profiteering, and uphold fairness of judgment regarding prizes. It was therefore decided to finance the Exhibition through public subscription.

The Royal Commission, chaired by Albert, with an executive committee drawn from the Society of Arts, was therefore careful to sound out the public's feelings. As early as summer 1849, Albert instructed men from the Society of Arts, including Henry Cole, to tour the country and sound out opinion.[1] Though Albert's advisers tried to prevent it, Cole discovered that stressing

Albert's—and therefore also Victoria's—support for the Exhibition brought great applause and support for the project.[2]

Other marketing strategies became obvious. In Manchester, the campaigners found the Exhibition's potential for marketing British goods abroad was recognized. Additionally, the Exhibition apostles reported that the Exhibition might appeal to British patriotism, and that this should also be exploited. Businessmen recognized that the Exhibition would teach "not the manufacturers only how to make, but the public how to buy." It was also believed that "moral good would result from that assemblage of rival manufacturers who would be induced by the Exhibition" and that it would "rub the sharp corners of many nations off." The Exhibition, it was therefore discovered, appealed to the cosmopolitan and pacifist aspects of Victorian Britain.[3]

A discourse about the Great Exhibition had begun, dominated by themes and symbols reflecting its aims and society's preoccupations. This grew in January 1850 with the creation of hundreds of local committees around the country so "that the whole Kingdom should be thoroughly educated to understand the several objects and scope of the Exhibition, and have their sympathies properly aroused towards it."[4] Within this national discussion about the Exhibition, set themes were exercised and propagated. The repetition of themes and symbols at local committee meetings and in the national press supported the development of an Exhibition movement. Public support for the project was boosted.

By March 21, 1850, Albert felt ready to appear at the head of the Exhibition campaign by personally speaking to a meeting at the Mansion House in London. The sense of occasion, with mayors from around the country, produced an attention to symbolic and decorative detail hitherto unmatched. Though the Egyptian Hall of the Mansion House was often used for banquets, there had never been "any occasion on which it presented so striking and peculiarly magnificent and appropriate an appearance as on the present . . . the novelty of the occasion itself had been taken advantage of to introduce a style of ornament and decoration at once novel and pleasing in the highest degree." Corinthian columns along each side of the hall were decorated with shields of arms from several countries, cities, and towns, "intermixed with trophies formed of the chief articles of product for which the several localities are celebrated, and the implements used in the districts." The great windows were decorated with transparent pictures redolent of the Exhibition. The eastern window, above the principal table, was "filled in with two colossal figures, representing Peace and Plenty encircling an immense globe of the world with a wreath of laurel; and beneath this group was a large picture representing the Port of London, with ships arrived from every quarter of the earth, disembarking the produce of the several countries." The western window enclosed "a colossal allegorical figure of Britannia, holding in her hand a ground plan of a building for the approaching grand exhibition. Four angels surrounded Britannia and trumpeted forth to the various parts of the world that she was willing to receive the works of art and manufacture of all nations and to reward the most meritorious."[5] Verbal imagery was being reproduced in visual representation.

Albert's speech at the banquet was an intellectual feat. Overcoming a foreigner's shyness of public speaking and his propensity to remain in the background, he now combined the themes and arguments used in support of the Exhibition into a logical, visionary whole. Now a key text for anyone studying the nineteenth century, Albert's speech brought together the great movements of the time and blended the forces of the old with those of the new.[6] Education, science, religion, free trade, national pride, cosmopolitanism, and pacifism were all woven into one to produce a new, all-encompassing theory of historical progress. Albert enjoined his listeners to put themselves at the vanguard of this movement, just as Karl Marx had done in a different sense three years previously.

Albert's themes were then recapitulated. The next speaker, the Archbishop of Canterbury, pointed out that

> whilst we are ministers of religion we are at the same time citizens, and we do not cease to be patriots (cheers); and as citizens and as patriots we take a lively interest in whatever tends to promote the national prosperity . . . I rejoice in this the more because it will tend to carry into effect one of the most glorious characteristics of our holy religion—good will among men (loud cheers).

Other speakers included, significantly, the architect of free trade, Sir Robert Peel, the fervently patriotic (but commercially liberal) foreign secretary, Lord Palmerston, and the foreign diplomats.

The Mansion House banquet also marked the foundation of an identifiable Exhibition "movement," integrating a variety of interests and preoccupations and combining different arguments, themes, and symbols. The proceedings and speeches were reported and reproduced widely in the press and in pamphlet form. The liberal *Economist* viewed the banquet as "the most important meeting in connection with the progress of industry, the spread of healthy feeling and sound knowledge, the encouragement of kindliness, humanity, and brotherly love, that ever was held in the metropolis, or perhaps the world."[7]

Opposition to the Exhibition and its inclusive but modernizing program remained and even grew as the Exhibition movement came together. Protectionists, landed interests, aristocrats, and radical socialists began to coalesce and even, in an act of supreme irony, to organize their own banquets. In June

1850 this opposition reached a peak, with a looming vote in Parliament about the proposed site of the Exhibition in Hyde Park threatening to throw the whole project off course.

When Sir Robert Peel was killed unexpectedly at the end of June in a riding accident, parliamentary opposition was blunted. Albert, however, was quick to perceive the national mood of shock and possibly remorse among Peel's opponents. He began selling the Exhibition as Peel's project at the follow-up to the Mansion House banquet held in York on October 25, 1850. Here Albert thrilled the country with a speech on the merits of the Exhibition. But he also spoke of "the one alloy to my feelings of satisfaction and pleasure . . . the painful remembrance that one is missing from amongst us who felt so warm an interest in our scheme, and took so active a part in promoting its success; the last act of whose public life was attending at the Royal Commission." The press responded. The *Illustrated London News* compared Albert's fight for the Exhibition with Peel's for free trade. Albert's tribute to Peel, it judged, "was well-earned, and is justly due; and though it reach not 'the dull cold ear of death,' will fructify in the minds of the living, and cheer the rising generation of statesmen in the arduous and too often thankless career which lies before them."[8] In Peel, the Exhibition had a martyr. Albert, meanwhile, was his anointed apostle.

The press warmed to Albert for the first time: forgiving him his idealism, his secondary position to the Queen, and even his German background. This was not only due to his adoption of Peel's mantle. The *Morning Chronicle* noted that the York banquet reversed old traditions of royal relations with the provinces. "He comes to it," the paper noted, "not at second-hand from the mansion of some neighboring landed lord, but direct from the presence of the sovereign herself, prepared to express as from her own royal mouth the interest she feels in the trade and industry of all her people."[9] Royal attendance at regional public events, it was quickly appreciated, exhilarated the country. The tradition of public visits by monarchs to the provinces dates from this point. The *Illustrated London News* expressed Albert's rising popularity as a result of his association with the Exhibition. "At every successive appearance of His Royal Highness before the public," it said, "he has exhibited qualities which the English people know thoroughly how to appreciate."[10]

The positive experience of these tentative royal forays, a desire to maintain public support, and the realization that the monarchy was good for the Exhibition and vice versa supported the decision to hold a public opening ceremony for the Great Exhibition. As the Exhibition approached, the newspapers learned that only a private tour of the building was intended.[11] A furor erupted. As the *Daily News*—crucially, a popular liberal paper—put it: "A more impolitic, a more absurd, or a more ludicrous resolution the Commissioners could not have come to."[12] Looking back, it is easy to underestimate the novelty and the dangers of a public royal occasion, however. Nothing like it had been attempted before. Assassination attempts on monarchs were frequent. Moreover, it was planned that some 25,000 season-ticket holders should enter the building on May 1. The decision to proceed with a public ceremony was so important that Russell—the Prime Minister—was consulted. Ultimately, however, it was Albert and Victoria who took the brave decision to appear before the public. This momentous act rested, however, upon experience of the banquets, a fear of the consequences should there *not* be a public opening, but also, the prospect of promoting both the Exhibition and the monarchy.

ANALYZING THE OPENING CEREMONY

The decision to have a public opening just one week before the Exhibition was due to begin produced a sudden rush to construct a ceremony. The decision that Victoria should not travel to the Exhibition in her state coach was taken quickly (Russell believing this would demean other state ceremonies).[13] Albert only now approached the Archbishop of Canterbury, believing "that the blessing of Almighty God should be invoked upon the undertaking in a short prayer."[14] Cole appears to have produced at this point the idea that Albert should present Victoria with a report on the Royal Commission's progress. A musical dimension to the opening was hurriedly arranged.

The fact that the opening ceremony drew on the experience of preceding months is obvious. The intermingling of the courtly with the industrial and modern began then. So did the involvement of the Church. That Victoria should not only appear before her own subjects, but before the massed diplomatic corps, was an adaptation of mayoral banquets, though it proved rather a radical one. Diplomats revolted—partly goaded on by autocratic Austria and Russia as a protest against liberal Britain—but also revealing a fault line between the cosmopolitan agenda of the Exhibition and prevailing nationalist perspectives.

The Exhibition's organizers and participants also exploited much older traditions. A throne—admittedly donated by the East India Company—was placed on a dais in the arched transept of the Exhibition. Victoria was to be seated upon it, surrounded by her own, and foreign, subjects. The similarity of this scene to the opening of Parliament or the Coronation was obvious. Meanwhile, despite Russell's worries about the coach, it was essentially agreed that the opening of the Exhibition should be a state one. Victoria and Albert were to travel to the Crystal Palace in open-top coaches followed by foreign royalty, on public display. The national anthem was to be played on their arrival. All were to wear court dress—a stipulation to which only the radical likes of Richard Cobden objected.[15] At the end of the ceremony, Victoria was to declare the Exhibition open, and guns were to be fired in military salute from St. James's Park. The National Anthem was then to be played again by the bands of the Scotch Fusilier and Coldstream Guards.

The religious dimension also drew on ancient rites. Once a prayer had been agreed on, the setting of the transept and the presence of the Queen encouraged the trappings of a national church service. Organ and choir music played, using organists and choirs from St. Paul's Cathedral, Westminster Abbey, the Chapel Royal, St. George's, Windsor, the Royal Academy of Music, and the Sacred Harmonic Society. The choice of the "Hallelujah Chorus" from Handel's *Messiah*, to be sung after the Archbishop of Canterbury's prayer, was significant. The oratorio, a blend of religious and secular tradition, extended ancient church traditions to this display of mammon.

Yet in many respects the opening ceremony was novel. When Victoria and Albert entered the building through its north entrance, they were entering a structure (constructed only months before), which architecturally was positively revolutionary. The Exhibition was housed in the Crystal Palace, a building constructed especially for it in Hyde Park, London. Again, buildings up to this time had mainly been built out of stone or wood. The Crystal Palace, however, was a celebration of the latest technology in architecture. It was constructed from mass-produced metal parts and glass. There was a practical side to this. People were still unsure at the beginning how large the Exhibition would turn out to be, so building out of regular parts meant the Crystal Palace could be as large or as small as required. Yet most people viewed the building as fantastical and almost dreamlike. Nothing that large had ever been constructed before in such a short space of time (six months). Glass had been a scarce commodity and highly taxed until recently, so the Crystal Palace expressed opulence and great wealth. There was also something obviously monumental about it. It was 1,851 feet long, and at its center there was an arched transept, giving it a cathedral-like atmosphere. Inside, the visitor was greeted by full-grown elms, which had simply been covered over by the building, the sound and smell of perfumed fountains, and yellow and blue columns which faded into a blue horizon as they led off into the distance.

The gathering within the Crystal Palace combined old and new. Alongside figures of the political establishment at the opening ceremony were the aristocratic courtiers of old, leaders of industry, and the representatives of the countries of the world. Beyond them were the 25,000 or so season-ticket holders allowed into the building to witness the spectacle.

Essentially, older ceremonial tradition was being stretched to embrace a new, modern, industrial scenario. The embodiment of this was the procession formed to tour the building—a type of royal inspection of the Exhibition—before Victoria declared it open. Royal Heralds headed it. After that came the Crystal Palace's architect and contractors; Superintendents of Works; Financial Officers of the Royal Commission; the Building and Financial Committees of the Royal Commission; its Executive Committee; Foreign Commissioners; Secretaries to the Royal Commission, the Royal Commission; Victoria's Master of Ceremonies; Foreign Ambassadors; members of the British Government; the Bishop of London; the Archbishop of Canterbury; White Wands (the Comptroller of the Royal Household); the Vice-Chamberlain; the royal party (including Victoria's immediate family); the Prince and Princess of Prussia; the Duchess of Kent; Prince Henry of the Netherlands; Prince Edward of Saxe-Weimar; Gold Stick in Waiting; Master of the Horse; Groom of the Stole; Captain of the Gentleman at Arms; and so on. Never before had there been such a procession fusing royalty, aristocracy, religion, industry, and international representatives into one moving mass.

FORGING A MODERN CONSENSUS: THE RECEPTION OF THE OPENING CEREMONY

The opening ceremony of the Great Exhibition is a familiar subject in British history. Many aspects of it—royalty mingling with the public and the industrial elite—have become accepted, everyday practice. The startling mixture of old ceremonial tradition with new situations no longer strikes us. Yet at the time they caused public indignation. The protectionist newspaper, *John Bull*, representing a group pushed aside by the Exhibition's organizers, was one of the commentators to take exception. Prior to the opening it had already deemed the religious aspects of it "wholly inadmissible . . . Our Church is not, and we trust never will be, given to undertake a part in public shows and festivities. The sobriety of her solemn ritual is reserved for solemn occasions."[16] Finding it hard to admit the success of the event, it grumbled that the reception of Victoria "was not altogether as enthusiastic as on other occasions; a circumstance which the free trade journals attribute to the disappointment of the crowd because the Queen did not ride in a state coach." It went on: "We warn the Free Traders not to try the patience of the English people too hard, lest they provoke to animosity and disgust those who are at present disposed to treat a questionable undertaking with forbearance."

Among aristocrats and monarchists there was also a good deal of nervousness and concern about the possible fate awaiting Victoria and Albert at the Crystal Palace. Frederick William IV of Prussia tried to forbid his brother attending, for fear of assassination. Queen Victoria's mother "felt so nervous and anxious,"[17] while Lady Lyttelton admitted later to Victoria, "I own I was not without anxiety—and was visited by many fears & doubts."[18]

Most opponents of the Exhibition appear to have been silenced by the ceremony's success, however. The goal of the Royal Commission to make the opening ceremony inclusive, and the demonstration of social unity and harmony between old and new produced elation. Russell congratulated Prince Albert on "the triumphant success of the proceedings of this day . . . the general conduct of the multitudes assembled, the loyalty & the content which so generally appeared."[19] Lord Carlisle noted that "the immense, orderly, pleased masses without, were as striking as all the rest."[20]

As hoped, the Exhibition ceremony was a major boost to the fortunes of the monarchy. None other than Lord Palmerston, Victoria and Albert's political foe, felt moved to congratulate them on "a day the result of which must be no less gratifying to Your Majesty, than honorable to the nation whose good fortune it is to have Your Majesty for its sovereign."[21] Equally, it served its purpose in strengthening public support for free trade and the morale of the government in the face of protectionists led by Lord Stanley. The likelihood of Russell's resignation began to diminish from May first onwards.

The social harmony constructed at the opening ceremony rested on a symbolic acceptance by the monarch of industry—a dimension not lost on many foreign observers. King Leopold of Belgium, one of Albert's political mentors, wrote to Victoria, "I am glad that foreigners saw for once, that to the highest authority in the state even a great and free country like England may show real and great respect."[22] Lord Abercromby, British Minister in Turin, wrote to Lord Palmerston, "The British nation has practically shown on the occasion of the opening of the Exhibition what are the results of truly liberal institutions, of a reliance on the justice and power of the law, and of a respectful obedience to it."[23] As *Punch* incisively noted:

> It was a magnificent lesson for foreigners . . . to see how securely and confidently a young female Sovereign and her family could walk in the closest possible contact, near enough to be touched by almost everyone, with five-and-twenty thousand people, selected from no class, and requiring only the sum of forty-two shillings as a qualification for the nearest proximity with royalty.[24]

Not every aspect of the ceremony was the result of planning. Many commentators reported the appearance of the Duke of Wellington at the ceremony and the applause that greeted him. It seems a widespread necessity to incorporate such national institutions into the ceremony expressed itself here and produced a spontaneous ceremonial innovation at the group level. Another, more humorous, example of this was the Chinese ambassador, who threw himself at Victoria's feet and then was given pride of place in the subsequent procession around the building. It later turned out he was an impostor, a Chinese man at the Exhibition to advertise the presence of another major tourist attraction in London, the Chinese Junk on the Thames. But he was accepted and accommodated into proceedings on the back of the public's cosmopolitan sympathies.

Newspapers reflected surprise at the sense of a new era, a millennial occasion, and a new chapter in history generated by the opening. Many (even those such as *John Bull* and the *Times* previously critical of the event) responded by beginning serialized histories of its development. A large number of commentators, apparently coincidentally, spoke of the opening as a "fairy-tale." Meanwhile, a veritable flood of poetry on the subject was now produced. Was it the relief of the public that social division in Britain had been averted that produced this sudden outpouring of symbolical commentary? Or was it simply that the Great Exhibition had managed, through its rhetoric, symbolism, and ceremony, to tap in to some of the most powerful movements of the age? The *Times* reported, "May-day witnessed a sight the like of which has never happened before, and which, in the nature of things, can never be repeated. They who were so fortunate as to see it hardly knew what most to admire, or in what form to clothe the sense of wonder, and even of mystery, which struggled within them." It went on, "Some saw in it the second and more glorious inauguration of their Sovereign; some a solemn dedication of art and its stores; some were most reminded of that day when all ages and climes shall be gathered round the throne of their Maker; there was so much that seemed accidental and yet had a meaning, that no one could be content with simply what he saw."[25]

THE IMPORTANCE OF CEREMONY: THE LEGACY OF THE GREAT EXHIBITION

Nearly everyone recognized that something quite special had happened on May first, and almost immediately efforts were made to try and repeat it. Organizers borrowed heavily from the opening ceremony's arrangements for a *fete* in Birmingham in June, held in honor of foreign commissioners, and again at the closing ceremony of the Exhibition on October 15, 1851. Throughout the summer of 1851, plays, concerts, music-hall routines, and poems recreated aspects of the event. The opening of the rebuilt Crystal Palace in Sydenham, south London, in 1853 was not just marked by a ceremony similar in construction to that in 1851. It also created an arena perpetuating aspects of the ceremony, used for choral concerts and Handel festivals, and forming the springboard for the Victorian revival of oratorios.

Albert had succeeded in reviving the fortunes of the monarchy. It was no accident that President Louis Napoleon of France—soon Emperor Napoleon III—arranged a *fete* in Paris in August 1851 and tried to persuade Albert to travel there. Napoleon's efforts to siphon off the glory of the ceremony also produced the Paris International Exhibition of 1854. Generally, monarchs and governments in other countries absorbed the lesson of the opening ceremony. Henceforth, monarchs would feel less timorous about public appearances or associating themselves with the industrial classes.

The incandescence of the opening ceremony had burnt the symbols, associations, and rhetoric of the Exhibition movement on the public mind. The Exhibition had also brought into being a politically significant alliance of enlightened aristocrats, liberals, industrialists, reformers, and others, and a system of thought Albert had so succinctly expressed at his Mansion House speech in 1850. From 1851 Albert's status soared, and after his death there developed a veritable Albert cult. It is no accident that this cult, embodied in the great Albert memorial in Hyde Park, revolved around the icons and themes of the Exhibition.

Between 1851 and 1861, Albert and Victoria rode on the crest of a wave of popularity. Much of this stemmed from the fact that, through extending old ceremonial traditions to new settings, they had managed to associate the monarchy with the modernizing forces of liberalism, industry, and the middle classes. With Albert's death, the possibility of using royal ceremony to validate and promote new developments admittedly then receded. However, it is very likely that the experience of the public response to the royal opening of the Great Exhibition inspired Disraeli's decision to name Victoria as Empress of India in 1877. Disraeli, as a protectionist, had been on the sharp end of the Great Exhibition's popular success. He had witnessed the effect on the public of seeing Victoria "crowned" before the world at the opening ceremony and had learned from it. In the late 1870s, imperialism was supported by an increasing number of interests. By associating Victoria with it, Disraeli was once again extending the monarchy's support base and strengthening his own government. At the same time he was lending imperialists an official seal of approval.

There was another connection between the ceremonial of the Exhibition and imperialism, however. The Exhibition movement had involved many who believed that Britain had a moral and even religious duty to promote progress abroad and that its economic policies and political liberalism ought to be propagated. The Exhibition and the symbolism associated with it had presented a picture of the world where Britain led other countries and where colonialism was seen as Britain's moral right. In having Victoria crowned as Empress, Disraeli was attempting to pick up the movement once more. It turned out to be another successful innovation. There would be a strong similarity between the ideology of imperialism in Britain towards the end of the nineteenth century and that which had supported the Exhibition and shaped its opening ceremony.

SUGGESTED READINGS

Though there was great interest at the time of the Great Exhibition in its historical significance, it was not really until after the Festival of Britain in 1951 that academic research into the subject began. It was against the background of that event that works were produced such as Yvonne Ffrench, *The Great Exhibition, 1851* (London, 1950); Kenneth Luckhurst, *The Story of Exhibitions* (London, 1951); and Nikolaus Pevsner, *High Victorian Design: A Study of the Exhibits of 1851* (London, 1951). Even for a long time after this, accounts were generally uncritical and simply noted the Exhibition as one of the most impressive Victorian achievements without really explaining why. This was even the case with detailed works such as Richard Altick, *The Shows of London* (London, 1978) and Eric de Maré, *London, 1851: The Year of the Great Exhibition* (London, 1972). The Exhibition was still generally treated as an honored piece of national heritage. From the 1960s onwards, with the rise of more critical histories of capitalism and modernism, the Exhibition began to be viewed, however, as a symbol of hypocrisy, where the contradictions of the Victorian period and the polarities of wealth and poverty were on display for all to see. Gradually, this seems to have produced a more positive appreciation of the Exhibition's significance within the process of modernization in Britain. Exhibitions in general have begun to be seen as important phenomena culturally and economically as seen in David Gelernter, *1939: The Lost World of the Fair* (New York, 1995); John Findling, *Historical Dictionary of World Fairs* (New York, 1990); Johannes Huynen, *Trends in Trade Fairs* (Utrecht, 1973); and Werner Plum, *World Exhibitions in the Nineteenth Century: Pageants of Social and Cultural Change* (Bonn, 1977). There has been a more sympathetic treatment of the Victorians in the last thirty years or so. Asa Briggs led the way in reviving a positive appreciation of them and directed his focus to the Great Exhibition in chapter 2 of his *Victorian Things* (London, 1988). The Open University's Arts Foundation Course was also important in focusing attention on both the Victorians and the Exhibition, in particular through J. M. Golby's *Culture and Society in Britain, 1850–1890* (Oxford, 1986). The event, it has begun to be argued, helped bring together the ancient elites and traditions with new modes of production and the social classes produced by it. This is the thrust of both Jeffrey Auerbach, *The Great Exhibition of 1851: A Nation on Display* (New Haven, 1999) and John R. Davis, *The Great Exhibition* (Stroud, 1999). The Victorians' achievements in meeting the challenges of great economic and social change has begun to be respected, and the similarity of their predicament with our own is acknowledged. With this in mind, more research is now being done on focused aspects of the Great Exhibition, such as in Franz Bosbach and John R. Davis, ed.,*The Great Exhibition of 1851* (Munich, 2003) and Louise Purbrick, ed., *The Great Exhibition of 1851: New Interdisciplinary Essays* (Manchester, 2001).

NOTES

1. July 14, 1849, Minutes of a Meeting at Osborne House, John Scott Russell Papers, Volume 1, Royal Society of Arts (hereinafter RSA).

2. September 10, 1849, Cole to Colonel Phipps, Letters, Volume I, 1849, Royal Archives, held at the Archives of the Royal Commission of 1851.

3. October 1849, Report made to HRH Prince Albert . . . of preliminary inquiries into the willingness of Manufacturers and others to support periodical Exhibitions of the Works of Industry of all Nations, Volume I, Earliest Proceedings, John Scott Russell Papers, RSA.

4. Appendix 4, January 18, 1850, Royal Commission Minutes, Archives of the Royal Commission of 1851.

5. March 21, 1850, Grand Banquet to HRH Prince Albert at the Mansion House, London, in Honour of the Exhibition of 1851, Volume II, Earliest Proceedings, John Scott Russell Papers, RSA.

6. Full text in J. M. Golby, ed., *Culture and Society in Britain, 1850–1890* (Oxford: Open University Press, 1986), 1.

7. [undated] Document 15, Leaders from *John Bull*, the *Economist*, and the *Spectator*, Letters, Volume I, Royal Archives held at the Archive of the Royal Commission of 1851.

8. *Illustrated London News*, November 2, 1850.

9. *Morning Chronicle*, November 2, 1850.

10. *Illustrated London News*, October 28, 1850.

11. Perhaps after a leak by Cole: Henry Cole Diaries, National Art Library.

12. *Daily News*, April 17, 1851.

13. April 19, 1851, Lord John Russell to Prince Albert, F24, Royal Archives, Windsor.

14. April 22, 1851, Prince Albert to the Archbishop of Canterbury, F24, Royal Archives, Windsor.

15. April 27, 1851, Henry Cole Dairies, National Art Library.

16. [undated], Document 1, Letters, Volume VII, Royal Archives held at the Archive of the Royal Commission of 1851.

17. May 1, 1851, Duchess of Kent to Queen Victoria, F24, Royal Archives, Windsor.

18. May 3, 1851, Lady Lyttelton to Queen Victoria, F24, Royal Archives, Windsor.

19. May 2, 1851, Lord John Russell to Prince Albert, F24, Royal Archives, Windsor.
20. May 1, 1851, Lord Carlisle's Journal, Z.166, Royal Archives, Windsor.
21. May 2, 1851, Lord Palmerston to Prince Albert, F24, Royal Archives, Windsor.
22. May 5, 1851, King Leopold to Queen Victoria, F24, Royal Archives, Windsor.
23. May 10, 1851, Abercromby to Palmerston, F24, Royal Archives, Windsor.
24. *Punch*, 20 (1851), 190.
25. *Times*, May 1 and 2, 1851.

Chapter Eight

The Indian Rebellion of 1857: A Crisis in British Imperial Consciousness

David Savage

On the morning of June 9, 1857, alert readers of the morning papers in London would have seen a notice that some native soldiers (sepoys) in a garrison town in northern India had mutinied against their British officers. The soldiers had refused to bite the bullets used in their drill because they believed them to be covered with pig or cow grease. The incident had occurred in Meerut one month earlier on May 10. This was a major bit of bad news arriving by the quickest communication link between India and the imperial capital. Word of the mutiny had traveled by telegraph from Meerut to Agra to Bombay just before the rebels cut the wire. The news reached Bombay in time to be put on the next boat to Europe. When the India Mail arrived in Marseilles in the south of France after a voyage into the Red Sea, overland to Suez, and another voyage across the Mediterranean, telegraph lines again carried the message to London. English readers did not yet realize that they were distant witnesses to events that, as they unfolded, would produce a deep crisis in the consciousness of the British people about their own identity and their place in the world.

REBELLION IN INDIA

The news from India appearing in the British press was always a month or more behind events. Brief telegraphic summaries arrived first, followed sometimes weeks later by written official dispatches, private letters, English-language Indian newspaper accounts, and reports from a few correspondents

111

retained by the major London dailies. These reports began to pour in so that by midsummer the British public and politicians alike knew that they had a major crisis on their hands. Having burned the officers' bungalows in the cantonment at Meerut and killed many officers and their wives, the rebel troops had marched to Delhi where the sepoy garrison in that ancient city joined them. There they made an aging, powerless, and reluctant Mughal emperor symbolic head of the revolt. Within three weeks, garrison after garrison of troops across north and central India joined the revolt. In areas where British military rule collapsed, the sepoys were joined by large numbers of civilians who acted from a wide variety of motives. Heads of pre-British dynasties and landed notables who had lost ground under recent British land settlements assumed leadership of the revolt in areas where large numbers of rural peasants had joined the sepoys. Hindu and Muslim religious leaders called on their followers to defend their faiths against attempts by Christian missionaries and evangelical British officials to convert them. By mid-July much of north India in a swath from Delhi to Patna was under rebel control. Hundreds of European men, women, and children had been killed, and those remaining cowered in fortresses and fortified places in the principal towns.

India constituted the most populous and rich of Britain's imperial possessions. Domination of the Indian subcontinent had only recently been completed with annexation of Sind (1843) and the Sikh kingdom of the Punjab (1849), ending a period of conquest that had begun in the mid-eighteenth century. By the 1850s India was secured by a composite army of some 45,000 European and 230,000 Indian troops organized into three commands— Bombay, Madras, and Calcutta. The sepoy regiments that mutinied in 1857 were part of the Bengal Army headquartered in Calcutta.

CONTAINING THE REBELLION

The British press and Members of Parliament were nearly unanimous in demanding prompt military action to put down the revolt. This was the period of Britain's unchallenged industrial and naval supremacy, and the public had no reason to doubt the nation's ability to handle any challenge. The British public was accustomed to stories of soldiers and naval squadrons around the far-flung empire suppressing tribal revolts, expanding imperial territory into troublesome frontiers, and providing the coercive power that ensured the Pax Britannica. Furthermore, Britain and her French and Austrian allies had just completed a successful war against Russia in the Crimea. At this pinnacle of patriotic pride the British public expected a quick resolution of the revolt in India.

By good fortune a contingent of British troops, just completing a mission in Persia, was available for immediate dispatch to Calcutta under Brigadier-General Henry Havelock. They joined the British troops in Bengal and were reinforced during the spring and summer by officers and men from home, raising the non-Indian personnel in the Bengal Army from twenty-four thousand to over seventy thousand. A column of British troops marched westward from Calcutta under Colonel James Neill to be joined later by Havelock's troops while sections of the Bengal Army comprising British officers and Sikh soldiers stationed in the Punjab moved into the area of rebel control around Delhi.

BRITISH PUBLIC REACTION

The British public was told by the government that all would soon be restored to order. The *Times* on June 27 carried a telegraphic message received from Marseilles saying, "A force is marching sufficient to overwhelm the mutineers in every quarter. Oude [Oudh] is tranquil." Even with that the public was not easily reassured. The *Times* leader on the same day called for "action—sharp, stern, and decisive. An Imperial interest is at stake—nothing less than our dominion in British India."[1] The press continued full of alarm and patriotic posturing. The *Illustrated London News* on July 4, even before news of the spread of rebellion beyond Meerut and Delhi had reached Britain, wrote:

> Our house in India is on fire. We are not insured. To lose that house would be to lose power, prestige, and character—to descend in the rank of nations, and take a position more in accordance with our size on the map of Europe than with the greatness of our past glory and present ambition.[2]

Britons tended to see themselves not only as preeminent in military, industrial, and commercial strength but also as morally superior to their rivals. Patriotic sentiments of the kind quoted above were predicated on the assumption that Britain's role in the world was to lead the European advance of civilization itself. This sense of moral superiority was a rich amalgam of rationalist ideas of progress, free trade capitalism, and Christian providentialism. Moralists in the first half of the nineteenth century had accommodated their sentiments to individual enterprise and a national policy of free trade. The former promised personal advancement and the latter national leadership in a peaceful league of commercial trading partners. The British empire of the first part of the nineteenth century was an empire of free trade—the result of an ever-expanding search for markets and the use of force to secure them when peaceful means of persuasion failed. Freed from the impediment of backward governments, peoples in all parts of the world would surely aspire to join in this forward march of civilization.

The British sense of moral superiority was usually expressed in a decidedly Protestant Christian idiom with a litany of providentially guided accomplishments. At the insistence of evangelical Christians the British government had ended the slave trade in 1809 and abolished slavery from all parts of the empire in 1833. A crusade to suppress barbarous practices in other parts of the world attended the expansion of commercial markets. British naval patrols intercepted slavers of other nations in the Atlantic and Indian Oceans. At the beginning of the century the Anglican Church and other Protestant denominations established societies to send missionaries into an expanding empire opening the way for the spread of the Gospel. Little stood in the way of advancing Christian civilization. Indeed, it seemed that God had chosen the British to be the primary instrument for the spread of enlightenment and civilization to the rest of the world.

When it came to India the British public had every expectation that the powerful modernizing forces emanating from the West would dissolve old ways and remold Indian society. For instance, the British public was both attracted and repelled by the barbaric rite of sati, a practice in which a widow threw herself on the funeral pyre of her deceased husband. In 1829 the government overcame their reluctance to interfere with native social and religious customs and abolished sati. In the 1830s British rulers embraced the responsibility to enlighten the natives through the introduction of higher education in the English language. Thomas Babington Macaulay famously argued that English education would produce a class of Indians educated in English ways, "who may be interpreters between us and the millions whom we govern—a class of persons Indian in colour and blood, but English in tastes, in opinions, in morals, and in intellect."[3]

From the 1830s until the governor-generalship of Lord Dalhousie in the 1850s, a reformation of Indian administration was undertaken to bring it closer to British ways. Land and tax systems were overhauled; civil laws were codified; railroads and telegraph lines were laid, and new territories annexed—most fatefully the kingdom of Oudh in the central Gangetic plain in 1856. Above all, the British Raj had brought peace and order to the entire subcontinent. Even imperial governors who were nervous about the wisdom of moving too rapidly to reform Indian society were able to embrace the imperial purpose of bringing good government to the people they ruled. In the 1850s there were few critics of British hegemony in the East. There was certainly little sense at home of the power of ethnic or religious loyalties to resist the onrush of progress and civilization. From the perspective of 1850 it seemed that British dominance was both natural and providential. There had been struggle and resistance in the past, but from mid-century it seemed that the empire in India rested on the acceptance, if not active collaboration, of the native population. When a large portion of her Indian subjects rose in rebellion, Britons felt betrayed.

ATROCITIES AND CALLS FOR REVENGE

What turned the Indian Rebellion of 1857 into much more than a setback for the British military and a deep sense of betrayed trust were the events of the summer of 1857. In June and July the recently annexed kingdom of Oudh with its principal cities of Kanpur (Cawnpore) and Lucknow rose in revolt, and a rebel leader emerged in the person of Nana Sahib. In Lucknow the white inhabitants and many of their servants built entrenchments around the British residency and waited for rescue. In Kanpur some nine hundred European men, women, and children fortified themselves in an entrenchment hastily built for the purpose. Meanwhile, Colonel Neill marched upriver, taking terrible revenge on inhabitants in his path. On June 27 Nana Sahib offered safe passage downriver to Allahabad in exchange for the surrender of the Kanpur garrison. Some 450 persons walked out of their entrenchments to the banks of the river and began to board the boats waiting there. Guns then fired from both banks, and the boats were set on fire. All but 130 were killed: a few escaped and the rest were taken prisoner. The women and children who survived were rounded up and imprisoned in the Bibighar, a house built for the Indian ladies of a former British officer. On July 16 just prior to the arrival of Havelock's relief column, the women and children held in the Bibighar were murdered, and their bodies thrown into a nearby well.

The British reading public began to be inundated with graphic accounts of Indian atrocities and British countermeasures. Unapologetically the *Times* printed a letter from an artillery officer in Peshawar.

> We had a night alarm a short time since. I awoke and heard 'boom.' 'boom,' hearing guns fired (for so it seemed) at regular intervals from the fort, we thought the city had risen. . . . This was caused by the explosion of little mines in the city in honour of a wedding. Well, next morning the persons concerned and those who worked at the mines were tied up and received such a flogging as they will not easily forget. In these times of danger and treachery we don't bother ourselves about the quirks of law, but hang, shoot, or flog as the circumstances arise. We stand no nonsense here. The General swears he will maintain discipline.[4]

Even before the massacre at Kanpur, brutal revenge was being exacted by Colonel James Neill marching with his column westward toward Oudh.

Graphic accounts of British atrocities were not kept from the reading public. The *Daily News* reported "every native that appeared in sight was shot down without question. In the morning Colonel Neill set out parties of his regiment . . . and burned all the villages near where the ruins of our bungalows stood, and hung every native that they could catch, on trees that lined the road."[5]

News of the Kanpur massacre did not reach Britain until late August. Anxiously awaiting news of Havelock's relief of Kanpur and Lucknow, the public instead heard of defeat and massacre. At first the public had to piece together what had happened from brief telegraph messages sent when ships reached Mediterranean ports. Then detailed accounts arrived. These were occasionally written by eyewitnesses. More often they were based on wildly exaggerated rumors that circulated among the British-Indian community and were printed in the Bombay or Calcutta newspapers. Whatever negative reaction there might have been from early accounts of the brutal behavior of British forces was wiped out by the horror of Kanpur. The well at Kanpur became the emblem of Indian fiendishness and depravity.

> The history of the world affords no parallel to the terrible massacres which during the last few months have desolated the land. Neither age, sex nor condition has been spared. Children have been compelled to eat the quivering flesh of their murdered parents, after which they were literally *torn asunder* by the laughing fiends who surrounded them. Men in many instances have been mutilated and, before being absolutely killed, have had to gaze upon the last dishonour of their wives and daughters previous to being put to death.[6]

THE UNSPEAKABLE CRIME OF RAPE

An elaborate myth constructed of rumor and sexual fantasy began to take shape. Stories that the *Times* called "too foul for publication" hinted at the unspeakable crime of rape. A missionary writing from Calcutta after the news of the surrender of the garrison at Cawnpore to Nana Sahib, reported that the rebel leader "has made prisoners 25 to 30 English Ladies who are now kept forcibly by the wretch for the basest of purposes!!!—But my pen refuses to proceed."[7] Exemplary Victorian ladies became the symbolic victims of the entire native uprising. Even private correspondence from the time reveals the depth of horror Britons felt from the reports they read in the press. "I can think of nothing but these Indian massacres. . . . I can hardly bear to look at a woman or child—even my own beloved ones sometimes. It raises such horrible images, from which I can't escape. What does it all mean?"[8] There is little doubt that this sexualization of the narrative of the rebellion sanctioned the use of force and violence in repressing the rebellion. Civilization itself became gendered. British soldiers became the avengers of Victorian woman-hood.[9]

Kanpur was turned over to Colonel Neill, newly promoted to the rank of brigadier general, as Havelock moved on to the relief of Lucknow. Neill was seen by many to be the ideal instrument of divinely sanctioned punishment. A prominent missionary and fellow Scottish countryman wrote of Neill: "His Scottish Bible-training had taught him that justice was as absolute an attribute of Deity as mercy, and that magistracy was an ordinance of God designed to be a terror to evildoers."[10] Neill ordered that all suspected of complicity in the massacres

> be selected according to their rank, caste, and degree of guilt. Each miscreant, after sentence of death is pronounced upon him, will be taken down to the house in question [the Bibighar], under a guard, and will be forced into cleaning up a small portion of the blood-stains; the task will be made as revolting to his feelings as possible, and the Provost-Marshall will use the lash in forcing any one objecting to complete his task. After properly cleaning up his portion, the culprit is to be immediately hanged, and for this purpose a gallows will be erected close at hand.[11]

In order to insult both major religious communities, "All the Brahmins will be buried, and the Mohammedans burned."[12]

Reports of the measures taken, including descriptions of condemned prisoners being forced on their hands and knees to lick up the bloodstains around the Bibighar, began to appear in the British press. "We stuffed pork, beef and everything which could possible break his caste down his throat," wrote one soldier, and "tied him as tight as we could by the arms and told the guard to be *gentle* with him. . . . The guard treated him *gently*. I only wonder he lived to be hung which I had the pleasure of witnessing."[13]

Most captured rebels were summarily shot or hung. However, in areas where some order had been restored, more deliberate methods of execution and counterterror were employed. The whole garrison of Peshawar was called out to the execution ground, forming three sides of a square, to witness victims being blown from the muzzle of guns. An officer who carried out such an execution wrote:

> The first man led out was a fine looking young sepoy. . . . I had his wrists tied tightly, each to the upper part of a wheel of the gun. Then I depressed the muzzle, until it pointed to the pit of his stomach, just below the *sternum*. . . . Then I ordered the pot-fire to be lighted and gave the word 'Fire!' There was a considerable recoil from the gun, and a thick cloud of smoke hung over us. As this cleared away we saw two legs lying in the front of the gun. . . . From six to eight seconds after the explosion . . . down fell the man's head.[14]

There was scarcely a murmur of protest at these severe measures in Britain or among the British citizens in India. The well at Kanpur had made the press nearly unanimous for vengeance and stern retribution. The *Examiner* wrote, "It is satisfactory to learn that our troops have already exacted some retribution; but it is devoutly to be hoped that a more terrible measure of vengeance is in store for these human devils, and especially for Nena himself, whose barbarities are as revolting as any recorded in Indian history."[15]

BRITISH MILITARY HEROES

The process of mythmaking produced gallant heroes as well as barbarous villains and virtuous victims. The prime figure to emerge was General Henry Havelock. A not particularly effective military leader by most subsequent accounts, General Havelock was nonetheless elevated in the popular imagination to the status of avenging hero. In many ways Havelock was the ideal Victorian hero. He "appears as a self-made man, product of the career open to talent, who typifies the virtue and authority of a middle class that believed its time had come."[16]

> The middle classes of this country may well be proud of such men as these, born and bred in their ranks—proud of such representatives, such reflections of their own best and most sterling characteristics—proud of men who were noble without high birth, without the pride of connexions, without a breath of fashion, and without a single drop of Norman blood in their veins.[17]

Stories also began to circulate affirming Havelock's place as a serious Christian. He was a Baptist, married to the daughter of Joshua Marshman, editor of *Friend of India*, an influential newspaper in Calcutta. He was said to have preached to prayer groups of converts among the rank and file of his soldiers and was notorious for his long-winded orations on the parade ground. One missionary, trying to absolve his kind from blame for causing the rebellion, told an audience: "Many taunts at first had been uttered against preaching colonels and Christian officers in India, but those scoffings had ceased now that it was known that General Havelock . . . was also a pious and God-serving Christian.[18] Havelock died of dysentery in January after he had led his army to the relief of Lucknow. Even though the city had to be retaken a second time, Havelock's victories assured him a place in the annals of British military heroism throughout the Victorian era. His statue erected by a grateful public still stands in Trafalgar Square in London.

A CRISIS OF CONSCIENCE

The Indian Rebellion of 1857 forced the British public to examine its Protestant conscience about the nation's role as an imperial power. There were a few public voices of dissent concerning the harsh measures being taken to repress the rebellion,[19] a very few anti-imperial voices from the labor left,[20] and a few more who recoiled from the evangelical moral posturing that characterized so much public rhetoric,[21] but the events occurring in far-away India did nothing to shake the overwhelming belief that Britain was the preeminent civilizing force in the world. Yet that firm conviction made it all the more necessary for British Christians to examine their collective conscience to discover why things had gone so badly wrong. Nowhere was this self-critical attitude more in evidence than in the sermons preached on October 7, 1857.

That Sunday was declared by the Queen to be a Day of Fast, Humiliation, and Prayer. Nonconformists protested the principle of the state church calling the nation to prayer but fell in with the mood of the time and participated fully. The sermons preached that day and reproduced in newspapers and periodicals afterwards, assured Britons that their nation, as the most truly reformed nation, like Israel of old, was chosen and favored by God to be a light to all people. India was placed under British rule by God Himself so that "England's light might shine in India's darkness." Almost no clergymen doubted the essential justice of British rule in India. Yet Britain's failure to live up to her high calling as a chosen and favored people was the principal theme of the sermons on that day of national humiliation. Britain's failings were many, and preachers did not lose the opportunity to chastise her for drunkenness, adultery, the pandering of government to popery, and all of the sins of mammon. But the shortcoming most frequently cited that day was the failure of the nation in its duty to civilize and Christianize India. Some preachers pointed out that India had been gained by conquest and treachery, that greedy commercial interests conspired to keep Christian influence from offending the natives, that the national sin of the opium trade continued, and, closer to home, that the churches themselves had failed to supply the means for the conversion of India. For these sins the rebellion was a punishment and a warning. "If national judgments result from national sins, you and I must take our share. You and I helped to produce the massacre at Delhi—you and I to fill that hideous well at Cawnpore. National sin is but the aggregate of individual sin."[22] The atrocity stories that had circulated in the press for weeks were offered as proof of Britain's erroneous judgment in placing trust in unregenerated Indian character. Britain was fully justified in suppressing the rebellion and ruling India with increased military force. Indeed, clergymen saw the hand of providence at work in the fact that British troops were already on the way to China when the rebellion broke out and could be diverted to India, and that the Anglo-Persian war had ended just in time to release Major General Havelock for the deliverance of India.[23] Whatever their theological or ecclesiastical differences, the preachers, and presumably their listeners, were united in their understanding that the awful events in India were in some way of God's making, and, for that reason, full of significance and meaning. The tales of murder and rapine that had filled the news since June left none in doubt that God was on the side of British arms. Clerical prestige was placed firmly on the side of a ruthless repression and maintenance of the Raj. Clergymen of all denominations were certain that God still had work for Britain to perform in India.[24]

In this atmosphere of righteous indignation and moral certainty, the British missionary societies launched a campaign to atone for Britain's sins by undertaking with renewed determination the civilization and evangelization of India. They raised additional funds, sent out a new and enthusiastic cohort of missionaries and tried, but failed, to persuade the government to sanction the mandatory teaching of the Bible in Indian schools. They ran into obstacles from government officials worried that earlier attempts to change and reform Indian society had been a principal cause of the rebellion and fearing to cause any further offenses against native sensibilities, put a stop to the missionary crusade for Bible instruction. This was an early sign of a set of policies for governing India that were crafted in the immediate aftermath of the revolt and that set the tone for the remainder of the century.[25]

THE AFTERMATH OF REVOLT

Criticism of prerebellion policies led to the abolition of the East India Company and the assumption of direct rule by the British government. The Company Board of Control and Governor General in Calcutta were replaced by a secretary of state for India responsible to the British Cabinet and a viceroy in Calcutta appointed by the British government. The end of company rule gave symbolic recognition that India was a colony of conquest and was seen by many to be a challenge to the liberal idea of progress and reform that had prevailed in the first half of the century. The Indian army was reconstructed—increasing British forces by a third to sixty thousand and reducing the number of sepoys to one hundred twenty thousand. Separate native regiments were recruited locally so that they would form separate communities and not become a nascent national army. Within this army the British came to value the services of what they considered "martial races"—particularly the Sikhs of the Punjab who had helped suppress the rebellion in Delhi and the Gurkhas of Nepal. This was a practical move in the aftermath of revolt; it was also a reflection of a growing recognition of the importance of ethnic identity both as a matter of respect for native institutions and as a policy of dividing communities within India from each other—a policy of "divide and rule."[26]

There was no further annexation of territory. The many princely states that had not yet been annexed and brought under direct British administration were allowed to remain with their rajas and maharajas and native administration under the supervision of a British resident. Likewise there was to be no interference with the religion and customs of the natives—certainly no Bible instruction in government schools. This was made clear by a royal proclamation that was to guide policy in these sensitive cultural matters. The proclamation announced the Queen's reliance "on the truth of Christianity," yet disclaimed "alike the right and the desire to impose our convictions on any of our subjects. We declare it to be our royal will and pleasure that none be in anywise favoured, none molested or disquieted by reason of their religious faith or observances, but that all alike shall enjoy the equal and impartial protection of the law."[27]

In the aftermath of revolt a new respect for native customs, or at least a fear of offending native sensibilities, led to the creation of ethnic regiments in the army, the preservation of Princely States, and religious toleration. It did not, however, curtail the government's continued sponsorship of English-medium education in schools directly managed by the government and through grants-in-aid to missionary schools. The civilizing mission—bringing to the natives of India the best that British civilization could offer—continued unabated.

The British public did not soon forget the horrors of the rebellion, although they completely elided the counterterror of British troops. The "Mutiny," as it was almost always referred to, became a centerpiece of popular literature. Writers like Charles Dickens and Flora Annic Steel, and a host of lesser writers, produced more than fifty novels dealing with the Mutiny before the end of the century. The tropes of civilization versus savagery and masculine heroism in defense of innocent women and children that suffused this writing contributed to a hardening of racial attitudes in the general public and undoubtedly sanctioned the willingness to use force in the maintenance of British rule in India and elsewhere in the empire.

In important ways the extension of imperial rule over the peoples of Asia had always been predicated on notions of racial superiority, and there is little doubt that the fighting and killing during the Rebellion was conducted by both sides along a racial and cultural divide. In these circumstances the entire conflict could be seen in racial terms, and when it was, the racial characterizations could be breathtaking in their scope. The Scottish missionary, Alexander Duff, places the rebels squarely in the negative center of a common Orientalist stereotype.

> Throughout all ages the Asiatic has been noted for his duplicity, cunning, hypocrisy, treachery; and coupled with this . . . his capacity of secrecy and concealment. But in vain will the annals even of Asia be ransacked for examples of artful, refined, consummate duplicity, surpassing those which have been exhibited throughout the recent mutinies.[28]

The Rebellion hardened the lines of separation in India. Race determined status and position. As one reporter observed shortly after the rebellion, "At the gateway of the bridge there is a guardhouse, and Sikh sentries are on duty who examine all natives and force them to produce their passes; but on seeing my white face they present arms. My skin is the passport—it is a guarantee of my rank."[29] The next half-century saw a physical and cultural distancing as whites took to exclusive social clubs and spent the hot weather in hill stations where all natives except household servants were forbidden access. Observers noted a change of attitude among the white population in India. G. O. Trevelyan, after a tour of India in 1863, tried to defend an ancient Indian culture against the tendency of British-Indians to refer to the natives as "damned niggers." Yet he too perpetuated the standard stereotypes of racial character. He referred to the "want of stamina" and the "absence of energy among the inhabitants." "Honest, faithful performance you will expect from him in vain." He has "no notion of truth and falsehood." But Trevelyan, as a descendent of T. M. Macaulay, held on to the liberal faith in the power of education to transform even backward races. With time and training "the Hindoo is capable of speaking the truth, just as he is capable of reading Gibbon, wearing peg-top trousers, and drinking bottled ale."[30]

So contradictory attitudes persisted into the remainder of the century. One attitude was a holdover from an earlier, more naïve era—a liberal faith that all people given time and opportunity will grasp the value of self-improvement and will see the advantages of modern civilization. They may not convert to Christianity, but they will come more and more to value and imitate progressive British civilization. Such attitudes retained not a little bit of paternalism, and the idea of trusteeship—the idea that Britain had a moral obligation to train Indians and other less advanced peoples in the arts of civilization—became fixed in British liberal imperial consciousness. In the words of the *Saturday Review*, India must be ruled as "a great moral trust held by us for the civilization of the world."[31] This faith in the advancement of civilization was manifest in policies that continued to protect Christian missionary enterprise, foster growing numbers of educational institutions, and permitted the admission very gradually of educated natives into the ranks of the administrative apparatus of their own country.

Set off against these modernizing policies was a keen sense that the Indian native was a long way from being fit for self-governance. The British Raj came to rest on what one scholar has called "the illusion of permanence."[32] The Rebellion had given a clearer sense that empire was of necessity despotic—the only kind of governance that people at a lower level of civilization will respect. The Rebellion "will teach the English people a useful lesson," opined one London weekly, "We are justly proud of our own liberty, but rather too fond of imagining that a similar liberty is fit for all the nations of the earth. . . . India is not our colony, but our conquest."[33] The British Raj in the latter part of the nineteenth century was wrapped in a cloak of fabulous spectacle reinvented in imitation of Mughal splendor. Furthermore, despotic government became more professional and efficient. Developments in scientific statecraft required ever more precise knowledge of the mores, manners, and social stratification of the governed. Beginning with the first systematic census in 1851, new social sciences were developed: for example, anthropometry (racial classification by skull measurement), ethnography of caste, classifying castes as martial or criminal, and the like. These were accompanied later in the century by a trigonometric mapping of the entire subcontinent and by archaeological explorations and restorations of monuments from India's ancient past. Firm scientific administration satisfied the needs of British business and enterprise and was considered good for the natives as well, providing them with the best government they had ever had. British governors "knew" the natives they governed and knew best what they wanted and needed.

The Rebellion in India in 1857 was the most serious challenge to their imperial authority that the British people experienced in the nineteenth century. Given the incomplete modern revolution in communications, the anxiety and fear that ran through the British-Indian community took the form of exaggerated rumor, was distilled into an image of savagery and horror, and was transmitted to the British public at large. The ensuing national excitement had the effect of arousing a rather complacent public to keen interest in the exotic, if sometimes repulsive, lands of England's overseas enterprises and laying the political foundation for further imperial expansion later in the century. Modern media at home turned the Indian Rebellion into Britain's first popular colonial war.

SUGGESTED READINGS

Histories of the Indian Rebellion of 1857 differ in the name they apply even to itself. British historiography for a long time almost always referred to it as the "Mutiny." Indian nationalist historians for a time referred to it the first "Indian War of Independence." Most modern scholars now call it a rebellion or an uprising, denoting that it was much more than a mutiny of sepoy soldiers and something less than a fully national struggle. Good general accounts, almost entirely from the British perspective, are Christopher Hibbert, *The Great Mutiny: India, 1857* (London, 1978); Andrew Ward, *Our Bones Are Scattered: The Cawnpore Massacres and the Indian Mutiny of 1857* (New York, 1996); and Saul David, *The Indian Mutiny, 1857* (London, 2002). A balanced and scholarly account from the Indian perspective is Rudrangshu Mukherjee, *Awadh in Revolt, 1857–1858: A Study in Popular Resistance* (London, 2002). General assessments of the impact of the Indian Rebellion on British public perceptions and policy are found in many sources. Some of the most interesting are Francis Hutchins, *The Illusion of Permanence: British Imperialism in India* (Princeton, 1967); Thomas Metcalf, *Ideologies of the Raj* (Cambridge, 1995); and David Washbrook, "After the Mutiny: From Queen to Queen-Empress," *History Today* 47 (September 1997). Useful information on press coverage of events as well as the elevation of General Havelock to hero status is in Graham Dawson, *Soldier Heroes: British Adventure, Empire and the Imaginings of Masculinities* (London 1994). The question of violence and counterviolence is examined by Rudrangshu Mukherjee, *Spectre of Violence: The 1857 Kanpur Massacres* (New Delhi, 1998). On the Christian public response see Brian Stanley, "Christian Responses to the Indian Mutiny of 1857," in *The Church and War,* ed. W. J. Sheils (Oxford, 1983); and David W. Savage, "Evangelical Education Policy in Britain and India, 1857–1860," *The Journal of Imperial and Commonwealth History* 22 (September, 1994). The literary legacy of the rebellion is treated in a chapter in Patrick Brantlinger, *Rule of Darkness: British Literature and Imperialism, 1830–1914* (London, 1988). Flora Annie Steel's novel *On the Face of the Waters* (London, 1887) was probably the most widely read fictional account of the rebellion. The highly gendered nature of the rebellion narrative is revealed by Jenny Sharpe, "The Unspeakable Limits of Rape: Colonial Violence and Counter-Insurgency," *Genders* 10 (Spring, 1991). Two widely read contemporary British retrospectives give a flavor of the struggles of conscience regarding the rebellion and British rule in India. William Howard Russell, *My Indian Mutiny Diary* (London 1860) is by the leading international reporter of the *Times,* and G. O. Trevelyan, *The Competition Wallah* (London, 1864) is by a member of a leading British Liberal family.

NOTES

1. *Times*, June 7, 1857.
2. *Illustrated London News*, July 4, 1857.

3. T. B. Macaulay, Education Minute, Feb. 2, 1835, quoted in Peter Burroughs, "Imperial Institutions and the Government of Empire," in *The Oxford History of the British Empire: Vol. III, The Nineteenth Century,* ed. Andrew Porter, 181 (Oxford: Oxford University Press, 1999).

4. Letter dated June 26, *Times,* August 22, 1857.

5. *Daily News,* August 25, 1857, quoted in Rudrangshu Mukherjee, *Spectre of Violence: The 1857 Kanpur Massacres* (New Delhi: Penguin Books India, 1998), 28–29.

6. *Times,* September 17, 1857.

7. July 17, 1857, Incoming Letters, North India (Bengal) Box 9/Folder: Calcutta 1857, London Missionary Society Archives, School of Oriental and African Studies, London.

8. Charles Kingsley to F. D. Maurice, September 3, 1857, in *Charles Kingsley: His Letters and Memoir of His Life* (London: H. S. King & Co., 1877), II, 34–35.

9. See Jenny Sharpe, "The Unspeakable Limits of Rape: Colonial Violence and Counter-Insurgence," *Genders* 10 (Spring 1991).

10. Alexander Duff, *The Indian Rebellion: Its Causes and Results in a Series of Letters* (London: J. Nisbet and Co., 1858), 245, quoted in Andrew Ward, *Our Bones Are Scattered: The Cawnpore Massacres and the Indian Mutiny of 1857* (New York: H. Holt and Co., 1996), 454.

11. Orders of General Neill quoted in John William Kaye, *A History of the Great Revolt,* (London, Repr. of 1880), II, 398–99.

12. Orders of General Neill quoted in Kaye, *Great Revolt,* 398–99.

13. Major Bingham, quoted in Christopher Hibbert, *The Great Mutiny: India, 1857* (London: Allen Lane, 1978), 210.

14. F. C. Maude, *Memories of the Mutiny,* (London: Remington and Co. Limited, 1894), I, 274, quoted in Mukherjee, *Spectre of Violence,* 42.

15. *Examiner,* August 29, 1857.

16. Graham Dawson, *Soldier Heroes: British Adventure, Empire and the Imaginings of Masculinities* (London: Routledge, 1994), 107.

17. *Times,* November 14, 1857, quoted in Dawson, *Soldier Heroes,* 107.

18. *Times,* October 3, 1857, quoted in Dawson, *Soldier Heroes,* 108.

19. The public voices were few, indeed. In 1925 an exposé of British brutality was published by Edward Thompson, *The Other Side of the Medal* (London: L. & Woolf, 1925).

20. *Reynold's Newspaper,* representing the nonsocialist left, and especially Ernest Jones, an aging Chartist, sympathized with the national aspirations of the rebels. See James Bryne, "British Opinion and the Indian Revolt," in *Rebellion 1857: A Symposium,* ed. P. C. Joshi (New Delhi: People's Pub. House, 1957).

21. The *Saturday Review* was patriotic but caustic about evangelical rhetoric.

22. Sermon of Rev. Henry Melvill quoted in *Saturday Review,* October 24, 1857.

23. Salahuddin Malik, "God, England, and the Indian Mutiny: Victorian Religious Perceptions," *Muslim World* 73 (April 1983).

24. Brian Stanley, "Christian Responses to the Indian Mutiny of 1857" in *The Church and War,* ed. W. J. Sheils (Oxford: Blackwell, 1983).

25. David W. Savage, "Evangelical Education Policy in Britain and India, 1857–1860," *Journal of Imperial and Commonwealth History,* 22 (September 1994).

26. Thomas Metcalf, *Ideologies of the Raj* (Cambridge: Cambridge University Press,

1994); Sudipta Sen, *Distant Sovereignty* (New York: Routledge, 2002); Robin J. Moore, "Imperial India, 1858–1914," in Porter, *Oxford History of the British Empire: The Nineteenth Century.*

27. Queen's Proclamation quoted in Savage, "Evangelical Education Policy," 447–448.

28. Duff, *Indian Rebellion*, 54.

29. William Howard Russell, *My Indian Mutiny Diary* (London, 1860), 166.

30. G. O. Trevelyan, *The Competition Wallah* (London: Macmillan, 1864), 218–223.

31. *Saturday Review*, October 24, 1857.

32. Francis Hutchins, *The Illusion of Permanence: British Imperialism in India* (Princeton: Princeton University Press, 1967).

33. *Illustrated London News*, September 12, 1857.

Chapter Nine

Charles Bradlaugh, Militant Unbelief, and the Civil Rights of Atheists

Timothy Larsen

BEFORE PUBLIC ATHEISM

Most Britons today would not be concerned if, for example, their university professor, their Member of Parliament (MP), or one of their employees happened to be an atheist. Britain in the early years of the nineteenth century, however, was a very different world in this regard. During the first decade of the nineteenth century, there were only two universities in England, Oxford and Cambridge, and one had to assent to Anglican doctrine even to be awarded an undergraduate degree, let alone to become a Fellow or a professor. All Members of Parliament took a Protestant, Christian oath: Roman Catholics, Jews, and atheists therefore could not serve as MPs. There was no organized atheist movement. Indeed, it is doubtful that there were very many atheists to organize. A formidable list could be created of all the celebrated writers from the last hundred years who were atheists, but the first half of the nineteenth century seems to have produced only one public atheist in Britain whose work was admired beyond a radical subculture: P. B. Shelley. Moreover, Shelley's advocacy of atheism as an undergraduate was deemed a sufficient reason to have him expelled from the University of Oxford. The journey from the Oxford that expelled Shelley to the one that gives endowed chairs to avowed atheists, from the House of Commons that enforced a Protestants-only rule to the one that has since proven itself capable to accept an atheist as the leader of one of the main political parties (and therefore a suitable candidate for the office of prime minister), reached its most decisive stage in the life and efforts of Charles Bradlaugh (1833–1891).

FROM ANGLICAN TO ICONOCLAST

Bradlaugh grew up among London's lower classes. His father was a confidential clerk to a firm of solicitors, and Bradlaugh was one of seven children. Bradlaugh's parents considered themselves Anglicans. They thought that Sunday school would be good for their children; however, they saw no compelling reason why they should make a habit out of regular church attendance for themselves. Charles Bradlaugh, however, was not willing to take religion complacently in his stride. The turning point came when he was fourteen or fifteen years old. The bishop of London had decided to come to their district to confirm some of its young people. Bradlaugh was himself a Sunday school teacher by then, and the clergyman in his parish could discern that he was unusually bright and able. Therefore, Bradlaugh was set to work to learn the doctrines of the church in order that suitably admirable findings might result from the bishop's examination of candidates. It was not to be, however, as the church's doctrines, and indeed the Bible itself, did not pass the teenager's own inspection. Instead, Bradlaugh's faith was unsettled by the contradictions he found there. He confided his concerns to his minister, the Reverend John Graham Packer, and was rewarded not with reasoned arguments but rather with alarm, retaliation, and abuse. Bradlaugh was removed from his position as a Sunday school teacher, and his father was solemnly warned that his son was thinking like an atheist. Bradlaugh therefore gave up going to church. Packer had failed to become a Christian intellectual guide for him. Instead, Bradlaugh found his way into radical plebeian circles in London and began an informal education in freethought, with numerous stimulating conversation partners. By the age of sixteen he was himself delivering freethinking orations and being noticed in the press as a sort of boy infidel. His father disapproved, and Bradlaugh left home.

At the age of seventeen, Charles Bradlaugh joined the army in order to pay off his debts. Back in London and civilian life again at the age of twenty, he found work with a firm of solicitors, first as an errand boy, then as a clerk. Bradlaugh learned the law and the ways of the law. He had a lawyer's instincts and would spend much of the rest of his life tenaciously fighting to advance the legal rights of atheists. He has been accused of being litigious, but such a charge needs to be set in its proper context. His was not the litigiousness of a prickly or thin-skinned man but rather that of a popular champion of a cause. He knew that a propitious test case could establish a right for the first time and, if necessary, he was quite ready to provoke one. The odium that was then attached to atheism can be measured by the fact that his sympathetic employer had a quite reasonable fear that having a clerk in his firm who was known to be an atheist would drive away clients. Bradlaugh therefore agreed to use a pseudonym when writing against Christianity or in lieu of his real name in the advertisements for his skeptical lectures and debates. His commitment to a forthright attack on the Bible and Christian doctrine was aptly expressed in the *nom de plume* he chose: Iconoclast. Certainly by the end of the 1860s, Bradlaugh had emerged as British's most notorious atheist.

BRITAIN'S MOST NOTORIOUS ATHEIST

Indeed, Bradlaugh was arguably the very first Briton to spend an entire adult life as an avowed, public, populist atheist. His friend, John M. Robertson, writing in 1895, helped to put Bradlaugh's career in context by reminding his readers, "Explicit Atheism is only in our day become at all a common opinion."[1] Freethought in the eighteenth century had taken the form of deism rather than atheism. Deists attacked the Bible and numerous Christian doctrines such as the notion of miracles and the deity of Christ, but they still affirmed the existence of the Almighty. For popular freethinkers in the Victorian age—not least Bradlaugh himself—Thomas Paine (1737–1809) was a sort of patron saint of the cause. His *Age of Reason* had laid out the contours of the critique of the Bible that served Bradlaugh well in a lifetime of anti-Bible writings, lectures, and debates. Still, Paine was a deist who presented the *Age of Reason* as an effort to clear away untenable faith claims so that a rational religion with God as creator as its central tenet might take its place, thereby not advancing, but rather staving off, a move toward atheism (amply exemplified from his place of writing—revolutionary France). The great popular champion of freethinking around the middle of the nineteenth century was George Jacob Holyoake (1817–1906), but in the early 1850s he coined the term "secularism" to describe his own position precisely so that he could reject the label "atheism." Bradlaugh, however, coming on Holyoake's heels, chose to wear the loathsome "atheist" label prominently as a badge of honor.

ORGANIZED ATHEISM

Charles Bradlaugh more or less single-handedly created British atheism as an organized movement. The first major step was the launching in 1860 of a newspaper, the *National Reformer*. There had been a couple of unapologetically atheistic papers prior to this one, but they had been short-lived and ill-fated (or, in the case of the first such venture, the *Oracle of Reason*, 1841–1842, successfully hounded out of existence through prosecutions). The

National Reformer survived as long as Bradlaugh himself did, truly flourishing for several decades of that period and making its mark as a strong, radical voice. This was despite the fact that the main chain of booksellers in the Victorian era, W. H. Smith & Son, refused on principle to carry it, and it was harassed by the government on several occasions. Bradlaugh declared of his paper in 1862, "Editorially, the *National Reformer*, as to religious questions, is, and always has been, as far as we are concerned, the advocate of Atheism."[2] How few people were yet willing to travel down this road is illustrated by the fact that Bradlaugh originally had as his coeditor another popular, skeptical lecturer and writer, Joseph Barker, but within a year or two Barker had abandoned freethinking and rediscovered an evangelical faith. The *National Reformer* let atheists—and potential atheists—know that they were not alone, that their ideas could be articulated and defended, and where to go to find like-minded people.

In 1866, Bradlaugh founded the National Secular Society. This body allowed popular freethinkers across the country to network and organize directly. At its most successful, the Society reached a peak of 120 local branches spread across Britain, with perhaps as many as six thousand members.[3] As more than one scholar has observed, the National Secular Society resembled nothing so much as a small religious denomination.[4] Local branches offered fellowship and camaraderie to freethinkers who might otherwise have felt marginalized and isolated. On a national level, the Society helped to ensure that the rights and views of atheists were advanced.

"KILL THE INFIDEL!"

If the National Secular Society was not unlike a church, Bradlaugh himself, during the early years, was reminiscent of one of the original Methodist itinerant preachers as he took his controversial message from town to town with little or no remuneration and in the face of harassment and persecution. Sometimes no one in a particular town would rent him a hall in which to hold his meeting. Occasionally, an owner who had signed a contract with him would then receive pressure from local clergymen or government officials and therefore decide not to honor it. In Liverpool, the mayor (falsely) informed the owner of a hall that if he let Bradlaugh speak there he would be breaking the law. In Huddersfield, the owner of the hall he had rented had second thoughts and locked him out. In Wigan, a local clergyman apparently thought that Bradlaugh should not even sleep in their town, let alone speak in it, and succeeded in getting Bradlaugh thrown out of his hotel room. In Blyth, no innkeeper would take him in. In Plymouth, even though it was standard practice for lecturers on other subjects to speak there, and he had only uttered one banal sentence, he was arrested for inciting a breach of the peace when he began to speak in a public park. In Guernsey, a man was arrested for distributing freethinking literature written by "Iconoclast." When the author came to support his imprisoned admirer, he was met by a mob that shouted, "Kill the Infidel! Murder the Infidel!"[5] When he was slandered on one occasion, Bradlaugh sued for libel. There was no question that he was right in point of law, but the prejudice against atheists was so pronounced that he was only awarded one farthing (one fourth of a penny) in damages, despite having spent £100 in costs. This prompted him bitterly to ask the question, "Outlaw or Citizen? Which Am I?"[6] And so it went on and on.

Much of this persecution was in spite of the law rather than because of it, but legal discrimination against atheists was also considerable, and Bradlaugh set out to have it overturned. One major source of injustice was that witnesses in a court of law were required to swear a Christian oath. If an atheist refused to take the oath on conscientious grounds or if a judge decided that a witness's skeptical opinions made him or her ineligible to swear such an oath, then the atheist could not obtain legal redress for crimes against him or her. Bradlaugh reminded the orthodox that this was not necessarily to their advantage, "At present, and according to English law, any person might murder a bishop in the presence of half-a-dozen Atheists, and escape justice, because none of those Atheists would be legally competent to bear testimony as to the murder."[7] Less fantastical scenarios, however, were no less outrageous. When G. J. Holyoake's nine-year-old boy was killed by a reckless driver, he was not allowed to give evidence at the inquest because he could not take the oath. In 1862, Bradlaugh solemnly warned potential public atheists that their road had been made into an unpleasant one by their opponents:

> I can offer you no inducements to come here. I admit that to be a Freethinker is to be an outlaw, according to the laws of England. I admit that to profess your disbelief renders you liable at the present moment to fine and imprisonment and penal servitude. I admit that that is the statute law of England. I admit that if you are free enough to say you are an infidel, your evidence may in a court of justice be rejected, and that so you may be robbed.[8]

When Bradlaugh sued someone who owed him money from a business transaction, the judge not only refused to allow him to testify because of his religious opinions but also declared the case undefended, decided for the other party, and added for good measure that Bradlaugh ought to consider himself fortunate not to have been sent to jail! Another such court case involving Bradlaugh, however, led (with his prompting) to new legislation, the Evidence Amendment Act, 1869, that allowed atheists to affirm rather than swear "if the presiding judge is satisfied that the taking of the oath would have no binding effect upon his conscience." Thus Bradlaugh, by his determination to be a public atheist and the tactics of his legal mind, had been the catalyst for a major advance in the civil rights of atheists.

ATHEISM AND PARLIAMENT

Charles Bradlaugh is most remembered, however, for his long, bitter, and ultimately triumphant fight to be allowed to take his seat as a Member of Parliament, his avowed atheism notwithstanding. Throughout the nineteenth century in Britain, a legally bolstered Anglican hegemony was steadily eroded as the principle of religious equality before the law was increasingly implemented in a wide variety of areas. Atheists, however, were the very last class of men, in terms of religious restrictions, to gain the right to serve as MPs. In 1829, this right had been conceded in the case of Roman Catholics. The Society of Friends, whose members were commonly known as Quakers, was a Protestant sect that maintained a conscientious, religious opposition to all oaths. The first Quaker entered Parliament in 1833 when a decision was made to allow members of that religious minority to affirm in lieu of the oath. There was a prolonged, contentious struggle over the admission of Jews to Parliament. Nevertheless, Jewish emancipation was finally secured in 1858, and Baron Lionel de Rothschild duly took his seat as a member for London. Bradlaugh first ran as a candidate to represent the people of Northampton in Parliament in the 1868 election. He lost, but he doggedly continued cultivating a base of support in the town and putting himself forward at each election. He finally won the 1880 election.

In 1866, Parliament had enacted that Quakers, Moravians, and Separatists (that is, Protestant sects that objected to all oaths for religious reasons), were allowed to affirm rather than swear. After listing these three groups, the act then added vaguely, "and every other person for the time being by law permitted to make a solemn affirmation or declaration."[9] Bradlaugh had been regularly affirming rather than swearing in courts of law for almost a decade by that time on the strength of the Evidence Amendment Act, 1869, and the Evidence Amendment Act, 1870, and therefore he reasoned that atheists now fell under the general phrase in the 1866 act on parliamentary oaths as people whom the law now permitted to affirm. When the 1880 Parliament assembled, he informed the Speaker of the House that he wished to affirm on this basis. A select committee was then formed to discover whether or not this was permissible, and it ruled that it was not. Bradlaugh therefore then put himself forward to take the oath. A Conservative member complained that

Bradlaugh was ineligible to take the oath, and another committee was formed to decide on that point.

"SO HELP ME GOD"

These were uncharted waters. On the one hand, there was no precedent for challenging a member who wished to take the oath regarding his suitability on religious grounds. People who were well-known to be religious skeptics such as Lord Bolingbroke and John Stuart Mill had taken the oath without any objections. On the other hand, no one had ever tried to affirm and, having been refused, decided to take the oath instead. It was assumed that asking to affirm was tantamount to saying that one could not conscientiously take the oath. No Roman Catholic, Quaker, or Jew had ever attempted to submit to an unaltered oath: each group had agitated for changes and stayed outside the House until they had been secured. It seemed to many as if Bradlaugh was following expediency at the expense of principle. After all, the oath contained the words "So help me God" and included the act of kissing a Bible, a book that Bradlaugh had practically made a career out of disdaining. Even many of those who believed in his right to sit in Parliament were disappointed with his willingness to take the oath. Perhaps most damagingly, G. J. Holyoake expressed his disapproval. Bradlaugh himself, however, argued that he had never objected to taking the parliamentary oath but had only expressed a preference for affirming. He denied that "So help me God" could be uttered in good conscience only by a theist, claiming it could be said as "merely a form of asseveration."[10] The committee ruled that he was not allowed to take the oath, while expressing a hope that he might be able to affirm after all. This impasse was then formally underlined by a motion that passed in the House on June 22, 1880, which stated that Bradlaugh should not be allowed to either affirm or take the oath. In short, no way was opened to allow him to take his seat. He was, however, permitted to speak from the Bar of the House (symbolizing that he was an outsider to that chamber). His eloquence on this occasion was conceded even by some of his enemies. Bradlaugh argued that he had a right and a responsibility to represent the people who had elected him. He therefore refused to leave the House. Charles Bradlaugh was then taken into custody, thereby becoming the last person in British history to be imprisoned in the Clock Tower (commonly known today as "Big Ben").

His imprisonment ended the next day, but his parliamentary struggle had only just begun. On July 2, 1880, the House effectively overturned its own motion of a few weeks earlier (as well as the ruling of the first select committee) and passed a motion that Bradlaugh be allowed to affirm. He did so and went on to serve as a full member of Parliament for about nine months. His taking of his seat had been immediately challenged in the courts, however, and, having lost both the case and an appeal, he was barred from Parliament once again by the end of March 1881. Over the next several years, Bradlaugh was not allowed to sit in Parliament even though he continued to win every election. He tried everything he could think of, even the ruse of swearing himself in before any objection to his taking the oath could be made.

Parliament debated the matter repeatedly and at length. These debates show only too clearly the virulent attitudes at that time of many Britons toward atheists. MPs referred to Bradlaugh as "an infidel blasphemer" and "the wolf" who was "at the gate," and "the human embodiment of the reverse of virtue."[11] Of his supporters amongst the general populace, Lord Randolph Churchill pronounced, "For the most part, they were the residuum, the rabble, and the scum of the population; the bulk of them were persons to whom all restraint, religious, moral, or legal, was odious and intolerable."[12] A pamphlet was circulated among his constituents that endeavored to persuade them that he was not a suitable person to represent them in Parliament: "Our objection to Mr. Bradlaugh is that he is socially lawless, devoid of moral sense, untruthful, morally unclean, a coarse blasphemer, and an avowed atheist."[13]

Even more telling, however, was the phenomenon of MP after MP denying that there was an atheist community at all. The Irish members tended to make this point with added jocularity. William O'Brien, member for Mallow in County Cork, averred:

> I believe the number of people who agree in all things with Mr. Bradlaugh is not much greater or more choice than the number of people who would like to go about the streets naked, and I do not apprehend that in this climate the one creed is ever more likely to be popular than the other.[14]

Several members expressed doubts regarding the very existence of true atheism. If atheists could annoy Christians by denying that God existed, then Christians could likewise annoy skeptics by denying that atheism existed! Nevertheless, this argument did reveal how little progress atheism had yet made in the country: it was still possible for its very existence to be repeatedly challenged in the nation's most representative assembly.

ATHEIST MEMBERS OF PARLIAMENT

Bradlaugh won the 1885 election just as he had done four previous ones, but this time the situation proved different. There was a new Speaker of the

House, Sir A. W. Peel, and he simply reversed the policy of the previous Speaker, allowing Bradlaugh to take the oath, and the president of the National Secular Society was suddenly an MP. This happened in January 1886. Bradlaugh remained an MP for Northampton with all the rights and privileges thereof until his death in 1891. He steadily worked to change the law so that he and future atheists with political aspirations could affirm rather than take the oath. Bradlaugh's Affirmation (or Oaths) Bill finally passed through the House of Lords in December 1888 and was enacted into law. The last religious disability finally had been removed from the House of Commons. The march of the principle of religious equality was now complete on that front.

CHRISTIAN ALLIES

What was at stake in this struggle over the parliamentary oath? The prime minister himself, W. E. Gladstone, a deeply Christian man, came to argue that there was no Christian logic in drawing the line at mere theism, in arguing that it did not matter what kind of religion a person had or what god they worshipped so long as they were religious in *some* way and acknowledged *some* deity. What are religious oaths for? Are they there in order to decrease the likelihood that people would speak or act dishonestly? This notion seemed predicated on the assumption that people would cheerfully lie to one another but only if the name of God was not evoked. Bradlaugh had a rather unvarnished summary of this logic:

> The oath has a value only in the case where a man is so destitute of moral principles that he would readily bear false witness against his neighbour, but is so miserably superstitious that he will tell the truth under oath from fear of hell fire.[15]

Moreover, if the oath had not kept skeptics out in the past (or then current ones such as John Morley), then why was it deemed so essential? Bradlaugh's offense, it would seem, was being such an avowed atheist: he was too plain-speaking, too blunt, too willing to deliver iconoclastic ideas straight to the masses. In other words, social class was an underlining issue. Discreet skepticism might be allowed, but it must not be baldly articulated in front of the children. Bradlaugh's eager efforts to export atheism to the masses certainly did not help him win friends in respectable circles, but it is also true that his ideas were inherently offensive to the religious sensibilities of many Britons.

From still another vantage point, however, it is important to realize that Bradlaugh would not have triumphed without the goodwill of numerous Christians. Most coherently and forcefully, the Nonconformists were champions of religious equality. Nonconformists or Dissenters were Protestants in denominations other than the Church of England and its reluctantly estranged sister, Wesleyan Methodism. Many Nonconformists, especially those in the Congregational, Baptist, Unitarian, and Quaker denominations, believed strongly that the state should not discriminate on the basis of religious opinions. They had a strong pressure-group organization, the Society for the Liberation of Religion from State Patronage and Control. Commonly known as "the Liberation Society," Edward Miall, a Congregational minister, had founded it in 1844 as the British Anti-State Church Association. Nonconformists had campaigned for the admission of Jews to Parliament, and they offered clear and influential support to Bradlaugh during his struggle. Henry Richard, MP for Merthyr Tydvil and a deeply religious evangelical Congregationalist, for example, argued in the House of Commons that Bradlaugh's exclusion was grounded in the dangerous fallacy that religion could be protected by punitive legislation. Nonconformist MPs voted overwhelmingly, indeed almost exclusively, on Bradlaugh's side throughout the entire struggle, and numerous devout Anglicans joined them as well.

BLASPHEMY

The right to sit in Parliament was won, but there was still much more to do. Bradlaugh resigned the presidency of the National Secular Society due to ill health in 1890, the year before his death. His greatest sadness on this occasion resulted from the fact that he had hoped to serve in that office until "the laws relating to Blasphemy were erased from the Statute Book."[16] The twentieth century, of course, has come and gone, and blasphemy is still an offense in British law. Blasphemy is a much contested and elusive concept but, however one defines it, no one denies that the laws against it in an English context privilege Christianity in general (and the Church of England in particular). Atheists must watch what they say, when they say it, and how they say it when expressing their opinions, lest they be prosecuted. A whole parade of freethinkers was tried for blasphemy in the nineteenth century. Bradlaugh himself managed to evade this fate, but his successor as president of the National Secular Society, G. W. Foote (1850–1915), was not so fortunate. Foote launched a new journal, the *Freethinker*, in 1881. It was initially published by Bradlaugh's Freethought Publishing Company, and its prosecution was partially motivated by a desire to attack Bradlaugh. The *Freethinker* had fun tweaking the sensibilities of Christians. One article was entitled, "What Must I Do To Be Damned?"—a witty inversion of the biblical question that had served as a title for innumerable evangelical sermons, "What Must I Do

To Be Saved?"[17] The *pièce de résistance* was a series of "Comic Bible Sketches," cartoons that parodied the life of Christ as well as other biblical characters, passages, and themes. Foote was found guilty of blasphemy and given a twelve-month prison sentence with hard labor. The judge, Mr. Justice North, was well-known to be a devout Roman Catholic. Foote responded to his sentence with the devastating retort, "My lord; I thank you; it is worthy of your creed."[18] A waggish journal quipped, "Mr. Bradlaugh has been successful in keeping himself out of prison: but hasn't he somehow managed to put his Foote in it?"[19] Charles Bradlaugh did more than any single person to help to transform Britain from a society where freethinkers were discriminated against in all kinds of ways to one where avowed atheists were treated equally before the law at many crucial points, but Iconoclast's agenda is yet to see its full completion.

SUGGESTED READINGS

Charles Bradlaugh has been the subject of a whole series of biographies, but the two most useful ones are the one by his daughter, Hypatia Bradlaugh Bonner, *Charles Bradlaugh: His Life and Work,* 2 volumes, second edition, (London, 1895), and the most recent one, David Tribe, *Charles Bradlaugh, M.P.,* (London, 1971). They are both sympathetic treatments. Bradlaugh's struggle to become an MP has been the subject of a full study, Walter L. Arnstein, *The Bradlaugh Case: Atheism, Sex, and Politics among the Late Victorians* (Columbia, MO, 1983 [originally 1965]). For organized freethought in nineteenth-century Britain, see Edward Royle, *Victorian Infidels: The Origins of the British Secularist Movement, 1791–1866* (Manchester, 1974); Edward Royle, *Radicals, Secularists and Republicans: Popular Freethought in Britain, 1866–1915* (Manchester, 1980); and Shirley A. Mullen, *Organized Freethought: The Religion of Unbelief in Victorian England* (New York, 1987). For a history of British atheism, see David Berman, *A History of Atheism in Britain: From Hobbes to Russell* (London, 1988). Two recent studies have explored the theme of blasphemy in a British context, David Nash, *Blasphemy in Modern Britain: 1789 to the Present* (Aldershot, 1999); and Joss Marsh, *Word Crimes: Blasphemy, Culture, and Literature in Nineteenth-Century England* (Chicago, 1998). For the role of Nonconformists in advancing the rights of atheists and the principle of religious equality before the law in Britain, see Timothy Larsen, *Friends of Religious Equality: Nonconformist Politics in Mid-Victorian England* (Woodbridge, Suffolk, and Rochester, NY, 2002). For more on religious equality as well as an exploration of popular freethinking perspectives, including a chapter on Bradlaugh's anti-

Christian views, see Timothy Larsen, *Contested Christianity: The Political and Social Contexts of Victorian Theology* (Waco, TX, 2004).

In terms of primary sources, Bradlaugh wrote his own account of the first years of "the Bradlaugh Case": Charles Bradlaugh, *The True Story of My Parliamentary Struggle* (London: Freethought Publishing Company, 1882). The official record of that struggle may be found in *Hansard's Parliamentary Debates* (Third Series). In terms of the legal situation of atheists, another valuable source is Charles Bradlaugh, *The Laws Relating to Blasphemy and Heresy: An Address to Freethinkers* (London: Freethought Publishing Company, [1878]). The best introduction to Bradlaugh's critique of Christianity is his most sustained work in that area, Charles Bradlaugh, *The Bible: What It Is* (London: Austin & Co., 1870). Finally, his daughter produced a useful compilation of cases of legal discrimination against freethinkers, Hypatia Bradlaugh Bonner, *Penalties Upon Opinions; or Some Records of the Laws of Heresy and Blasphemy,* second edition (London, 1913).

NOTES

1. Hypatia Bradlaugh Bonner, *Charles Bradlaugh: His Life and Work,* 2 volumes, second edition (London: T. Fisher Unwin, 1895), II, 115.

2. Bonner, *Charles Bradlaugh*, I, 129.

3. Edward Royle, *Radicals, Secularists and Republicans: Popular Freethought in Britain, 1866–1915* (Manchester: Manchester University Press, 1980), 133–36.

4. For a sustained exploration of this theme, see Shirley A. Mullen, *Organized Freethought: The Religion of Unbelief in Victorian England* (New York: Garland, 1987).

5. Bonner, *Charles Bradlaugh*, I, 192.

6. Bonner, *Charles Bradlaugh*, I, 290.

7. Charles Bradlaugh, *The Bible: What It Is* (London: Austin & Co., 1870), 239.

8. Bonner, *Charles Bradlaugh*, I, 209.

9. Walter L. Arnstein, *The Bradlaugh Case: Atheism, Sex, and Politics among the Late Victorians* (Columbia: University of Missouri Press, 1983), 67.

10. Charles Bradlaugh, *The True Story of My Parliamentary Struggle* (London: Freethought Publishing Company, 1882), 40.

11. *Hansard's Parliamentary Debates* (Third Series) CCLIII, 411, 1289, 1297.

12. *Hansard*, CCLXXVIII, 1442.

13. Arnstein, *Bradlaugh Case*, 97–98.

14. *Hansard*, CCLXXVIII, 1761.

15. Charles Bradlaugh, *The Laws Relating to Blasphemy and Heresy: An Address to Freethinkers* (London: Freethought Publishing Company, [1878]), 29.

16. Bonner, *Charles Bradlaugh*, II, 107.

17. Acts 16:30 in the Authorized (King James) Version.

18. David Nash, *Blasphemy in Modern Britain: 1789 to the Present* (Aldershot: Ashgate. 1999), 144.

19. Joss Marsh, *Word Crimes: Blasphemy, Culture, and Literature in Nineteenth-Century England* (Chicago: University of Chicago Press, 1998), 151.

Chapter Ten

In Fits and Starts: The Education Struggle in Nineteenth-century Britain

Eric G. Tenbus

The necessity for political reform in Great Britain during the nineteenth century was paramount. The movement toward democracy generated considerable interest throughout the century, causing both parliamentary and public debate, as well as sporadic incidents of popular violence, as the political realm reluctantly and slowly expanded. Initially, the beneficiary of political reform was the middle class, the masters of the Industrial Revolution whose increasing wealth was not matched by political participation. In 1832, that participation was guaranteed as they finally gained entrance into the political arena through the Reform Act. The arduous struggle of the working classes for political enfranchisement, however, was not truly viable until the Chartist Movement was born in the late 1830s when thousands of workingmen joined together to demand political rights.

In the midst of the decade-long Chartist struggle, as authorities grew frightened of the increasing size of the movement and its threatening physical force faction, one visionary saw an opportunity for the government to defuse the Chartist menace while simultaneously improving the lives of the working class. Scoffing at the Chartist belief that universal suffrage would solve all social ills, James Kay, secretary of the Committee of the Council on Education, argued in a widely read 1839 treatise that the growing threat of social upheaval or even revolution could only be averted through improved education: "The sole effectual means of preventing the tremendous evils with which the anarchical spirit of the manufacturing population threatens the country is . . . [to give] the working people a good secular education."[1]

Despite his paternalistic attitude of using education to keep social order, Kay's opinions underscored the importance of educational reform as a necessary accompaniment, or perhaps prerequisite, to political reform. While the policymakers in 1839 were not yet ready to extend democracy that far—the working classes would have to wait until 1867 and 1884 for franchise extension—it was clear to men like James Kay that much good could come from educational reform in general. As the century progressed, more Victorians came to believe that educational reform was the natural complement to political reform because those with political power feared sharing it with those who had received little or no schooling; thus, it became necessary to educate those who would receive the franchise via political reform. Complicating matters and making educational reform a daunting and often complex task, however, was a religious establishment unwilling to relinquish its grip on an education system it had created and a laissez-faire economic environment that wished to reduce the size, cost, and influence of government.

EDUCATION IN EIGHTEENTH-CENTURY BRITAIN AND THE STIRRINGS OF REFORM

Education in eighteenth-century Britain was primarily reserved for the nobility and gentry, as well as the upwardly mobile, yet relatively sparse, merchant classes. It was not compulsory nor was it a responsibility of the government. The notion of state-sponsored education, especially of the poor, was simply an idea that had not yet blossomed and would not until the next century. During the Enlightenment, however, some Europeans advocated placing a greater emphasis on education for all levels in society. Yet that belief was resisted by the dogged certainty of others that any education of the working class would engender feelings of unhappiness within their station in life, which, these social watchdogs cautioned, would lead to idleness, resentment, and, ultimately, sedition.

While formal education in eighteenth-century Britain rarely reached the lower orders, this was not to say that the poor did not have opportunities for instruction. There were fee-paying dame schools usually run by unqualified elderly women which, at their very best, provided very uneven education and were more closely related to modern "day-care" establishments. More prevalent were the free charity schools that were established by philanthropists and were predominantly associated with local parishes, and, thus, were tied to religion. In most charity schools the teachers were required to be members of the Church of England, and the curriculum was religiously inspired. Subjects might include reading, writing, and arithmetic as well as instruction in some practical task that could lead to future employment, including spinning, sewing, knitting, and gardening. Despite increasing criticism at the turn of the century on the deficient pedagogy within these schools, they served an important purpose in meeting the educational needs of the lower orders, however meagerly, at a time when there were few other alternatives. One final educational opportunity was the Sunday school phenomenon which emerged late in the eighteenth century as the location where most children were receiving any modicum of education. The success of these schools was a reflection of an industrial age dependent upon child labor as attendance did not interfere with the child's work during the week. Religion saturated the curriculum as all of the Christian churches rushed to meet the educational and spiritual needs of their respective flocks. It has been argued that, more than the other types of schools, the Sunday schools helped to set the stage for the educational reforms of the nineteenth century by offering a free, denominationally flavored education to all children which was fully cognizant of and attentive to the industrial demands of the country.[2]

Early in the nineteenth century, as the need for increased education within the rapidly expanding industrial centers grew more desperate, two educationists independently developed systems of elementary education that could meet the needs of a burgeoning population and do so economically. Both Andrew Bell, an Anglican clergyman, and Joseph Lancaster, a Quaker headmaster, developed a classroom approach that came to be called the monitorial system. In this system, the headmaster instructed the monitors, the trustworthy older students, who then taught the material to the younger students. Much like the division of labor in the factories, this system efficiently compartmentalized the education so that classrooms could handle much larger enrollments without having to hire more trained teachers. Thus, the perfect system for a utilitarian age was providing a rote, mechanized education for the mechanized, industrial society.

Outside the classroom, two organizations that came to exert a dominant influence in nineteenth-century education were the National Society and the British and Foreign School Society founded in 1811 and 1814, respectively. The former was premised on the Bell system and provided funds for schools in which the education was required to include the doctrine of the Established Church while the latter found its inspiration in Lancaster's model and supported schools open to students of any denomination. An intense rivalry commenced between the two educational societies that foreshadowed the emerging religious problems, especially after the state acknowledged that it had a role in supporting public education.

THE STATE ENTERS THE FRAY

That acknowledgment first came to light in 1807 when Samuel Whitbread introduced legislation in the House of Commons to create publicly funded parochial schools run on the monitorial system. Efforts of the Church of England to continue their dominance in elementary education, combined with the nagging fear among MPs that increased education might lead to greater disenchantment among the working class, led to the bill's failure. The next major legislative initiative for state-supported education came from the Whig stalwart Lord Brougham in 1820. His plan would have created a vast system of rate-supported primary schools nominally under Anglican control. All teachers would have been required to be members of the Established Church, and the local clergyman would have had the right to inspect the schools. The curriculum would have required religious education, but not of the sectarian kind. Despite the progressive nature of this bill in drawing the state into establishing a regular system of primary education, it was opposed both by the Anglicans and the Nonconformists. Churchmen wanted Anglican religious instruction, while Nonconformists believed the entire design was skewed too heavily in favor of the Anglican establishment.[3] Brougham eventually withdrew the bill.

Educational progress finally came as a result of major political reform. The four-year period from 1828 to 1832 saw the culmination of efforts to expand the political nation and bring democratic changes to Great Britain; this reform released shock waves through society that would eventually engulf education. The 1828 repeal of the Test and Corporation Acts gave Nonconformists full political citizenship by jettisoning those laws which had prevented them from holding national or local office. Although these laws had not been enforced since the mid-eighteenth century, the result was to energize Dissenters, as well as Roman Catholics, who soon lobbied for the repeal of similar laws that excluded them from the political nation. Catholic Emancipation followed in 1829 and, for the first time since the seventeenth-century, Catholics could again sit in Parliament. Finally, the long-awaited political reform came in 1832 when Lord Grey was able to push through the Reform Bill that directly expanded representation in Britain by enfranchising the middle class and the industrial towns in which they lived. While the majority of the population was still excluded from the machinery of government, the addition of the middle class to the electorate and Parliament, many of whom were not Anglican, brought added pressure to address elementary education in Britain.

The momentum of reform continued unabated the following year. Parliament passed a Factory Act which, while upholding the principles of laissez-faire and not affecting adult working hours, imposed restrictions on child labor and, importantly, required factory owners to provide children under thirteen with at least two hours of education per working day. With that precedent set, John Arthur Roebuck introduced to the House of Commons in 1833 an ambitious education bill that proposed creating a compulsory national education system for children six to twelve to be overseen by a new cabinet minister for education. Importantly, he justified the bill by arguing that the recent expansion of democracy to the middle class would eventually expand to the working class: "I wish the people to be enlightened, that they may use the power well which they will inevitably obtain."[4] While the mood had certainly shifted in favor of some state support for education, his bill was still too radical a departure from the status quo and far too expensive. The bill failed, but, as a consolation, Parliament approved an annual grant of £20,000 towards school construction. Given England's educational deficiencies, this was a paltry sum, but the initiative revealed a Parliament not totally indifferent to the plight of education. Viewed as a supplement to private funding, however, the grants would only go to those communities that could raise half the necessary funds themselves. As a result, the grants tended to support the wealthier environs, while neglecting the poorer areas that were in greater need. The grants were distributed through the two education societies: the Anglican National Society and the Nonconformist British and Foreign School Society. Not all churches were eligible, however; English Catholics would have to wait another fourteen years before they could receive state education grants.

JAMES KAY-SHUTTLEWORTH AND THE COMMITTEE OF THE PRIVY COUNCIL ON EDUCATION

After six years of parliamentary grants, the young Queen Victoria created an official ministry for education, the Committee of the Privy Council on Education, to oversee the administration of the money. Justifying this action, Home Secretary Lord Russell wrote that despite the efforts of the education societies, "still much remains to be done," including increasing the number of qualified teachers, perfecting the method of teaching, and initiating an inspectorate. Russell admitted these deficiencies were the result of "the neglect of this great subject among the enactments of our voluminous legislation."[5] Yet even with a growing Nonconformist presence in Parliament and an increasing secular liberal voice that called for a separation between religion and education, the Established Church continued to run the show. It controlled appointments to the new school inspectorate and devised the regulations for religious instruction. These were privileges that Nonconformists resented.

The first secretary of the Committee of the Council on Education was Dr. James Kay, later to become Sir James Kay-Shuttleworth. Dr. Kay had studied at the University of Edinburgh and, upon completion of his medical degree in 1827, took a position as a physician in that nucleus of the Industrial Revolution, Manchester. Enveloped in extensive poverty, the slums of Manchester caused Dr. Kay to reflect on the role of the government in providing ameliorative solutions. In 1832, Kay published *The Moral and Physical Condition of the Working Classes Employed in the Cotton Manufacture in Manchester*, a pamphlet that placed the onus of reform squarely on the shoulders of the state. More specifically, Kay argued that better education should lead the way out of the dismal state of affairs he witnessed in Manchester. "The education of the poor must be substantial," he wrote. "The poor man will not be made a much better member of society by being only taught to read and write. His education should comprise such branches of general knowledge . . . [that] would elevate his tastes above a companionship in licentious pleasures."[6] His solution was a comprehensive national system of education to meet the needs of the working classes. Kay's widely circulated pamphlet garnered much attention and ultimately led to an official governmental inquiry into the adequacy of elementary education in Lancashire. This pamphlet revealed that Kay's interests were transitioning from medicine to larger social ills. Soon after, he gave up his position as a physician to become an Assistant Poor Law Commissioner after the national poor law system was created in 1834 by the Poor Law Relief Act.

In his years as an Assistant Poor Law Commissioner, Kay gained national experience beyond Lancashire, and his work and words on educational matters soon caught the eye of Prime Minister Viscount Melbourne and Home Secretary Russell. When the decision to create the Committee of the Privy Council on Education was made in 1839, Kay was a natural choice as its first secretary. Initially, Kay proved to be an eager, if not overambitious, advocate for education as he attempted to extend the power of the Committee beyond the limits originally intended. There was a sense of alarm in Kay's justification for such exertion as he truly believed that, in light of the recent Chartist agitation, only education could mollify the rising "anarchical spirit of the manufacturing population" that threatened Britain with revolution.[7]

Kay wanted the Committee's role to be more than simply providing funds for the construction of schools via the national education societies, which Kay viewed as potential obstacles in the poorer regions. After considerable resistance from the Cabinet, Kay agreed to a moderate extension of authority. For example, only affiliates of either society could submit applications for funding, with special allowances made for poverty-stricken areas. Such allowances would prove to be rare. And within a few years Kay and the Committee found that their greatest problem was no longer in convincing the state that it must support education, but in increasing support for working-class education without angering either the Anglicans or the dissenters and their respective societies.[8] As Kay admitted in 1839, the pursuit of any educational solution "rouses the advocates of the antagonist principles involved in questions of civil and religious liberty, which have caused political struggles" every time.[9] Hence, the emergence of the "religious difficulty."

In 1843 Sir James Graham's Factory Bill again propelled education to the forefront of the national legislative agenda. With recent violence in the manufacturing districts as a backdrop, Graham proposed to extend the limitations on child labor, set up district schools under the control of the Church of England, and, with a nod toward dissenters, permit non-Anglican children to skip instruction in the Established catechism and liturgy. Rather than satisfying dissenters, the bill enraged and motivated them. Both Nonconformist Protestants and Catholics rallied their constituencies throughout the industrial belt and brought forth over two million petition signatures against the bill's passage. Despite the promise of further amendments, such as a conscience clause to protect religious freedom in education, the opposition was far too suspicious of any educational system placing Anglicans in charge, either as teachers or trustees.[10] Kay-Shuttleworth, as he was now known after his marriage to Janet Shuttleworth in 1842, supported the bill even though he, too, distrusted the supremacy of the Established Church in educational affairs. Yet his biographer believes that Kay-Shuttleworth was perhaps convinced that Nonconformists would be satisfied with the conscience clause and that this was the best system they might be able to achieve.[11] However, in the face of such fierce opposition, Graham eventually dropped the bill and returned the next year with a successful Factory Bill without the education provisions.

Kay-Shuttleworth's greatest contribution to the protracted evolution of education came in 1846 when the Committee announced an ambitious pupil-teacher training program, the goal of which was to ultimately replace the now outdated and suspect monitorial system. As author of this plan, Kay-Shuttleworth believed it would improve the quality of education in the elementary schools, while, at the same time, increasing governmental support and control. He was correct on both accounts. In this scheme, the best students were apprenticed to their schools from the age of thirteen to eighteen, during which time they received training before or after school and helped teach during the school day. After the apprenticeship, they could win scholarships to attend a training college. Once graduated and certified, teachers would earn a higher salary and even a pension with fifteen years service. Kay-Shuttleworth's plan meant a dramatically increased financial commitment from the government to pay teacher trainers, to finance, in part, the training colleges, to support the higher salaries, and to create the pension system. With this augmentation of the state's role in educational provision, Kay-Shuttleworth had successfully expanded the role of the Committee beyond its original mission—administrational oversight of building grants. Parliament responded with a substantial educational allocation of £100,000 for 1846. Not only did his reforms improve teacher training, they also created a minimum of standards to which all schools must conform. Required annual state inspections would enforce adherence to such standards in regards to staff, equipment, and classroom discipline, and a poor inspection could result in the grants being withheld. With Kay-Shuttleworth's guidance, Great Britain had achieved a new level of state support for education, and the Committee's authority from London over education throughout the country was increased dramatically.

Despite Kay-Shuttleworth's administrative triumphs, his tenure with the Committee would soon come to an abrupt end. The year 1847 brought a battle over management clauses for schools receiving governmental assistance. The new clauses shifted control away from the local clergymen, and thus set the Secretary and his Committee at odds with the Established Church. The fact remained that many still believed that a national system of education, which Kay-Shuttleworth was developing, should be overseen by the national church. Those clauses also made provisions for Roman Catholic schools to be admitted to the state grant system, which was an unpopular move in the eyes of many Anglicans and dissenters. It was also in that same year that Kay-Shuttleworth's accounting practices came under parliamentary scrutiny. Parliament could not understand how he had spent more than his allotted annual grant, and his reply to an official inquiry was that he had simply used his surplus from the previous year. This was a surplus of which Parliament knew nothing and, if they had, they may have reduced his grant in light of the pervasive laissez-faire philosophy dominating the Treasury under Charles Trevelyan. Many in Parliament began calling the Secretary Kay-Shuttleworth an electoral liability. Frustrated by continued harping over his expenses, unclear as to his future status within the emerging education bureaucracy, and hampered by poor health which was often exacerbated by his micromanagement style and extremely long hours, Kay-Shuttleworth retired from public duty in 1849. The man who had contributed the most to the development of a modern educational system in Great Britain was now removed from the scene, while the challenges this system would face were just beginning.

EDUCATION MEETS
MID-VICTORIAN FRUGALITY

Although the architect was gone, the system he built matured under the guidance provided by the blueprint of 1846. The pupil-teacher system grew to fifteen thousand active participants by 1859, and there were thirty-five train-ing colleges that had produced some seven thousand "certificated" teachers. Not surprisingly, the education budget mushroomed and state funding increased from the £100,000 grant in 1846 to £840,000 in 1862. While this pleased educationists, cost-conscious, mid-Victorian politicians fretted over the seemingly unending appetite for increased funding of the Education Department, which was finally created as a separate entity in February 1856. With costs soaring, a Royal Commission was convened in 1858 under the guidance of the Duke of Newcastle to investigate the status of popular educa-tion in Great Britain with an eye toward reducing costs.

After three years of investigation, the Newcastle Commission, to which Kay-Shuttleworth testified in 1860, reported with mixed results. On the posi-tive side, the number of children attending school had increased to one in seven, a figure that had risen from one in fourteen at the end of the Napole-onic Wars. But of greater concern were irregular attendance figures and the relatively short duration of children's education. According to the report, only 29 percent of children over age ten attended inspected schools; that number dropped to 19 percent for children over age eleven.[12] Nonattendance figures skyrocketed in industrial areas where communities struggled to raise the funds to meet the required halfway point before they could begin receiv-ing grants. These same communities also faced the allure of the local factory that was often greater than the parents' belief in the efficacy of education for their children. Children were more useful as wage earners. Kay-Shuttleworth warned the Commission that the popular idea of offering aid to schools based upon examinations was dangerous because it would sacrifice "the moral and religious training, [and] the intellectual training . . . [by] restricting the instruction to a mechanical drill in the reading, writing and arithmetic."[13] Such cheerless findings, combined with an ever-increasing urge in Westmin-ster to curb the spending of the bureaucracy, led the vice president of the Education Department, a laissez-faire Liberal named Robert Lowe, to con-coct a simplified and, hopefully, more thrifty system that, when implemented in 1862, would become an onerous yoke around the British educational neck for the next forty years.

Lowe's new system—the Revised Code—altered the means of funding ele-mentary schools. Henceforth, school funding would be based on average attendance and a satisfactory examination report from the school inspector; this effectively created a system contemptuously called "payment by results." Since Her Majesty's inspectors only examined children in reading, writing, and arithmetic, other subjects that had been introduced under Kay-Shuttleworth's direction were discouraged and, as a result, the curricula of elementary schools narrowed significantly. The long-term results of the

Revised Code became apparent later when elementary education evolved into a rote process that ensured children could pass their inspection examinations. Meanwhile, teachers and school managers were tempted to and did falsify attendance figures so as to not lose grant money. Moreover, Lowe's changes eliminated Kay-Shuttleworth's prized pupil-teacher grants that led to a decrease in their number at a time when the emphasis on attendance caused those figures to rise significantly; the result was increased class size. Lowe had predicted of his new education system, "If it is not cheap, it shall be efficient; if it is not efficient, it shall be cheap."[14] His words were prophetic. By 1866, the education grant had decreased over £200,000 and attendance figures generally increased. Mid-Victorian thrift had prevailed. But educationalists, even retired ones like Kay-Shuttleworth, were keen to point out that the new system was harming education. The former secretary of the Committee wrote in 1868, "The intentions of the authors of the Revised Code have not been fulfilled by the greater proficiency of the scholars in the rudiments of reading, writing, and ciphering."[15] A cheaper, but perhaps less effective education system struggled on and by the end of the decade would face the most comprehensive changes of the century.

Before those changes, however, came Prime Minister Derby's bold "leap in the dark": the Tory Reform Act of 1867. This act expanded the franchise to the upper level of the working class by admitting borough householders who paid rates (property taxes); artisans, clerks, shopkeepers, and others received the vote for the first time, thereby nearly doubling the electorate. This enlargement of the political nation elicited memories of the 1832 Reform Act and some politicians, once resigned to the new parliamentary reform, echoed sentiments reminiscent of 1832: if the newly enfranchised class was to enter the political realm, they must have the necessary education so as to properly wield their newfound rights. Or as Robert Lowe stated with a mixture of bitterness and trepidation, it was now absolutely necessary to "compel our future masters to learn their letters."[16] Kay-Shuttleworth, retired for nearly twenty years, used the passage of the Reform Bill and his influential name on educational matters to bring education to the forefront of the government's agenda. In a pamphlet titled *Memorandum on Popular Education*, he offered advice on how the education system could be brought into better alignment with the expansion of democracy. He also boldly criticized the government's recent handling of education, namely the implementation of the Revised Code. In his call for further education reform in light of the Reform Bill, he wrote:

> Various powerful motives have promoted the growth and improvement of primary education, especially since 1846. But the recent extension of the franchise superadds

one which has never before operated with the same force. There is now a clear political necessity to fit the electors for the right exercise of their power.[17]

THE RELIGIOUS OBSTACLE

With greater pressure from the likes of Kay-Shuttleworth to provide more comprehensive education for the enfranchised working class, educationists began preparing for a legislative showdown following the Reform Act of 1867. First and foremost in the minds of those concerned with education was the enduring religious difficulty. The Church of England ran most elementary schools, mainly due to tradition and its financial advantage of being the state church. Additionally, all education legislation came under the intense scrutiny of and was heavily influenced by church officials. Since, in theory, most Anglicans and dissenters were unwilling to separate religion from education, the question was not whether religion should be part of the curriculum, but whether religious education should be sectarian (read: Anglican) or not. At the very least, Nonconformists wanted a conscience clause that would allow their children attending Anglican schools to opt out of religious instruction. A notorious mid-century religious census revealed to the surprise and horror of the Church of England that close to half of Britain's population preferred another church. Thus, it was clear that the Established Church was no longer as popular as it had been in the past. Whether or not they could maintain their domination over education was an open question.

By the mid-1860s, a growing percentage of dissenters wanted even more radical reform. They supported completely secular education because they did not like state funds supporting the predominantly Anglican schools. To these dissenters, it would be better to sever sectarian religious instruction from elementary schools altogether and leave it for their Sunday schools where they could control it. Moreover, a smaller, more extreme minority clamored for secular education purely on ideological grounds. However, the goal of the secularists was daunted by the fact that education had always been the preserve of religious bodies in Great Britain; the system that existed in the 1860s was the creation of the churches. It would be unfathomable to simply exclude religion from a system the churches had built.

THE EDUCATION ACT OF 1870 AND THE
CREATION OF THE DUAL SYSTEM

In 1868, as pressure was mounting to provide a free, compulsory, nondenominational, and for some, a secular system of education, William Ewart Gladstone became prime minister. His vice president of the Education Department was W. E. Forster, who introduced a bill to Parliament in February 1870 to radically alter the education system. In Forster's words, the bill was intended to only "fill up the gaps" in the current system of denominational schools, not to replace it. Since Forster interpreted the biggest problem as a paucity of schools, he proposed to create a system of schools run by locally elected boards in only those areas where the existing denominational system was deficient. The churches would be given a mere six months to meet those deficiencies, after which time a local school board could be elected and a school built and maintained from local rates. Each new school board would then decide whether or not to include religious instruction in their schools and, if they did, it had to be nondenominational. In effect, the bill would establish dual (and competing) systems of education: a new, rate-supported, and nondenominational system, and the long-standing, denominational, grant-assisted system. The bill provoked much popular interest and parliamentary wrangling and finally was approved into law after six months of intense debate.

DISSATISFACTION AND THE STRUGGLE FOR EDUCATIONAL EQUALITY

As is the case with most compromises, there was much criticism of the Education Act of 1870. It did not make elementary education free or compulsory, nor did it solve the religious difficulty. However, the Act did set the precedent that the state would provide schools in areas where the voluntary denominational schools could not so that children, no matter how poverty-stricken, would not live beyond the reach of a basic, nondenominational education. Despite the liberal ideology of limited government so prevalent at the time in the minds of politicians, especially that of Prime Minister Gladstone, the Act expanded government's role in education once again. The ever-vigilant Kay-Shuttleworth followed the introduction and passage of the bill with great interest, and it had his support. Forster even paid tribute to the retired secretary during the ensuing debate as the "man to whom, probably more than any other, we owe national education in England."[18] Kay-Shuttleworth also could monitor the bill's progress through his son, who had just recently been elected to Parliament and who, ironically, made his first parliamentary speech in support of the bill that continued the work of his father.

Kay-Shuttleworth published his final essay on education in 1876. In it, he reflected back on the workings of the dual system since 1870, and his anxiety about the course of education was palpable. Surprisingly, he now feared for the continued existence of the denominational schools and criticized the rapid growth of the board school system, which, he believed, might put the denominational schools out of business. With church schools educating two out of three school children but the best equipment and buildings and higher salaries going to board schools, Kay-Shuttleworth argued that should the church schools be ruined, the board schools would never be able to absorb their two million plus children. Therefore, the man who once fought the Anglican church over its virtual monopoly on elementary education now argued that the denominational schools were vital to the continued efficient operation of the education system and should be protected. He believed they had earned that right.

By the 1880s many religious leaders, Anglican and dissenter, feared that Kay-Shuttleworth's warning was coming true. The Catholic Archbishop of Westminster, Henry Edward Manning, a leading advocate for the preservation of the denominational schools, wrote in 1878, "Unless the efficiency of our voluntary Christian schools can be maintained, the School Board system, which [was] brought in as a supplement, will become the National system; and the Christian . . . schools will cease to be the system, and become the supplement."[19] Manning later served on the Cross Commission, which was initiated in 1886 to investigate the efficacy of elementary education since 1870. The Cross Commission's findings indicated that all was still not well in education. Manning and others like him who believed in the importance of the denominational schools issued a majority report that requested assistance from the rates, which only their competition—the board schools—received. A minority report argued vehemently against the majority's request.

Thus, the religious difficulty was still an obstacle, and the battle now was waged to achieve equal footing within the dual system. Denominational school supporters complained that since church property was taxed to support the board schools, their own schools should share the rates, too. Their opponents answered that it was not consistent with the modern liberal state to underwrite completely the teaching of denominational education, which is what putting the church schools on the rates would accomplish.

The course of education in Great Britain after the seminal Education Act of 1870 was anticlimactic and was primarily peppered with the state's attempt to tinker with the dual system. Attendance was finally made compulsory in 1880 for children aged five to ten. Eleven years later, school fees were abolished and, for the most part, elementary education became free. Lastly, Robert Lowe's much derided system of "payment by results" was discontinued in 1897. The piecemeal tinkering ended in 1902 when the Conservative Balfour administration altered the system significantly with another Education Act. The Conservatives were much more sensitive to the challenges faced by the denominational schools in competing with the board schools than were the Liberals. The 1902 Balfour Act abolished the haphazard school boards established since 1870 and placed the board schools under new local education authorities, or LEAs, which were created systematically across the country. Importantly, the act finally allowed rate aid for denominational schools, but put those schools under partial control of the LEAs. While the troublesome dual system was not thoroughly dismantled, the closest thing to a truly national system of education was ultimately established one year after the death of the queen who had given her name to an era so important in the history of British education.

The unofficial father of the British education system did not live to see these later reforms. Kay-Shuttleworth died in 1877 without much national notice. He remains one of those historical characters whose achievements are better appreciated long after his time has passed. While he considered himself to have failed individually after his falling out with the Committee, and he never achieved the social status that he believed his talents were owed, Kay-Shuttleworth, more than anyone else in Victorian Britain, caused the country to take notice of the importance of a sound education for an expanding democracy. Overall, encouraged by the movement for political reform, supporters of educational reform battled the powerful forces of laissez-faire economy and carefully maneuvered through the minefield of religious discord to finally lay the foundation for a national system of education.

SUGGESTED READINGS

The historiography of education in modern Britain is varied and somewhat dated. A good starting point would be with one of the general histories of education such as the still excellent narrative by H. C. Barnard, *A History of English Education from 1760* (London, 1969), which examines both primary and secondary education, or the somewhat less analytical but still comprehensive account from Mary Stuart, *The Education of the People: A History of Primary Education in England and Wales in the Nineteenth Century* (London, 1967). Other general examinations include the more ponderous chronicle of educational changes in S. J. Curtis, *History of Education in Great Britain* (London, 1967), and a more up-to-date examination in David Wardle, *English Popular Education, 1780–1975* (Cambridge, 1976). To better understand the political machinations involved in the early stirrings of education reform, one should try D. G. Paz, *The Politics of Working-Class Education in Britain, 1830–50* (Manchester, 1980). Picking up where Paz left off, Donald K. Jones examines in detail later stages of the political effort in *The Mak-*

ing of the Education System, 1851–81 (London, 1977), which covers the momentous episodes of the Revised Code, the Education Act of 1870, and the changes of 1880–1881 that made attendance compulsory. The interplay of religion and politics in the course of education development is found in greater detail than in the general histories in John S. Hurt, *Education in Evolution: Church, State, Society and Popular Education, 1800–1870* (London, 1971) and James Murphy, *Church, State, and Schools in Britain, 1800–1970* (London, 1971). An interesting and intensive study of the Education Act of 1870 is found in Eric E. Rich, *The Education Act, 1870: A Study of Public Opinion* (London, 1970), while the long-term effects of the board school system are covered in N. J. Richards, "Religious Controversy and the School Boards, 1870–1902," *Journal of Educational Studies* 18 (June 1970). Maurice Whitehead, "A View from the Bridge: The Catholic School," in *From Without the Flaminian Gate: 150 Years of Roman Catholicism in England and Wales, 1850–2000* (London, 1999); and John T. Smith, *Methodism and Education, 1849–1902: J. H. Rigg, Romanism, and Wesleyan Schools* (Oxford, 1998) offer examinations of how two denominations, Catholics and Methodists respectively, were engaged in the movement to improve education. A different approach can be seen in David F. Mitch, *The Rise of Popular Literacy in Victorian England: The Influence of Private Choice and Public Policy* (Philadelphia, 1992), which investigates one of the successes of education reform in the nineteenth century. Finally, to learn more about the leading educationist of his day, there are two biographies: the dated but still useful account by Frank Smith, *The Life and Work of Sir James Kay-Shuttleworth* (London, 1923); and the more exhaustive treatment in R. J. W. Selleck, *James Kay-Shuttleworth: Journey of an Outsider* (Portland, 1994).

NOTES

1. James Kay-Shuttleworth, *Recent Measures for the Promotion of Education in England* (1839), as cited in *Sir James Kay-Shuttleworth on Popular Education*, ed. Trygve R. Tholfsen (New York: Teachers College Press, 1974), 91.

2. H. C. Barnard, *A History of English Education from 1760*, 2d ed., rev. (London: University of London Press, Ltd., 1969), 2–11.

3. Elie Halevy, *The Liberal Awakening, 1815–1830*, trans. E. I. Watkin (New York: Barnes and Noble, Inc., 1961), 106–7.

4. Barnard, *A History of English Education*, 68.

5. Lord Russell to Lord Lansdowne, as cited in James Kay-Shuttleworth, *Four Periods of Public Education as Reviewed in 1832, 1839, 1846, 1862,* reprint (Brighton: Harvester Press, Ltd., 1973), 445–6.

6. Frank Smith, *The Life and Work of Sir James Kay-Shuttleworth* (London: John Murray, 1923).

7. Kay-Shuttleworth, *Recent Measures*, 91–95.

8. Denis G. Paz, *The Politics of Working-Class Education in Britain, 1830–50* (Manchester: Manchester University Press, 1980), 104–6, 113.

9. Kay-Shuttleworth, *Recent Measures,* 81.

10. See J. T. Ward and J. H. Treble, "Religion and Education in 1843: Reaction to the 'Factory Education Bill,'" *Journal of Ecclesiastical History* 20 (April 1969): 79–110.

11. R. J. W. Selleck, *James Kay-Shuttleworth: Journey of an Outsider* (Portland: Woburn Press, 1994), 206–7.

12. Barnard, *A History of English Education*, 109.

13. James Kay-Shuttleworth to Earl Granville, April 24, 1861, as cited in Smith, *Life and Work*, 262.

14. Barnard, *A History of English Education*, 112.

15. James P. Kay-Shuttleworth, *Memorandum on Popular Education,* 1868, reprint, (New York: Augustus M. Kelley Publishers, 1969), 18.

16. Asa Briggs, *The Making of Modern England, 1783–1867: The Age of Improvement* (New York: Harper & Roe, Inc., 1965), 521.

17. Kay-Shuttleworth, *Memorandum*, 6.

18. Smith, *Life and Work*, 291.

19. *Times,* July 1, 1878, 10.

Chapter Eleven

A Woman's Right to Be Herself: The Political Journeys of Three British Suffrage Campaigners

June Hannam and Myriam Boussahba-Bravard

On October 13, 1905, Annie Kenney and Christabel Pankhurst attended an election meeting in the Manchester Free Trade Hall. The speakers were prominent members of the Liberal Party—Winston Churchill and Sir Edward Grey. In the crowded hall Annie Kenney stood up and asked, "If you are elected will you do your best to make Women's Suffrage a government measure?" No answer was given and the two women were forcibly removed from the meeting. After a scuffle with police, they were charged with obstruction and, on refusing to pay a fine, were sent to prison for a short period. Their actions gained considerable publicity for the cause of women's suffrage and excited the imagination of contemporaries. They also initiated a more intense phase in the history of the British suffrage movement that was to be marked by new methods, including militancy. Women took part in demonstrations and processions and sold newspapers in the street. Some were prepared to take direct action that could lead to arrest and imprisonment, including the disruption of meetings, breaking windows with stones, pouring tar into post boxes, and burning down buildings such as churches. By their actions they challenged prevailing views about appropriate feminine behavior and put forward new models of what it meant to be a political woman.

THE POLITICAL JOURNEYS OF TERESA BILLINGTON-GREIG, ANNIE KENNEY, AND HELENA SWANWICK

Why were women prepared to defy conventions and to disrupt the pattern of their day-to-day lives for the cause of women's suffrage? What explains the political choices that they made over tactics and methods? What meaning did the suffrage struggle have for their personal lives? We now know that the suffrage movement was a complex one in which women made a variety of choices that could change over time. One way to explore that complexity, in particular the interrelationship between personal and public life, is to examine the political journeys made by individual women. This chapter, therefore, will focus on three suffrage campaigners: Annie Kenney, Teresa Billington-Greig, and Helena Swanwick.[1] They were all connected by the events of 1905. Annie Kenney took part in the action, Teresa Billington-Greig was responsible for publicizing the event, and Helena Swanwick was inspired by it to become a suffrage campaigner. All three became well-known leaders of the movement but have been overshadowed by Emmeline and Christabel Pankhurst in accounts of the suffrage campaign. They also provide an interesting contrast with each other since they came from different generations and social backgrounds and also joined different suffrage organizations. On the other hand they all sought a "woman's right to be herself" and tried to make sense of their own experience through autobiographical writings.

Annie Kenney (1879–1953), who started to work in the textile mills of Lancashire at the age of ten, was the fifth of eleven children in a family that had fallen on difficult times. She became one of the most well-known speakers in the Women's Social and Political Union (WSPU) founded in 1903. Under the overall leadership of Emmeline and Christabel Pankhurst, the WSPU pioneered the use of militant methods. Its members were known as suffragettes to distinguish them from constitutionalist suffragists who preferred to conduct their protest from within the law. Teresa Billington-Greig (1877–1964) was also active in the WSPU. She was born in Blackburn, Lancashire, into a working-class family, although her mother's family had owned a department store. She became one of the paid organizers of the WSPU, but in 1907 she helped to form a new group, the Women's Freedom League (WFL) that carried out militant direct actions, such as boycotting the 1911 population census or encouraging married women to refuse to pay their taxes, but rejected actions such as the destruction of property. In 1911 she left the WFL and became a freelance writer. Helena Swanwick (1864–1939), the daughter of Oswald Sickert, a German artist, was born in Bavaria but the family eventually settled in England, the birthplace of Helena's mother. Helena was educated at Girton College, Cambridge, where she met and married Frederick Swanwick, a lecturer at Manchester University. She joined the North of England Society for Women's Suffrage, a branch of the National Union of Women's Suffrage Societies (NUWSS), formed in 1897 under the presidency of Millicent Fawcett, and became an active speaker.

What attracted women from such different backgrounds to the suffrage movement? Annie Kenney said very little about the relationship between her early life and her later political commitments in her autobiography, but at a women's meeting in Germany in 1908 she did discuss the different ways in which men and women had been treated in the factory where she worked as a young woman. She also suggested that these differences occurred within the home as well. "When work was over it was the mother who rushed home to prepare the tea and do the housework. I used to ask myself why this was so. Why was the mother the drudge of the family and not the father's companion and equal?"[2]

YOUTHFUL REBELLION

In reflecting in their autobiographical writings on their initial engagement with feminist politics, Teresa Billington-Greig and Helena Swanwick put far more stress on their early family life as playing a key part in influencing their later politics. They emphasized their "rebelliousness" as young women and their search for some kind of autonomy. Nonetheless, it should be noted that they looked back on their early lives through the lens of a later involvement in suffrage politics, which then affected the narrative framework within which they told their stories. Teresa Billington-Greig rebelled against both of her parents, who quarreled incessantly and undermined her confidence by viewing her as "ugly." She despised her father for being insincere in his Catholic allegiance and also her brother who was "proud of being the only boy."[3] In the 1890s she was a girl who read avidly and debated everything passionately, but she was critical of the education that she received at her Roman Catholic school. The Billington parents had little tolerance for the plans of their younger daughter to become a teacher. She was expected instead to help in the home and also to work part-time as a dressmaker's assistant, which she feared would "leave me no time at all for study" and would "just swallow up my life."[4]

At seventeen she left home and eventually found a job as an assistant teacher in a Manchester Roman Catholic school. Unqualified and inexperienced, she decided to sit for a teaching certificate, which she passed within four months, thanks to the support of two female heads of her school. The tacit contract was that she in turn would help others in need and in her autobiographical fragments she recognized the importance of the informal help offered to earnest and promising students who were handicapped by their circumstances. At eighteen Teresa was independent. She supported herself through her teaching job, lived on her own, and planned to fulfill her lifelong ambition of writing. "I did not regard teaching as a future life-work (sic). It was not my goal, only a stepping stone on the way."[5]

Helena Swanwick also had a difficult childhood—she was separated from her family through illness and disliked the school that she was sent to in France. She also resented the ways in which she was treated differently from her brothers but was able to link her personal resentments with a wider political perspective when, as an adolescent girl, she began to read John Stuart Mill and Shelley. She recalled that

> it was greatly encouraging to find my own personal inarticulate revolts linked up with what I now recognized as a world movement. I had felt and resented the assumption that, whereas education was of importance for my brothers, it was of no account for me. I resented also that I was required to render them personal services which they need not reciprocate. When they had done their lessons, they went to play, but when I had done mine, I very often had to mend their clothes.[6]

She was infuriated when her mother refused to allow her to go out unchaperoned in case she was subject to male attentions and therefore raged at a society that "shut up the girls instead of the men."

For the women discussed here, it is difficult to disentangle experiences of work and family life, and their own desire for economic independence, from the development of their feminist politics. Teresa Billington-Greig found that her working life was compromised by her political principles. It was difficult for her to reconcile her dislike of religion with the obligation to teach the subject, and the matter was only resolved when she was found a position in a Jewish school. In April 1904 she founded, and was the first honorary secretary of, the Equal Pay League, a feminist pressure group within the National Union of Teachers, but was dismissed by the technical education board when she asked to be paid according to the job and not to female rates. Her ability to earn an independent living, her political commitment, and her emotional fulfillment all came together when she was appointed as a paid organizer of the socialist group, the Independent Labour Party, and then of the WSPU.

Helena Swanwick was in a different position because she did not have to earn a living, but she was determined to gain university qualifications, "not at all relishing the idea of living as a dependent at home."[7] Her parents did not see the point of a girl going to university and refused to pay anything towards the costs of her higher education. She was enabled to fulfill her ambitions by winning a scholarship and also because her godmother decided to make up the balance of her expenses. Helena was appointed a lecturer at Westfield College, London, but after her marriage earned a little money from coaching, lecturing for Manchester University extension classes, and by writing articles and stories that appeared in magazines. She then began to write for the *Manchester Guardian*, first as a book reviewer and subsequently as the author of articles on domestic subjects.

PURPOSEFUL LIVES

From their early years, therefore, all three of the women discussed here had recognized that women were restricted compared to the men in their social circles and sought to be economically independent. They also took an interest in public affairs outside the home. Annie Kenney was involved in the labor movement in Oldham, Lancashire, and sang in the Oldham Clarion Vocal Union. Teresa Billington-Greig took an interest in social questions, and in her quest for self-education and self-discovery was excited by the atmosphere of debate that she found in the Manchester Ancoats Settlement, 1896–1904. Through the Settlement she met others keen on social reform and compared her new acquaintances with an ideal intellectual and political family. It was here that she learned the art of public speaking and came in contact with women such as Eva Gore Booth and Esther Roper, who were members of the North of England Society for Women's Suffrage and had links with the labor movement. In 1903, when she faced a dilemma about whether to teach religion, she came into contact with Emmeline Pankhurst, a member of the Education Committee, who encouraged her to give less time to the Settlement so that she could become more active as a propagandist for socialism and women's suffrage. The two causes were closely linked in Lancashire, since the WSPU initially grew out of the Independent Labour Party (ILP) in Manchester. Teresa Billington-Greig became a member of the WSPU soon after it was formed and then spent much of her time speaking to trade union and socialist groups in the area in favor of women's suffrage. Emmeline Pankhurst and Keir Hardie, a leader of the ILP, were then responsible for her appointment as the first woman organizer of the ILP.

Fifty years later she saw her involvement in socialism as naïve: "It was compounded largely of ethics and humanitarianism, to be fulfilled in a dual society which would destroy masculinism and cast aside all creeds and crutches to rely on reason, love and fair dealing."[8] The labor movement's emphasis on denouncing the exploitation of male workers while women were penalized in their working and personal opportunities simply because they were female, reinforced the indignation of young women such as herself.

> This could not but turn the enquiring eyes of women upon their own condition, which they found was always at the bottom economic level of their class. A newly engaged shop assistant boy would find himself poorly paid, but it would be taken for granted that he should receive half as much again, or even twice as much, as a newly engaged girl.[9]

Helena Swanwick was also interested in social questions. She helped to start and then to run two social clubs for men and women and also helped out in a club for working girls. As a married woman she found it difficult to spend too much of her time on such activities since "whatever work I undertook outside the home had to be subject to the two great restrictions of time and money. It is too little realized how difficult it is for a woman with no spare money to pay the expenses of travel and other subscription necessary for most public work."[10] She believed that all the political parties were dishonest in their attitudes towards women and later claimed that her dislike of committee work put her off from getting involved in formal politics.

The three women were drawn to suffrage politics in slightly different ways, although they were all influenced by meeting suffrage leaders. Annie Kenney was persuaded by a friend from the local labor movement to attend a meeting of the Trades Council where Teresa Billington-Greig and Christabel Pankhurst were to speak. In her memoirs she claimed that she had never really thought about women's suffrage until she was carried along by the emotional appeal of Christabel Pankhurst.[11] This version of events fitted in well with the role that she was eventually to play in the WSPU of Christabel's faithful follower. As noted above, her meeting with Emmeline Pankhurst was crucial for Teresa Billington-Greig who then developed an interest in the suffrage movement as an integral part of her socialist activities. Helena Swanwick initially took little interest in women's suffrage, although claimed later that all the books that she had to review for the *Manchester Guardian* opened her eyes to the ways in which men viewed women and helped to make her receptive to feminist ideas. It was after reading about the arrest of Annie Kenney and Christabel Pankhurst in 1905 that "my heart rose in support of their revolt." She felt that "I could not keep out of this struggle at this time. It did not attract me; it bludgeoned my conscience."[12] Nonetheless, knowing a good deal about the Pankhursts meant that Helena Swanwick felt that she could not work with them, and therefore she joined the North of England Society of Women's Suffrage.

PROPAGANDISTS FOR WOMEN'S SUFFRAGE

All three women worked tirelessly for the suffrage cause so that their personal lives and their political activities were difficult to separate. Annie Kenney and Teresa Billington-Greig carried out a wide range of activities for their "militant" organizations. When she first joined the WSPU Annie Kenney spoke several times a day in the Manchester area and was viewed as so effective that she was sent to help Sylvia Pankhurst to "rouse" London. She campaigned among women workers in the East End and also took part in deputations to the prime minister. A character sketch written by W. T. Stead in the *Review of Reviews* compared her to Joan of Arc and described her as a "woman of refinement and of delicacy of manner and of speech. Her physique is slender, and she is intensively nervous and high strung. She vibrates like a harp string to every story of oppression."[13] In 1907 she was sent as an organizer to the West Country and from her base in Bristol addressed numerous meetings, in particular during elections, helped to form new branches of the WSPU, and staged flamboyant public events and demonstrations. From 1912, when Christabel Pankhurst had fled to Paris to avoid arrest, she effectively ran the WSPU in London. She was arrested several times and went on hunger strikes. After release under the Cat and Mouse Act she would recover in a sympathizer's home, address meetings, try to evade the government, and then would be rearrested—all of which is described in graphic detail in her memoirs. Her husband later claimed that her health never fully recovered from her hunger strikes.

Teresa Billington-Greig was also a good organizer and attractive speaker. In 1906 she went to London as a paid organizer for the WSPU where she set up local groups; wrote to newspapers; organized demonstrations, meetings, and debates; and gained a reputation as a compelling speaker. She was a large woman "with a round pleasant face" and adopted a Grecian hairstyle with plaits around her head. Sylvia Pankhurst claimed that she had "a great zest and enjoyment in life," while Annie Kenney noted the way in which she crushed opponents with the "sledgehammer of logic and cold reason."[14] Teresa Billington-Greig was also arrested and imprisoned on numerous occasions in these early years, but after disagreements with the Pankhursts she left the WSPU in 1907 and formed a new organization, the Women's Freedom League (WFL). For four years she gave most of her energies to the WFL, addressing meetings and writing weekly leaders in the *Vote*, the official newspaper of the League. After being injured in a train accident in 1911 she left the WFL and became a freelance lecturer and writer.

Most accounts of the extent to which suffrage activism could transform, and take over, women's lives focus on the militant wing of the movement, and yet all suffragists were faced with new forms of political activity that could be difficult to deal with. Helena Swanwick's autobiography provides a vivid account of the problems of a propagandist working within the "constitutional" side of the movement. Speakers often faced hostile crowds who could become menacing and were frequently pelted with food and dirt so that their clothes were ruined. Swanwick claimed that

> I did cordially hate walking up the streets of a strange town ringing a dinner bell to
> announce a meeting. I hated worse having to stoop and chalk the time and place of
> a meeting on the pavement. But perhaps my most fervent detestation was for the
> diabolical device which sent us to polling booths, there to stand all day and collect

the signatures of Voters for our Voters' petitions. The cold! The weariness! The drunken loafers and impish children![15]

This did not stop Helena Swanwick from becoming a very active speaker—in 1908 she addressed 150 meetings in England and Scotland. Her speeches were based on sound reasoning, but she did not inspire the same devotion as some of the more charismatic suffrage speakers. One contemporary in the socialist and suffrage movement, Ethel Snowden, thought that she was "a person of quite extraordinary intellectual power, a little lacking in tenderness to those of lesser calibre." She did not "suffer fools gladly" but was courageous, hated "cant and humbug" and was one of the "most commanding personalities of the women's movement."[16] She did enjoy writing an article for a newspaper at speed and in 1909 became editor-manager of the *Common Cause*, the newspaper of the NUWSS, at a salary of £200. When she thought that the paper would benefit from being produced in London, she moved there with her husband, who was now retired, leaving her home in Knutsford, Lancashire. In 1912 she resigned the editorship but remained active on the executive group of the NUWSS and played an important part in helping to forge an alliance with the Labour Party just prior to the war. She finally resigned from the executive of the NUWSS in 1915, along with several others, because she wanted to take a firm stand in favor of a negotiated peace.

EMOTIONS, FRIENDSHIP, AND SUFFRAGE POLITICS

Suffrage campaigning, that involved working closely with other women, did lead to the development of intense emotional relationships and strong friendships that in turn helped to sustain the movement. Annie Kenney, for example, was devoted to Christabel Pankhurst, although her husband claimed that both women "idolised" each other.[17] She did not complain, therefore, when the Pankhursts constantly represented her as a mill worker, dressed in shawl and clogs. She had indeed worked in a mill, but had left that life behind, while her family had been a very cultured one, encouraging the children to read widely, including Spencer, Darwin, and Voltaire. In her memoirs Annie Kenney recalled that while in Manchester, "I had to speak at every meeting and I had to start by telling them I was a factory girl and a trade unionist." Teresa Billington-Greig claimed that "at one time the propagandists of the suffrage movement made much publicity on 'Annie Kenney, the Suffragette Mill Girl' lines which she deeply disliked. Yet she bore it with patience for many years. I believed she was right to object, for it presented her origin in a false aspect."[18] She was very upset when Emmeline and Fred Pethick-Lawrence, key leaders of the WSPU, were expelled from the organization in 1912 since she had been very close to them, but she stayed loyal to Christabel until the end.

On the other hand, in particular when she worked as an organizer in the West Country, it was Annie Kenney who inspired devotion from suffrage campaigners in the region, especially those from a higher social class than herself. This comes through clearly in the diaries of a local suffragette, Mary Blathwayt, who lived with Annie Kenney for a short period at the height of the campaign. In order to free Annie for propaganda work, Mary made sure that her stockings were mended and that her clothes were cleaned. The diaries record Annie's health problems in great detail, including toothache, sore throat, loss of voice, and extreme tiredness. She had her own room in the Blathwayt's house where she could recover after strenuous speaking tours. In the diaries she comes over as strong-minded, capable of exercising initiative, and influential in her opinions. She was the one, for example, who edited articles before they went into the local press and who gave advice about political tactics.[19] Mary Blathwayt in turn was devoted to Annie, while Teresa Billington-Greig claimed in the 1950s that Annie's influence over Emmeline Pethick-Lawrence was "so emotional and so openly paraded that it frightened me as I saw it as something unbalanced and primitive and possibly dangerous to the movement."[20] Involvement in the suffrage campaign changed her life in many ways—she was taken abroad on holiday by some of the WSPU leaders and while staying with the Blathwayts began to learn French, to play tennis, to swim, and to drive.

Other women found it more difficult to sustain personal loyalties, in particular when the desire for autonomy and independence conflicted with the loss of self that was implied in collective struggles. When political differences were combined with strong and difficult personalities, it is little wonder that splits were common. Teresa Billington-Greig, for example, who moved from active involvement in the WSPU to form her own group, the WFL, disliked what she saw as the increasingly autocratic style of the Pankhursts and also the way in which the WSPU was drifting away from the labor movement. In their turn the Pankhursts were alarmed by her criticisms of their leadership and tactics and tried to sideline her by sending her to Scotland at the end of 1906. Billington-Greig wanted democratic elections and consultation with members and wrote a constitution to be discussed at the autumn conference, but Emmeline Pankhurst managed to rally support and Teresa was ousted from the WSPU in 1907.

There were real political differences between the two women, but these were also enmeshed with the clash between two strong personalities. Looking back on her suffrage activities from the vantage point of forty years later,

Teresa Billington-Greig noted with some bitterness how she had given up everything for the cause: "I gave up my teaching, my Equal Pay work and my activity at the Manchester University Settlement and sacrificed my chance of a science degree to forward the woman's cause through the ILP." She attributed her decisions to the influence of Emmeline Pankhurst who had suggested that she work first as an organizer for the ILP and then that she transfer to organizing in the WSPU. Teresa claimed that Emmeline "was a very wonderful woman, very beautiful, very gracious, very persuasive. To work alongside her day by day was to run the risk of losing yourself. She was ruthless in using the followers she gathered around her as she was ruthless to herself."[21]

Teresa Billington-Greig was also difficult to work with. Throughout her life she withdrew from organizations because they did not live up to her expectations, in particular the insistence that the means to achieve the end had "to be impeccable." Her daughter recalled that "she was quite without small talk and she couldn't tell white lies and she couldn't hide the fact that she was bored." She was unable to work with people for long "because she couldn't compromise" and although she worked tirelessly for the WFL she was described as "autocratic and overbearing in Committee."[22] When Teresa finally left the League it was with some relief, since she felt liberated in being able to write and speak more freely.

Helena Swanwick, who campaigned for the constitutionalist group, the NUWSS, also made political choices that were closely bound up with her overall political philosophy and her sense of self. She approached her politics as a humanist, seeking liberation for all human beings—hence the title of her journal, the *Common Cause*. She claimed that she chose the name "to indicate my conviction that women's cause was men's, but also because I was frankly sick of 'Woman this' and 'Woman that'."[23] Helena Swanwick believed that those who blindly followed leaders were useless for democracy and argued that hero worship was "no preparation for democratic politics." Thus she criticized WSPU leaders for calling for women's votes while not allowing women to have any opinions. We now know that the situation was more complex than this. Many suggestions for militancy came from the rank and file who often took action without the knowledge or consent of the leadership, while being pushed into speaking roles or chairing meetings could propel women into greater public activism and self-confidence. Nonetheless, Swanwick's dislike of militancy was so great that she resigned from the editorship of the *Common Cause* because NUWSS policy was not to criticize the WSPU in public, and she wanted to argue that militancy was counterproductive.[24]

Teresa Billington-Greig also sought to approach women's suffrage from a rational perspective in order to provide a contrast with the hysteria that she believed was being encouraged by the WSPU. Free from organizational ties, she expressed her ideas in a number of articles and also wrote a key text, *The Militant Suffrage Movement, Emancipation in a Hurry* (1911), while the struggle was still raging. Claiming that she did not oppose militancy as such since "I am a feminist, a rebel, and a suffragist—a believer therefore in sex equality and militant action,"[25] she did denounce the Pankhursts for their lack of trust in the rank and file and the use of "feminine" strategies such as charm or charisma instead of the ballot. She condemned the publicity that aimed to fill the coffers of the WSPU while suggesting that inflammatory speeches made activists into fanatics. She disagreed with the use of violence as a means to pressure the government into becoming a ruthless torturer against helpless activists who were made into victims and thought that those seeking emancipation should not reenact the traditional female sacrificial role. For her such imagery morally and politically betrayed the women's cause. Like the constitutionalist Helena Swanwick she believed that women had to have experience in democratic procedures, otherwise they would gain no benefits from the vote.

DEBATING WOMEN'S EMANCIPATION: CROSSING THE BOUNDARY BETWEEN PRIVATE AND PUBLIC

Both Helena Swanwick and Teresa Billington-Greig took a broad view of women's emancipation and, in their writings, sought to look beyond the struggle for the vote. Helena Swanwick argued that sexual exploitation and economic oppression were intertwined, citing the fact that women could make more from prostitution than from other forms of waged labor. She preferred to emphasize cooperation between the sexes than to foster sexual antagonism and began to focus on issues of class inequality. She called for a democratic franchise for men and women and worked hard for the Election Fighting Fund, set up to enable the NUWSS to help the Labour Party at elections. As a freelance journalist Teresa Billington-Greig increasingly began to write essays about the economic and class basis of women's oppression, while her books included *Women and the Machine* (1913) and *The Consumer in Revolt* (1912). In the latter she introduced the category of the woman consumer who, while segregated in the family, was unable to exercise full economic influence. On the other hand she also pointed out that the labor movement concerned itself only with producers and sometimes conspired with employers against the interests of consumers. Her ambitious theoretical attempt to overlay class divisions with those based on consumers and producers was not taken up to any great degree by contemporaries.

Billington-Greig was a star in the suffragist years when her status of employee made her belong to a structured political group. Becoming freelance she achieved political freedom, but her isolation before the war prevented her theorizing from making any impact on her contemporaries and she became a figure who was marginal from the political struggle. The mainstream economic and political climate was not conducive to Billington-Greig's mode of analysis about women's emancipation when emphasis was being placed on the vote. Her intellectual production never stopped, but her suffragist sisters largely ignored her after 1911. This suggests that it is important to study the production and circulation of feminist ideas at a time when suffragism dominated the political milieu.

During the suffrage struggle Annie Kenney, one of the key propagandists for the WSPU, developed her closest emotional relationships with other women. In contrast, Helena Swanwick of the NUWSS and Teresa Billington-Greig of the WSPU and WFL gained a great deal of support from their husbands and sought to live out their feminist principles in their private, married lives. Fred Swanwick had decided not to marry before he met Helena, and she was prepared to remain his friend "for life." They realized, however, that there were so many obstacles to this in late Victorian England that they did eventually marry. Helena recalled that Fred would take her part when her mother objected to her professional work and after "twenty-four years of being 'ridden on the curb' in this way it was little short of heaven to live life with a man who was the most libertarian and unegotistic imaginable."[26] Teresa Billington-Greig was visited while in Holloway Prison by Frederick Greig, and they were married in a lay celebration (February 1907) after which they both adopted the name Billington-Greig. (This was common for couples who worked in partnership in this period in fighting for the suffrage.) Their wedding declarations for sexual equality in marriage echoed Teresa's arguments in *Woman's Liberty and Man's Fear* (1907) in which she described the male tyrant's agony when his slave is about to be emancipated. She distinguished tyrants from "thinking men" who were willing to enter negotiated partnerships with women; she reviewed the fields where women were discriminated against and unsurprisingly focused on work. For Billington-Greig the vote was only one aspect of emancipation and would not be significant if mentalities and habits did not change in family and work life. Thus although most of the autobiographies of suffragette campaigners, generally written in the interwar years, sought to emphasize women's exclusion from the public sphere and to underline the seriousness of their cause by focusing on their public activities, this did not mean that they were uninterested in the ways in which their struggle for the vote would impact on women's oppression within the home as well as in the public world, or that they did not dissolve the boundaries between public and private life in the lived experience of suffrage campaigning.

AFTER THE VOTE

What happened to the three women highlighted here once the vote had been won in 1918? Annie Kenney gave support to Christabel Pankhurst when she stood as a candidate for Parliament in the general election of that year, but in 1920 married James Taylor and, after the birth of a son, played no further part in political life. Teresa Billington-Greig opposed the First World War and provided hospitality for war workers and Belgian refugees. She soon found, however, that she was immersed in financial problems. Her daughter Fiona was born in 1915, and she had to take over her husband's role in his billiard tables firm first while he acted as a food controller in Glasgow and then in the early 1920s when his health broke. When he lost his job in the 1930s because of a pay dispute, she became the family's main wage earner and in 1939 found a teaching post in a small London private primary school. She still found time to get involved in politics, and her achievements were impressive. She returned to the WFL in the interwar years, working in particular to get women selected as candidates for parliamentary and local elections. When women achieved the vote on the same terms as men in 1928, she set up Women for Westminster and also took part in a number of groups, including Women Electricians, Women in Business, and the Women's Billiards Association. She never again, however, occupied the center stage and used her ill health as a reason to resign from the WFL in 1938.

In the 1920s she proposed a series of press articles on women, and for women, which were refused for publication. Her position echoed what she had written in 1911 in the Militant Suffrage Movement:

> (In the women's rebel movement) we have been playing for results. The woman has been sacrificed to the getting of the vote. If we turn away from this movement and condemn it we must be ready to pay the price. We shall not have publicity. We shall not have the world for an audience. We shall drop to the level of the common place and do our common place work.[27]

After the Second World War she brought together her autobiographical writings since she believed that feminists could learn from what had happened in the past. These showed that she had retained her critical edge since she complained that the personal stories of how women went to prison, told without historical or political context, led to a far too narrow conception of what the suffrage meant.

Of the three it was Helena Swanwick, the NUWSS activist, who continued to have a political career at a national and international level. Her work for the suffrage had attracted her to socialism, and this was reinforced during the First World War when she turned to peace work. She found that the Labour Party and ILP women's groups had "stood their ground as pacifists far better than the men's," and she was inspired by the ideal of international sisterhood.[28] After the war she continued her interest in peace, attending the Women's Peace Congress in Zurich in 1919 and editing *Foreign Affairs*, 1924–1928, the organ of the peace group, Union of Democratic Control. She committed suicide just after the outbreak of the Second World War.

Reaching a peak of intensity in the decade before the First World War, the women's suffrage campaign was a defining moment in British history when women asserted the right to take part as full citizens in the political life of their country. Their demands posed a particular difficulty for the Liberal government, in power during the crucial years 1906–1914, with its rhetoric of equality and support for fundamental human rights. At a deeper level suffrage activists also challenged prevailing views about women's identification with the private sphere of the home, conventional gender roles, and what it meant to be a political woman. In taking part in the movement, women's own lives were transformed and boundaries were blurred between personal life, friendships, political tactics and strategies, and concepts of women's emancipation. Suffrage activists took part in a common campaign with other women to ensure that they were not excluded from formal politics on the grounds of sex. At the same time they faced difficult choices when differences between women were exposed. The varied political journeys taken by Helena Swanwick, Teresa Billington-Greig, and Annie Kenney reveal the close interrelationship between personal life and feminist politics. They also reveal the complexity of the suffrage movement and suggest the need for caution in too readily accepting stereotypes that draw hard and fast distinctions between women in the movement, and in particular between militants and nonmilitants.

SUGGESTED READINGS

There is an extensive literature on the British suffrage movement, and therefore it is useful to consult general texts which provide an overview and a guide to further reading, for example, Paula Bartley, *Votes for Women, 1860–1928* (London, 1998) and Sandra Holton, "Women and the Vote" in *Women's History: Britain, 1850–1945,* ed. June Purvis (London, 1995). A valuable and comprehensive reference guide to all aspects of the movement, including topics such as the jewelry and newspapers of the suffrage campaign as well as sketches of the leading participants and their organizations, is Elizabeth Crawford, *The Women's Suffrage Movement: A Reference Guide, 1866–1928* (London 1999 and 2001). Early studies of the detailed politics of suffrage include Andrew Rosen, *Rise Up Women! The Militant Campaign of the Women's Social and Political Union, 1903–1914* (London, 1974); Constance Rover, *Women's Suffrage and Party Politics* (London, 1967); and Lesley Parker Hume, *The National Union of Women's Suffrage Societies, 1897–1914* (New York, 1982). The relationship between women's suffrage and the socialist and labor movements is discussed in Sandra Stanley Holton, *Feminism and Democracy: Women's Suffrage and Reform Politics in Britain, 1900–1918* (Cambridge, 1986), while Jill Liddington and Jill Norris, *One Hand Tied Behind Us: The Rise of the Women's Suffrage Movement* (London, 1978) is a pioneering study that highlighted the involvement of working-class women. June Hannam and Karen Hunt, *Socialist Women: Britain, 1880s to 1920s* (London, 2001) examines the complex political identities of socialist women who were also suffragists and explores attitudes towards adult suffrage. Recent collections of essays have drawn attention to the complexity of the suffrage movement, in particular the local dimensions of the movement, contested definitions of militancy, the relationship between the leadership and the rank and file, and the importance of the cultural dimensions of the campaign. These include June Purvis and Sandra Stanley Holton, eds., *Votes for Women* (London, 2000); Maroula Joannou and June Purvis, eds., *The Women's Suffrage Movement: New Feminist Perspectives* (Manchester, 1998); and Claire Eustance, Joan Ryan, and Laura Ugolini, eds., *A Suffrage Reader: Charting Directions in British Suffrage History* (London, 2000). A thought-provoking study of suffrage imagery is Lisa Tickner, *The Spectacle of Women: Imagery of the Suffrage Campaign, 1907–1914* (London, 1987). On the benefits of a biographical approach to understanding suffrage history, see Sandra Stanley Holton, *Suffrage Days: Stories from the Women's Suffrage Movement* (London, 1998). The ways in which participants of the suffrage movement, through their autobiographies and other personal narratives, constructed a version of suffrage history that has had a long lasting influence on the interpretations of historians has been highlighted in Hilda Kean, "Searching for the Past in Present Defeat: The Construction of Historical and Political Identity in British Feminism in the 1920s and 1930s," *Women's History Review*, 3, 1 (1994); Laura E. Nym Mayhall, "Creating the 'Suffragette Spirit': British Feminism and the Historical Imagination," *Women's History Review*, 4, 3 (1995); and Kathryn Dodd, ed., *A Sylvia Pankhurst Reader* (Manchester, 1991). For an account of the continuing struggle to achieve equal voting rights for women after 1918, see Cheryl Law, *Suffrage and Power: The Women's Movement, 1918–28* (London, 1997).

NOTES

1. For brief biographical sketches see Elizabeth Crawford, *The Women's Suffrage Movement: A Reference Guide, 1866–1928* (London: Routledge, 2001).

2. Tricia Davis et al., "'The Public Face of Feminism': Early Twentieth-Century Writings on Women's Suffrage," in *Making Histories*, ed. Centre for Contemporary Cultural Studies (London: Hutchinson, 1982), 312.

3. Billington-Greig papers, file on childhood, quoted in Brian Harrison, *Prudent Revolutionaries: Portraits of British Feminists between the Wars* (Oxford: Clarendon Press, 1987), 47.

4. Carol McPhee and Ann Fitzgerald, eds., *The Non-Violent Militant: Selected Writings of Teresa Billington-Greig* (London: Routledge & Kegan Paul, 1987), 56, 57.

5. McPhee and Fitzgerald, *Non-Violent Militant*, 70.

6. Helena Swanwick, *I Have Been Young* (London: Victor Gollancz, 1935), 82.

7. Swanwick, *I Have Been Young*, 115.

8. McPhee and Fitzgerald, *Non-Violent Militant*, 78.

9. McPhee and Fitzgerald, *Non-Violent Militant,* 80.

10. McPhee and Fitzgerald, *Non-Violent Militant*, 159.

11. Annie Kenney, *Memories of a Militant* (London: Edward Arnold, 1924).

12. Swanwick, *I Have Been Young*, 183.

13. W. T. Stead, "Miss Annie Kenney," *Review of Reviews*, June 1906, quoted in Crawford, *Women's Suffrage Movement*, 315.

14. Harrison, *Prudent Revolutionaries*, 48.

15. Harrison, *Prudent Revolutionaries,* 201.

16. Ethel Snowden, *A Political Pilgrim in Europe* (London: Cassell, 1921), 81, quoted in Johanna Alberti, *Beyond Suffrage: Feminists in War and Peace, 1914–28* (Basingstoke: Macmillan, 1989), 12.

17. Crawford, *Women's Suffrage Movement*, 319.

18. Crawford, *Women's Suffrage Movement,* 314, 313.

19. For a discussion of the diaries, see June Hannam, "'Suffragettes Are Splendid for Any Work': The Blathwayt Diaries as a Source for Suffrage History," in *A Suffrage Reader*, ed. Claire Eustance, Joan Ryan, and Laura Ugolini (London: Leicester University Press, 2000), 53–68.

20. Crawford, *Suffrage Movement*, 316.

21. McPhee and Fitzgerald, *Non-Violent Militant*, 104, 94.

22. Harrison, *Prudent Revolutionaries*, 51.

23. Swanwick, *I Have Been Young*, 207.

24. See the discussion of her ideas in Sandra Holton, *Feminism and Democracy: Women's Suffrage and Reform Politics in Britain, 1900–1918* (Cambridge: Cambridge University Press, 1918).

25. Harrison, *Prudent Revolutionaries*, 53.

26. Swanwick, *I Have Been Young*, 144.

27. Teresa Billington-Greig, *The Militant Suffrage Movement: Emancipation in a Hurry,* reproduced in McPhee and Fitzgerald, *Non-Violent Militant*, 221–22.

28. Cheryl Law, *Suffrage and Power: The Women's Movement, 1918–1928* (London: I. B. Tauris, 2000), 16.

Chapter Twelve

Mary Butler, Domesticity, Housewifery, and Identity in Ireland, 1899–1912

D. A. J. MacPherson

The last quarter of the nineteenth century saw profound changes in the economic and social position of women in Ireland. As traditional female employment in agriculture and the textile industries declined, women employed a number of strategies for survival and well-being. Unpaid domestic work vied with increased educational and occupational opportunities, both in Ireland and abroad. In rural Ireland at the end of the nineteenth century, women came more and more to eschew work in the fields for unpaid work in the domestic sphere: by 1901 only 430,000 Irishwomen were in paid employment in contrast to 641,000 twenty years earlier.[1] Greater economic prosperity and structural changes in the rural Irish economy gave women the opportunity to swap backbreaking farmwork for the rather less physical, but no less demanding work as housewives.

The life and writings of Mary Butler illuminate the changing economic and social position of women in Ireland at the end of the nineteenth century. Mary Butler (1874–1920) was a fascinating woman and a prominent member of many organizations devoted to the regeneration of Ireland, including Sinn Féin, the Gaelic League, and the United Irishwomen. Her work and her journalism illustrate several important themes in the history of Irishwomen at the end of the nineteenth and beginning of the twentieth centuries: the increasing domestic role of women; how housewifery was seen as useful to the nascent Irish nation; and, consequently, how some Irishwomen saw their domestic prowess as a justification for their involvement in Irish public life through, in the example cited by Butler, participation in local School and Poor Law boards. Irishwomen's heightened domesticity was a subject of much comment in the Irish press and contemporary literature. Indeed, there was far more to the Irish housewife at the beginning of the twentieth century than mere domestic drudgery. Irishwomen flocked to classes on household economy, cooking, and cleaning in order to improve their household skills and become better housewives. Many Irishwomen saw the increasing professionalization of their housewifery through such classes as raising their status in Irish society and affording them opportunities to become involved in Irish public and political life. Butler personified the tension that sprang up at the end of the nineteenth century between a view of female domesticity that saw women's role in the home as a basis for intervention in the public sphere and a resurgent traditional (and markedly Catholic) notion that women should be confined purely to the home as wives and mothers.[2] Butler's writings on domesticity veer from one extreme to the other. As a profoundly Catholic woman, Butler saw women's role in the home caring for their children and menfolk in an almost spiritual light, yet she could also argue that the importance of this role meant that women should become involved in Irish public and national life.

WHO WAS MARY BUTLER?

Mary Butler was born in 1874 and spent most of her childhood between family homes in County Clare and Dublin.[3] Her background was that of a slightly *déclassé* Catholic, upper middle-class family, whose Dublin home was a reasonably grand Georgian town house in fashionable Upper Fitzwilliam Street.[4] Indeed, until her early twenties, Butler gave little indication of the part she would later play in the Irish revival of the early twentieth century. According to her sister Belinda's account of their childhood, Butler took "girlish pleasure" at the "balls, parties, theater going, pretty toilettes" that took up much of the social whirl of Dublin society.[5]

At the end of the 1890s, however, Butler underwent a conversion to the cause of "Ireland." Two incidents turned Butler from a Dublin society girl into an Irish nationalist. In September 1899 she heard a lecture by the San Franciscan Irish émigré priest, Father Peter Yorke, entitled "The turning of the tide."[6] Shortly after, Butler chanced across the work of John Mitchel, the famous Fenian writer who had been imprisoned by the British for his part in the abortive rising of 1848, and "rose up from the reading a convinced nationalist and with a fire burning in my heart which has never since been extinguished."[7] She soon became involved with "all the public Irish Movements" as her sister wrote and threw herself into the burgeoning Dublin "scene" devoted to literary and national revival.[8] In February 1899, Butler joined the National Literary Society that had been founded by the Irish poet, William Butler Yeats and company, earlier in the decade.[9] Indeed, Butler's literary efforts were some of the more intriguing contributions to the Irish revival. A volume of short stories, *A Bundle of Rushes*, appeared at the end of 1900 and was widely commended for its use of Irish paper, binding, printing, and subject matter.[10] (The importance of supporting Irish industries was stressed throughout Butler's work, and she saw it as an integral and indispensable part of a woman's domestic role, a point to which we shall return in greater detail below.) Six years later Butler produced her first and only novel, *The Ring of Day* (1906), an "unconsciously autobiographical" book, as Patrick Pearse, who would later lead the Easter Rising of 1916, wrote, which dramatized her own conversion to the national revival. As a review in the *Times* declared succinctly, "The central figure is a girl of the landlord class who first appears as part of a clever picture of Dublin society; until her emotions are stirred by 'John Mitchel's Jail Journal,' and 'fling her on the shore of Nationality.'"[11]

In 1900 Butler joined the Gaelic League, an organization founded in 1893 by Douglas Hyde for the promotion of the Irish language, culture, and industry and one of the very few Irish societies of the time to accept women on an equal footing to men. After the success of her paper, "Womanhood and Nationhood," read at the Central Branch of the Gaelic League in Dublin at the end of 1902, she was asked to join the executive of the League.[12] In addition to her involvement in the Gaelic League, Butler was prominent also in the early days of Sinn Féin, Arthur Griffith's organization dedicated to Irish economic self-sufficiency and cultural and political independence from Great Britain that arose in the first years of the twentieth century. She was a delegate at the first Sinn Féin convention held in 1905 and indeed was credited by Griffith with suggesting the name Sinn Féin.[13]

Mary Butler wrote several pamphlets for both the Gaelic League and Sinn Féin and in these she highlighted the importance of women's domestic role to the future of Ireland. In *Irishwomen and the Home Language* and an essay in the Sinn Féin *Irish Yearbook, 1908*, Butler argued that women could use their domestic skills to create the ideal Irish home, in terms of teaching their children Irish, encouraging Irish entertainments, and buying Irish food, clothes, and furniture and thereby have a positive influence on the life of the nation.[14]

DOMESTICITY IN BRITAIN AND IRELAND: THE HISTORIANS' VERDICT

Butler's idea that women could form the basis of the Irish nation had its roots in the rise of domesticity in Ireland at the end of the nineteenth century. Butler's writings concentrate on the domestic role of women and it was this role, as housewives and mothers, which had become increasingly prominent for Irishwomen. This topic, however, has only recently surfaced as an approach to the history of Irishwomen and the issue of women and work. What we did know about Irishwomen's work in the past was to be found buried in more general studies of Irish economic history on agriculture, demography, emigration, and industry. As the Irish historian Bernadette Whelan has argued, this approach has focused the history of women's work rather too fixedly on the famine of 1845–1849.[15] A rather skewed view of prefamine times as being some kind of golden age for women and work has thus emerged, with the second half of the nineteenth century characterized as a period of ongoing decline for women and their opportunities for work that extended well into the twentieth century.[16]

The last two decades of the nineteenth century, however, saw a dramatic change in the social and economic position of Irishwomen. Many women turned their backs on paid work and instead unpaid housework became their primary occupation.[17] Employment figures bear out this demographic shift—in 1881, 815,000 women were in paid employment; by 1911 the number had declined to 430,000; and the number of female agricultural laborers fell from 27,000 in 1891 to 5,000 twenty years later.[18] Yet, this did not mean that women lost power and status, quite the reverse. By moving into the home, women made the domestic sphere their own and used it as a base from which they gained power through their control of the household economy.

The reluctance of census enumerators to record female employment in rural Ireland (a common feature of most Western nineteenth-century censuses) is not enough to explain the enormous demographic shift in the nature of work that women undertook. Growth in the Irish rural economy between 1890 and 1914 aided women's transition to domestic work. By the end of the nineteenth century, the economic depression of the late 1870s had begun to abate and farm prices started to rise once more. Agricultural production increased by around 20 percent between 1890 and 1910, while the number of people employed in the farming sector declined from 936,000 to 780,000. Along with greater productivity came large investment from the state and private sources in rural Ireland, such as the Congested District Board (CDB), the Irish Agricultural Organisation Society (IAOS), and the Department of Agriculture and Technical Instruction (DATI). The prosperity of the countryside grew further with the development of cooperative credit societies, who by 1911 gave loans of over £56,000, and by the distribution of land effected by the Land Act of 1881, the Purchase of Land (Ireland) Acts of 1885–1888 and 1891–1896, and the Wyndham Land Act of 1903, which gave farmers security of tenure and greater capital for improvements.[19]

Moreover, structural changes in Irish agriculture contributed to the attractiveness of housewifery for women. Following the famine of the 1840s, farming turned its back on labor intensive tillage and came more and more to rely on pasture.[20] Increasing mechanization and the development of creameries, which took butter making out of the home, further limited women's opportunities to work in the agricultural sector. Thus, women worked less in the fields because there was not as much work to be done. Other traditional areas of female employment were also in decline. Opportunities for work in domestic service shrank as the demand for servants lessened towards the end of the nineteenth century. The textile industry, a mainstay of women's work, ceased to be an employment option for many women as the sector became increasingly formalized, and factory based. Irishwomen sought to sustain their economic contribution by turning their attention to housework and making the most of their worth in the domestic sphere.[21]

The increased prosperity of rural Ireland gave women the opportunity to relinquish their work in the fields and, instead, invest time and energy in the running of their homes. Furthermore, this was not a retrograde step for women to make. By devoting themselves to full-time housework women could play a crucial role in the Irish economy and thereby derive a great deal of power and status from control over household consumption and the welfare of family members. Housework was economically important. A recent study of female labor in Ireland has suggested that unpaid housework amounted to around 25 to 40 percent of gross domestic product.[22] Houseworkers, who were not necessarily housewives but could include single women (such as daughters) or unmarried women (such as mothers and sisters), took responsibility for the welfare of the family, managed the household, and were in charge of household consumption. It was women who would buy food, clothes, furniture, among other things, for the house, and such control over the household purse strings gave women great power.[23]

Moreover, the greater attractiveness of unpaid work in the home was not restricted to Irishwomen. A similar shift in female employment patterns was also evident in mainland Britain at this time. Housewifery was an integral part of most families' and communities' well-being. In a mining community, for example, tasks such as running baths for the miners and preparing meals were an essential part of industrial production. Housework was not simply defined by domestic drudgery. As the British historian Jose Harris argues, "Most working class women saw confinement to domesticity as a luxury to be sought after rather than an imposition to be shunned."[24] In Britain, women's employment opportunities came under similar pressures as those faced by women in Ireland. Home employment declined in the face of the expansion of industrial and factory systems outside the home and led to more and more women defining themselves as housewives and deriving a sense of status from so doing.[25] Indeed, many British women argued that their increased role in the home gave them reason to intervene in public life. Female participation in local government from 1869 onwards was seen as the domestic work of the nation. When women stood for local election "so that they might inspect workhouse beds and children's bodies for vermin, bring the damaged and delinquent child to school, campaign for clean milk, pure water, and no drink, they were reading local government, in the phrases of the time, as compulsory philanthropy, as municipal housekeeping, as domestic politics."[26] Women involved in local government work deployed the language of separate spheres to show how women's domesticity could nurture public life, arguing that they belonged in local government because they understood how public issues affected the home and family.[27]

DOMESTIC EDUCATION IN IRELAND

Domesticity was thus a promising option for Irishwomen at the end of the nineteenth century and became an important strategy for female survival taken up by a growing number of women in Ireland. According to the earliest available census data on the numbers of female houseworkers in the 1926 census, between 37 and 39 percent of all women aged 12 and above were classified as working in the home.[28] Using the census data from 1891 and 1911, it has been estimated that before 1926 the number of unpaid female houseworkers increased. In 1891, there were 993,000 unpaid houseworkers, which had risen to 1,082,000 by 1911.[29]

The power and status women could derive from their work in the home was confirmed by the attention given it in the press and the number of domestic education courses and schemes that sprang up under the auspices of the likes of the IAOS, the CDB, and the DATI at the beginning of the twentieth century. Mary Butler was interested in both of these areas of Irish life, writing many newspaper columns on the subject of domestic education and helping to set up a school for domestic instruction—St. Kevin's Park, which later became the chief domestic economy school of the DATI.[30]

The cause of domestic education for women's work in the unwaged sphere came to be championed by several government and private organizations. The task of teaching housework to Irishwomen was taken up by the Women's National Health Association (WNHA), the United Irishwomen (UI), the IAOS, the CDB, the DATI, the Board of Education and, in urban areas, the Irish Co-operative Women's Guild. Stemming from a desire to eradicate tuberculosis from Ireland, the WNHA was formed in 1907 by the Countess of Aberdeen (wife of the Lord Lieutenant of Ireland) and saw the women of Ireland as responsible for the health of the country. Women could prevent tuberculosis by improving their housekeeping; if the house was kept scrupulously clean, the risk of the disease catching hold would be reduced. And it was to the task of educating women that the WNHA set itself, offering itinerant classes, child care clubs, and by 1910 embraced a membership of 18,000.[31]

The UI, founded in 1910, had similar aims to the WNHA but promoted a broader role for women's domesticity than simply the fight against tuberculosis. The UI was part of the Irish rural reform movement, at whose vanguard stood the IAOS and with whom they had strong links. Horace Plunkett and George Russell (known as Æ), two of the leading lights of the IAOS, saw women as essential to the regeneration of rural Ireland. Plunkett argued that women's domestic role was essential to the later portion of his notion of "Better Farming, Better Business, Better Living" and Russell placed Irishwomen at the center of his ideas for the creation of a rural civilization in Ireland. The inaugural meeting took place on May 8, 1910, in the house of the organization's founder, Anita Lett.[32] This meeting led to the establishment of the first branch in Bree, County Wexford, followed by branches in the other counties of Leinster, and the counties of Waterford, Cork, Limerick, Clare, Galway, Mayo, Sligo, Donegal, Tyrone, Antrim, and Cavan with active membership prior to the First World War peaking at around 1,500.[33] The UI sought to teach cooking, promote temperance, propagate cooperative principles, and encourage women's involvement in such matters as dressmaking, horticulture, beekeeping, and raising poultry.[34] The founder of the UI, Anita Lett, detailed the work of the UI, examining the activities of the two permanent organizers in the twenty branches formed by 1912, "scattered from Donegal in the North, to Wexford in the South and to Kilkee and Connemara in the West."[35] The work accomplished by the UI included "training Nurses for rural districts, holding classes for girls on domestic economy, feeding school children—obtaining garden plots for laborers. Lectures on various subjects, holding of flower and industrial shows, needlework societies, besides concerts, dances, games, clubs and a host of minor things." Lett saw the day-to-day work of the UI as providing a framework in which women could contribute to the construction of an Irish national identity; the needlework classes taught women Irish designs using Irish lace; at concerts, Irish music would be performed and Irish games played.[36] Classes on domestic economy were seen as important if women were to maximize the potential influence of their control of the domestic sphere.

The largest domestic education classes, however, were organized by state bodies. The CDB started classes in 1898 within the "congested districts" of

Ireland, mostly the poor west of the country. Over five thousand women attended these classes, which typically would include lessons in basic cookery, laundry, and cleaning.[37] Following the example of the CDB, the DATI inaugurated its own schedule of domestic economy classes carried out by the department's itinerant instructresses. Each year up to fifteen thousand women attended these classes, which concentrated again on household skills of cooking, cleaning, and laundry work.[38] In addition, the DATI assumed control of many existing schools of domestic economy, including St. Kevin's Park, mentioned above. By 1900, local education boards, seeing the success of the CDB and DATI schemes, began to offer domestic education as part of their curricula, and at the outset of the Great War, almost half of all schools taught domestic economy classes.[39] Familial domestic work was thus seen as vital to women's contribution to the Irish economy, and the education schemes offered by these various bodies described above were designed to make the most of women's domestic skills.

MARY BUTLER: THE PRACTICE OF DOMESTICITY AND ITS PLACE IN IRISH IDENTITY

Like many middle-class Dublin women at the beginning of the twentieth century, Mary Butler devoted a substantial portion of her time to philanthropic work. Butler helped establish what her sister described as a Catholic equivalent of the Young Women's Christian Association. St. Kevin's House situated in Parnell Square was established in the first years of the twentieth century, and included domestic economy as a central component of its activities and housed around 110 young women and girls. Under Butler's influence, Irish classes and Irish entertainments were organized, and visiting speakers invited to speak to the girls including, at one occasion, Patrick Pearse. A related "holiday house and training school of domestic economy" were established at St. Kevin's Park, Kilmacud, near Stillorgan, at which Butler was involved with the organization of cookery classes. In 1904 the school became the official training school for instructresses in domestic economy for the DATI.[40]

Butler's work in the domestic economy school was the practical expression of her writings for the Gaelic League and Sinn Féin, as we have seen above, and, more appropriately, of her journalism; in her newspaper columns and articles we can see a clear snapshot of the domestic ideal in Ireland at the beginning of the twentieth century. Mary Butler wrote for many Irish papers, including the *Irish Daily* and *Weekly Independent*, the *United Irishman*, *Sinn Féin*, and the *Irish Peasant*. In addition she also wrote for the *Southern Cross*, an Argentinean newspaper published by William Bulfin for the large Irish émigré population in South America.[41] Butler concerned herself with two main themes: the importance of domestic education and the interpenetration between domesticity and Irish public and national life. She felt that Irish-women, by perfecting their domestic skills, could bring a great influence to bear on their households and their families and, by promoting the Irish language and Irish clothes, industries, and entertainments, women could help forge an Irish national identity.

Butler believed that if women were trained properly in domestic skills, they would then be able to educate their children and menfolk; women could teach their children Irish, promote Irish industries within the home, and help stem the tide of emigration by creating an Irish home and social life. In her column "Women's World" in the *Irish Weekly Independent*, Butler addressed the question of women's involvement in the revival of the Irish language. Irish-women, in Butler's assessment, were essential to maintaining the Irish language and that "on the women no less than on men of the family the duty is incumbent to preserve the language of the country—that great bulwark against the denationalizing and demoralizing influences."[42] Butler argued that it was a woman's "all-powerful influence" in the home that would best serve the Irish language and that "Irish mothers" should raise their voices "in the cause of godliness, and honour, and patriotism" in order to "teach their children to know and love their country." Butler made a direct connection between the Irish language and a woman's role, as a mother, in teaching her children how to be Irish.

Furthermore, Butler saw the need to supplement this national education with a firm grounding in the principles and practices of domestic economy; these two areas were, in her view, interdependent, and if Irish women were to be good patriots they also needed to be good housewives. Butler's 1900 article, "Education—National and Practical," argued the need for women to receive technical education and she conflated national and material causes.[43]

Economic and national issues were intimately linked, much as they were in the thought of Arthur Griffith and D. P. Moran, and, as Butler concluded, "Prosperity and patriotism go hand in hand."[44] Housekeeping was an economically productive task and could contribute to the well-being of the nation and, therefore, could be instrumental in the construction of "Irishness."

Butler used the meeting of "prosperity and patriotism" to put forward the notion that the home was the basis of Irish national life. In an article urging women to dress in "neat, serviceable, Irish tweed," she argued that women could help support Irish industries and thereby put an end to emigration, one of the defining issues of the industrial movement in Ireland. Irishwomen, therefore, could use their control over household consumption to buy Irish goods and clothes, and, in doing so, save the Irish nation.[45]

An anecdote from Mary Butler's unpublished memoirs illustrates how her commitment to the promotion of Irish industry extended to a practical, every-day level. Butler recalled a scene in which Belinda, her sister, demonstrated the Butler household's belief in "buying Irish":

> One day Sissie [Butler's pet name for Belinda] took a biscuit on her plate. Chatting animatedly she was about to lift a biscuit to her lips when suddenly she broke off in the middle of a sentence, a look of horror came into her eyes and she dropped the biscuit on her plate as if it had stung her. "What is the matter?" I asked anxiously. "It is a Huntly and Palmer biscuit," she announced. Of course we had ordered Jacobs biscuits [a well-known Irish make] but the grocer had sent the foreign article instead of the home make and the maid not noticing the difference had unpacked the biscuits and placed them in the table [. . .] I often smile when we think of that scene—Sissie dropping the English biscuit as if it were a poisonous reptile. She laughed heartily herself after the first shock of the discovery was over saying merrily "Just imagine how anglicised I might have become if I had eaten it. I've had a nar-row escape from infection."[46]

Despite the jocular tone, Butler saw the promotion of Irish industries as an integral part of women's domestic role and, as this incident demonstrates, was prepared to practice what she preached.

Butler, writing at the end of February 1900, made the important point that a woman's unpaid domestic work should be considered in the same light as paid employment, "We are all women workers, though we may not all be bread-winners."[47] Butler went on to suggest that a woman's most important work was in the home, "for the nation is made up of units composing fami-lies," and it was women's control of home life that determined the life of the nation, not any success they might have promoting women's rights.[48]

Butler saw a woman's influence on the nation as being most keenly felt in the home, and an Irishwoman would not be best serving the cause of Irish nationality by becoming involved in public life. This theme occurs repeatedly in Butler's column. Commenting on women's "Power of Influence," she made clear the importance of women's domestic role: "Very few women are suited to take part in public life, but very many in private . . . inspire some of the noblest deeds, the loftiest undertaking of humanity."[49] Remarking on women's involvement in the Gaelic League, Butler argued that women's involvement in national life should stem almost entirely from their domestic role.[50] Butler insisted that "women should take a part in the National life of the country" but this was to be achieved "not by mounting platforms and haranguing at the cross-roads, but by working quietly, unobtrusively, and steadily in private, among their own family and friends."[51] This attitude was similar to those Butler had expressed within the pages of the Gaelic League and Sinn Féin pamphlets, emphasizing the private, domestic role for women. Yet the crucial difference was the closer, more explicit connection between this domestic role and the construction of an Irish national identity. For Butler, women's influence in the home was immense, and by being good, patriotic housewives, Irishwomen could form the basis of the Irish nation.

Butler's distaste in these articles for female involvement in public life reflected the concerns of Catholic domestic ideology at the end of the nineteenth century. The hostility of the Catholic Church towards the idea that women could use their domesticity to transcend the limits of the home was a response to changes in women's economic and demographic position. Reacting to the increased occupational and educational opportunities open to women in the Ireland of the new century, the Catholic Church sought to reinforce their view of Irishwomen as devoted wives and mothers, who had no role in Irish public life. In an essay urging Irishwomen to discourage their husbands and sons from joining the British Army, Butler suggested that women's domestic abilities gave them ample reason to intervene in Irish public life.[52] Women should augment and maximize their domestic role by becoming active citizens in the public life of the nation, "They as much as men are citizens of this country and should take an intelligent interest in public affairs." Using the language of separate spheres, Butler argued that women should seek to participate in "Local Government, Poor Law Boards, and Urban and District Councils," where their presence could have an "elevating and purifying influence."[53] However, Butler concluded her essay by emphasizing women's maternal role. Children were women's "sacred trust" and through educating the young women, as mothers, had "an almost unlimited power in moulding the characters of our future citizens." Butler saw women, therefore, not simply as confined to the fireside, tending to the needs of their husbands; women's role in the home would only attain its full potential if Irishwomen also partook in the political and cultural life of the Irish nation. In a fashion, the interconnected nature of women's role in the home and their role in public life was almost axiomatic—if women were to furnish Ireland with homes imbued with a national spirit, then they would, by necessity, have to participate in the life of the nation. Butler's often contradictory use of the vocabulary of separate spheres demonstrates how the Irish domestic sphere was not an uncontested domain over which conservative, Catholic notions of home life held sway but was instead an arena in which women could assert power and influence over Irish public and national life.

CONCLUSION

The end of the nineteenth century saw domesticity play an increasingly important part in the lives of Irishwomen. The life and writings of Mary Butler demonstrate how, as more women turned to full-time work in the home, housewifery was seen as economically and, indeed, nationally vital. Through their command of the domestic sphere, Irishwomen derived well-being and fulfillment, and, in addition, great power; as women perfected their household skills in the numerous domestic economy classes that sprang up at the turn of the century, they could influence the nature of the home to an increasing degree. Domesticity became a central determinant of both female and national identity in fin-de-siècle Ireland and through an examination of the writings of Mary Butler, it is possible to see how housework came increasingly to define the position and role of Irishwomen.

SUGGESTED READINGS

Historical scholarship on women in Ireland has increased markedly in the past ten to fifteen years, and a number of works have challenged the assumptions of earlier work, such as Margaret MacCurtain and Donncha O'Corrain, eds., *Women in Irish Society: The Historical Dimension* (Dublin, 1978), which portrayed women as passive victims of an inherently patriarchal society. A number of good general works emphasize the complexities of Irish women's experience, from Maria Luddy, *Women in Ireland, 1800–1918: A Documentary History* (Cork, 1995) to Janice Holmes and Diane Urquhart, eds., *Coming into the Light: The Work, Politics and Religion of Women in Ulster, 1840–1940* (Belfast, 1994). The changing nature of women's work in Ireland is covered in a number of works. The earliest analysis came in Mary E. Daly, "Women in the Irish Workforce from Pre-Industrial to Modern Times," *Saothar* 7 (1981). A summary of more recent scholarship may be found in Bernadette Whelan, ed., *Women and Paid Work in Ireland, 1500–1930* (Dublin, 2000). Women's unpaid domestic work has been examined by two historians during the 1990s, Joanna Bourke and Caitriona Clear. Bourke's work is best summarized in *Husbandry to Housewifery: Women, Economic Change, and Housework in Ireland, 1890–1914* (Oxford, 1993). For the twentieth century, see Caitriona Clear, *Women of the House: Women's Household Work in Ireland, 1922–1961: Discourses, Experiences, Memories* (Dublin and Portland, OR, 2000). A critique of Bourke and Clear's work is D. A. J. MacPherson, "'Ireland Begins in the Home': Women, Irish National Identity and the Domestic Sphere in the Irish Homestead, 1896–1912," *Eire-*

Ireland 36 (Autumn-Winter 2001). For the issue of women and Irish identity after the First World War, see Louise Ryan, "A Question of Loyalty: War, Nation, and Feminism in Early Twentieth Century Ireland," *Women's Studies International Forum* 20 (1997). Material on the life of Mary Butler is rather sparse, but her work is discussed in Frank A. Biletz, "Women and Irish-Ireland: The Domestic Nationalism of Mary Butler," *New Hibernia Review* 6 (2002); Elin Ap Hywel, "Elise and the Great Queens of Ireland: 'Femininity' as Constructed by Sinn Féin and the Abbey Theatre, 1901–1907," in *Gender in Irish Writing,* ed. Toni O'Brien Johnson and David Cairns (Milton Keynes, 1991); Maria Luddy, "Women & Politics in Nineteenth-Century Ireland," in *Women and Irish History: Essays in Honour of Margaret MacCurtain,* ed. Maryann Gialenella Valiulis and Mary O'Dowd (Dublin, 1997); and in Timothy G. McMahon, "'All Creeds and all Classes.' Just Who Made Up the Gaelic League?" *Eire-Ireland* 37 (Autumn-Winter 2002). For an example of Butler's own writings, see her novel *The Ring of Day* (London, 1906).

NOTES

1. Joanna Bourke, "'The Best of All Home Rulers': the Economic Power of Women in Ireland, 1880–1914." *Irish Economic and Social History* 28 (1991): 36.

2. Of the few historiographical treatments of Butler's life and writings, none address this fundamental dichotomy, seeking instead to present Butler as an undifferentiated supporter of the traditional Catholic image of woman as the good wife and mother. See Maria Luddy, "Women and Politics in Nineteenth-Century Ireland," in *Women and Irish History. Essays in Honour of Margaret MacCurtain,* ed. Maryann Gialanella Valiulis, and Mary O'Dowd (Dublin: Wolfhound Press, 1997), 101–102; Frank A. Biletz, "Women and Irish-Ireland: The Domestic Nationalism of Mary Butler," *New Hibernia Review* 6 (Spring 2002): 59–72; and Elin Ap Hywel, "Elise and the Great Queens of Ireland: 'Femininity' as Constructed by Sinn Féin and the Abbey Theatre, 1901–1907," in *Gender in Irish Writing,* ed. Toni O'Brien Johnson and David Cairns (Milton Keynes: Open University Press, 1991), 24–28.

3. National Library of Ireland (NLI) MS 7321, Life of Mary Butler, 1.

4. NLI, MS 4577, Letter from Mere Columba, OSB, Abbaye of St. Michel de Kergonan, Morbihan, France, Nov. 6, Presented to the National Library including a letter from Arthur Griffith on the death of her sister Mrs. T. Nolan (née Mary Butler); L. MacManus, *White Light and Flame: Memories of the Irish Literary Revival and the Anglo-Irish War* (Dublin and Cork: Talbot Press, 1929), 34.

5. NLI, MS 7321, Life of Mary Butler, 10–11.

6. Máiréad Ní Chinnéide, *Máire de Buitléir Bean Athbheochana* (Dublin: Baile Atha Cliath: Comhar Teoranta, 1993), 1.

7. MacManus, *White Light and Flame,* 34; Ní Chinnéide, *Máire de Buitléir,* 29.

8. Ní Chinnéide, *Máire de Buitléir,* 1.

9. NLI, MS 646, Minute Book of the National Literary Society.

10. *Social Review*, December 29, 1900; *Lady's Pictorial*, January 5, 1901.

11. *An Claideamh Soluis*, September 29, 1906; *Times*, August 3, 1906.

12. *Daily Freeman*, November 15, 1902; NLI MS 7321, Life of Mary Butler, 21.

13. NLI MS 7321, Life of Mary Butler, p. 46. Sinn Féin is the Gaelic for "Ourselves Alone."

14. Mary E. L. Butler, *Irishwomen and the Home Language* (Dublin: Gaelic League, n.d.); "To the Women of Ireland," in The National Council, *The Irish Yearbook, 1908* (Dublin: Gaelic League, 1908), 336–339.

15. Bernadette Whelan, ed., *Women and Paid Work in Ireland, 1500–1930* (Dublin: Four Courts Press, 2000), 1.

16. For examples of this approach to the history of Irishwomen during the nineteenth century see J. J. Lee, "Women and the Church since the Famine," in *Women in Irish Society: The Historical Dimension*, ed. Margaret MacCurtain and Donncha O' Corrain, (Dublin: Arien House, 1978), 37–45; and David Fitzpatrick, "The Modernisation of the Irish Female," in *Rural Ireland, 1600–1900*, ed. Patrick O'Flanagan, Paul Ferguson, and Kevin Whelan (Cork: Cork University Press, 1987), 162–180.

17. Joanna Bourke, *Husbandry to Housewifery: Women, Economic Change, and Housework in Ireland, 1890–1914* (Oxford: Clarendon Press, 1993), 1.

18. Bourke, "The Best of All Home Rulers," 36.

19. Bourke, *Husbandry to Housewifery*, 17–21.

20. R. F. Foster, *Modern Ireland, 1600–1972* (Harmondsworth: Penguin Books, 1988), 333.

21. Bourke, *Husbandry to Housewifery*, 205–206.

22. Tony Fahey, "Measuring the Female Labour Supply: Conceptual and Procedural Problems in Irish Official Statistics," *Economic and Social Review* 21, 2 (1990): 163–191.

23. Bourke, *Husbandry to Housewifery*, 15–16.

24. Jose Harris, *Private Lives, Public Spirit: Britain, 1879–1914* (Harmondsworth: Penguin Books, 1994), 81, 72.

25. Bourke, *Husbandry to Housewifery*, 333.

26. Patricia Hollis, *Ladies Elect: Women in English Local Government, 1865–1914* (Oxford: Clarendon Press, 1987), 6.

27. Judith S. Lewis, "Separate Spheres: Threat or Promise?" *Journal of British Studies* 30 (January 1991): 109.

28. *Census of Population, 1926, ii. Occupations of Males and Females in Each Province, County, County Borough, Urban and Rural District* (Dublin, 1926), 13.

29. Bourke, *Husbandry to Housewifery*, 201–206.

30. NLI MS 7321, Life of Mary Butler, 14.

31. Bourke, *Husbandry to Housewifery*, 236–239.

32. Sarah McNamara, *Those Intrepid United Irishwomen: Pioneers of the Irish Countrywomens' Association* (Parteen, Limerick: S. McNamara, 1995), 20.

33. Joanna Bourke, "'The Health Caravan': Domestic Education and Female Labour in Ireland, 1890–1914," *Eire-Ireland* 24 (Winter 1989): 21.

34. "Among the Societies," "The United Irishwomen," *Irish Homestead*, May 28, 1910.

35. Anita Lett, *Women's Work in Rural Districts: From a Paper Read at the Alexandra College, Dublin, April 27, 1912* (Wexford: pr. by the People, 1912), 10.

36. "United Irishwomen," *Irish Homestead*, (November 5, 1910), 925.

37. British Parliamentary Papers, CDB, *9th Report, 1900* (Cd. 239), HC 1900, lxvii, 39–40.

38. British Parliamentary Papers, DATI, *4th Annual General Report, 1903–1904* (Cd. 2509), HC 1905, xxi, 5–6.

39. Bourke, *Husbandry to Housewifery*, 245–248.

40. NLI MS 7321, Life of Mary Butler, 14.

41. NLI MS 13810 (5), William Bulfin Papers, Letters to and from Mary Butler, October 28, 1903.

42. Mary Butler, "Women's World," "The Language of St. Brigid," *Irish Weekly Independent* (*IWI*), October 21, 1899.

43. Butler, "Woman's World," "Education—National and Practical," *IWI*, May 19, 1900.

44. Butler, "Woman's World," "Education—National and Practical," *IWI*, May 19, 1900.

45. Butler, "Woman's World," "Practical Patriotism," *IWI*, March 24, 1900.

46. Quoted in Ní Chinnéide, *Máire de Buitléir*, pp. 72–73. This story is also interesting for what it tells us about the essentially middle-class nature of the Gaelic League and the "Buy Irish" campaigns. Belinda Butler's narrow scrape with an English-made biscuit is seen as the error of their grocer and their maid.

47. Butler, "Woman's World," *IWI*, February 24, 1900.

48. Butler, "Woman's World," *IWI*, February 24, 1900.

49. Butler, "Woman's World," "Power of Influence," *IWI*, March 31, 1900.

50. Butler, "Woman's World," "A Duty and a Privilege," *IWI*, May 26, 1900.

51. Butler, "Woman's World," "A Duty and a Privilege," *IWI*, May 26, 1900.

52. Butler, "To the Women of Ireland," 336–339.

53. Butler, "To the Women of Ireland," 336–339.

Chapter Thirteen

G. K. Chesterton and British National Identity in World War I

Susan Hanssen

In the summer of 1914, despite German challenges to British imperial claims and naval superiority, there was no evident or long-standing Anglo-German enmity that made war between the two countries appear inevitable. Animosity between France and Germany had come to seem a natural feature of the European scene by the twentieth century, but many in Britain still considered France their historic enemy and cultural opposite as well. The declaration of war between Germany and Great Britain on August 4, 1914, appeared to be the result of a very circuitous series of diplomatic events, following the assassination of the Archduke Franz Ferdinand, heir to the Austrian throne. In retrospect—after four years of horrifying bloodshed—many considered the domino effect that the assassination of the Austrian crown prince had had on the European system of alliances a tragic farce.

As the wheels of general European mobilization creaked forward, the wheels of cultural mobilization also began to move. The British government asked Charles F. G. Masterman, a former journalist, Liberal MP, and cabinet member, to form a new Ministry of Information, which would bring together the best-known authors of the period.[1] Their task was to justify the war, express their support for the government, and encourage voluntary enlistment. They were also to counter the German propagandists who had begun immediately to call the British people traitors to the Anglo-Saxon race.[2] After the war, a significant group of British writers looked back on the experience as a kind of national "identity crisis." They recalled how many Victorians had hailed the "Teutonic" peoples as the vanguard of civilization and how many Edwardians had emulated German models of education and social reform.

Most British soldiers and civilians, however, did not experience the war as a national "identity crisis" nor abandon public expressions of patriotism after the war. The British public responded to the declaration of war with unprecedented enthusiasm, and their support did not waiver. Considering the horrors of the new kind of total war, the British public's united willingness to "see it through" remains one of the central mysteries of the war.

INTRODUCING G. K. CHESTERTON

G. K. Chesterton, a prolific journalist who achieved a kind of iconic status as spokesman for Christian England before the war, viewed the outbreak of war with Germany as a kind of cathartic renewal of English patriotism. Chesterton provides an interesting example of someone whose prewar political radicalism rolled back to reveal a resistant core of national piety in 1914. After years in which his political writing had tended increasingly in the direction of vehement radicalism, Chesterton seemed to have reached a turning point in his career. In 1913 he transferred his twelve-year run of Saturday opinion columns in the liberal *Daily News* to the socialist *Daily Herald.* He also began a series of articles on freedom of the press for the *British Review*, a weekly Roman Catholic journal. These 1913–1914 articles for the *Daily Herald* and the *British Review* are perhaps the most disaffected he ever wrote. But at the outbreak of war, when the *Daily Herald* became fiercely pacifist, Chesterton broke his connection with the paper, was recruited by Masterman for the Ministry of Information, and immediately began writing a series of articles supporting the war for the *Daily Mail*, one of the largest of the mass circulation dailies in Britain.

CHESTERTON AND BRITISH IDENTITY

Chesterton recognized that the war had enabled a new kind of understanding of what it meant to be British. His wartime writing attempted to answer, for himself and for the public, the question, "What was it that has made the British peoples thus defer not only their artificial parade of party politics, but their real social and moral complaints and demands? What is it that has united all of us against the Prussian, as against a mad dog?"[3] His answer, as it gradually emerged, was that the British had reacted against racial definitions of national character and acquired a new willingness to acknowledge the influence of a larger European cultural heritage in forming the liberal, antistatist elements in the British tradition. He observed that during the war England had discovered "a very broken, belated, and inadequate sense of having an obligation to Europe, but no sort of sense whatever of having any obligation to Teutonism."[4]

Chesterton's wartime writing renegotiated Britain's cultural relationship with her various allies—Russia, France, Italy, and the United States. Chesterton's first wartime work, the *Daily Mail* series of articles, republished as *The Barbarism of Berlin* (1914), attempted to explain how Britain could ally herself with the Russians, whom the German propagandists referred to as the "barbarians of the east." In a second book, *The Crimes of England* (1915), he tried to soften the British animosity towards France by pointing out that if the French tended towards creating an all-powerful, unified state, as the English traditionally asserted, England herself had not been immune to the temptation towards statism. Later the same year, in *Letters to an Old Garibaldian* (1915), Chesterton revived the memory of the Italian hero's triumphal tour through Britain to provide a context for England's alliance with Italy. In his last and most ambitious wartime project, *A Short History of England* (1917), he attempted to secure in advance the meaning of a possible Anglo-American alliance. The common thread in these works is Chesterton's attempt to knit England into a community of European nations defined by a tradition of Christian liberalism.

THE CHRISTIAN LIBERAL TRADITION

In *The Barbarism of Berlin,* Chesterton insisted that, however backward and Byzantine the Russians seemed politically, Russian patriotism lay within the Christian liberal tradition of the West because it included some notion of reciprocity and respect for the patriotism of other nations. Russian barbarism was a case of "old barbarism" overlaid with European traditions. The "new barbarism" of Teutonism, on the other hand, was incompatible with Western patriotism understood as a Christian virtue because "the claim of racial superiority is the last and worst of the refusals of reciprocity."[5] If there was any irony in the wartime alliances, Chesterton observed, it was that the thoroughly modern English had emerged unscathed from the influence of German pseudoscientists like Harnack and Haeckel, who made racial appeals to the English as "fellow Teutons" and had managed to tie themselves to the Russians based on some older and deeper bond.[6]

Chesterton elaborated reasons for England's "sluggish" belatedness in allying herself with European liberalism against Teutonism in *The Crimes of England*. He argued that the English came late to the struggle against Prussianism because they themselves "had also sadly strayed" from their native

Christian liberal tradition into the thickets of racial theory.[7] Chesterton wrote that England's greatest crime was her treatment of Ireland, which he considered a part of Britain's attempt in the midst of the Napoleonic wars, to transform their traditional eclectic polity into a unitary state ruled by an enlightened elite with the aid of German mercenaries.[8] He nevertheless insisted that William Cobbett and Charles Dickens gave voice to the true English spirit when they protested the illiberal tendencies of the nineteenth century.[9]

Letters to an Old Garibaldian was an ambitious attempt to reimagine Britain's cultural relationship with Italy. While in the two previous works he had explained what European character was not (a racial identity or a religious allegiance to the state), in his third wartime book Chesterton moved towards a more positive formulation. He noted the common ground in the controversies that marked their national histories—"the quarrel which (very tragically I think) has for some years cloven the Christian from the Liberal ideal"—but argued that the internal factions of Italian and English politics, the Catholics and Jacobins, the clergy and republicans, had joined in "an instant alliance" against the brutalities of race theory.[10] "They have only to look northward and behold the third thing, which thinks it is superior to both . . . Neither religion at its worst nor republicanism at its worst ever offered the coarse insult to all mankind that is offered by this new and naked universal monarchy . . . In citizen and Christian sinner there has always been something which your ancestors called *Verecundia*, which is at once humility and dignity."[11] In 1914, he believed, the British had united against Prussianism by a "universal flash of faith—or, if you will, suspicion."[12] He believed that the Napoleonic Wars, the Crimean War, and the Boer War had caused more internal controversy than the war with Germany: "For the first time, perhaps, what we call the United Kingdom entirely deserves its name. There has been nothing like such unanimity within an Englishman's recollection."[13] Chesterton therefore considered the wartime alliance between England and Italy a revelation of Europe united beneath divisions of race, nation, class, and party, defined by allegiance to the "liberty and laughter" flowing from a religiously-grounded belief in a common human nature.[14] Against the Germans, who saw only the myth of race, this European tradition upheld the belief that every man was "as an Italian more than Italian, as Englishman more than Englishman."[15] Having arrived at an understanding of a shared European identity, Chesterton began work on his history of England, a piece of wartime writing that exploded the boundaries of simple propaganda.

ENGLISH HISTORY AND NATIONAL IDENTITY

Chesterton's greatest contribution to the wartime renewal of British patriotism was his *Short History of England*, which took on the task of smoothing over the American Revolution and laying the groundwork for the Anglo-American wartime alliance by providing an account of cultural unity founded on language rather than race. Chesterton was explicit about what he hoped to accomplish in his *Short History*. In the introduction to the book, he wrote that he wanted to surpass J. R. Green's popular *Short History of the English People*, which had replaced the protagonists of older celebratory histories—the English Constitution and the British Parliament—with the Anglo-Saxon race. Chesterton realized that any attempt to disengage popular British history from Anglo-Saxon racism without dampening patriotic enthusiasm during wartime was a delicate task. He therefore proceeded by connecting with the traditional patriotic history in every crucial episode, providing a series of sympathetic rereadings of the familiar narrative. One reviewer for the *Church Times* noted that Chesterton built on the history acquired by "any intelligent schoolboy" and accepted "the importance of legend, as revealing the mind of the common people."[16] The *New Statesman* agreed that "it is curious to notice how often Mr. Chesterton can accept statements of historians and even their interpretations of particular events. It is in the cast which he gives to the whole that he differs from them."[17] The result was so effective a renegotiation of England's history that reviewers declared that future generations would refer to Chesterton as the "Sage of Fleet Street" or the "Sage of Beaconsfield" because he had achieved "the sort of history, as he might claim, that makes history."[18]

Chesterton began by dealing directly with the question of the racial origins of the nation. "The orthodox modern history, notably Green, remarks on the singularity of Britain in being alone of all Roman provinces wholly cleared and re-peopled by a Germanic race."[19] Chesterton dismisses race as a factor in English character and launches his narrative from the common ground of all European nations, saying, "In the barbarous twilight of history," before one can know with certainty "whether the Britons . . . were Iberian or Cymric or Teutonic," one finds that "they were Roman . . . The important thing about France and England is not that they have Roman remains. They are Roman remains."[20]

Chesterton thus began his story by redefining the "singularity of Britain," arguing that what made England unique was the fact that she was the last-born of the Roman provinces. "Pre-Christian Rome," he says, "was regarded as something mystical for long afterwards by all European men," because the attempt at republicanism was considered "the utmost Man had done."[21] But the conquest of far-off England proved that Roman republicanism was itself liable to corruption. The English slaves sold in Roman slave-markets were signs that the Roman ideal of a "small civic community" was already overextended. England only became a Roman province as Christianity appeared, preaching the doctrine of sin and redemption and suggesting that "even good government was not good enough."[22] As the power of the Roman Empire disintegrated, Chesterton says, England took her essential character from the Christian reaffirmation of the "loose localism" of the Roman ideal.[23] England, being the furthest and last-born province of the dying empire, remained relatively untouched by the alternative vision that would haunt medieval and modern Europe, the dream of a Holy Roman Empire, a sanctification of pagan reality rather than the pagan ideal.[24] England thus acquired a unique historic role in European history as bearer of republican and Christian liberalism. By making "the singularity of Britain" her allegiance to an ancient tradition, Chesterton avoided the deterministic quality that seeped into Whig history when racial or economic factors became the defining features of national character. As one reviewer wrote, other historians "could not get away from the belief that political and economic factors were the most important things in life, which is a very partial way of approaching the spirit of a people . . . Green made the English nation the subject of his book, while Mr. Chesterton makes it his hero."[25]

The rest of Chesterton's narrative is a tale of his hero's survival against odds. Chesterton evokes Alfred the Great and the Arthurian legend as signs that the English maintained their Roman and Christian heritage during the Dark Ages.[26] Because of his emphasis on the continuity of Roman-Christian culture through the Anglo-Saxon period, the Norman invasion of 1066 does not present any essential discontinuity in his narrative. William of Normandy "was what Julius Caesar was, what St. Augustine was: he was the ambassador of Europe to Britain."[27] The great Norman invasion was merely one of the "three great southern visitations which civilized these islands."[28] Chesterton envisions medieval England as still "full of local affections," the Christian tradition guarding the "mystery of locality" with pilgrimages and local patron saints.[29] This "freer element in Feudalism" resisted the urge towards centralization, imperialism, and utopianism.[30] "The feudal undergrowth prevented even a full attempt to build the *Civitas Dei*, or ideal medieval state."[31] For Chesterton the medieval barons resisting King John were not guardians of a peculiar Anglo-Saxon constitution against Latin corruptions so much as bearers of Europe's ancient Christian liberalism.

Turning to the early modern period Chesterton goes on to deny that the Reformation, the defeat of the Spanish Armada, or the Glorious Revolution represent significant breaks in the continuity of English identity.[32] In the progressive-Whig tradition, Elizabeth's reign and the triumph of the navy represented the beginnings of modern liberty, linked, especially in Froude and Green, to the rise of Protestantism, commercialism, and imperialism. For Chesterton, Elizabeth was a Little Englander, a new Alfred. He objects to "wooden cliches about the birth of the British Empire and the spacious days of Queen Elizabeth" as contradicting "the crucial truth" of the episode, which was that England was a small nation fighting against a vast empire.[33] Even Shakespeare, "the great poet of the spacious days," Chesterton says, "does not praise [England] as spacious, but only as small, like a jewel."[34] For Chesterton the defeat of the Spanish Armada is Little England's myth of miraculous survival rather than the British Empire's myth of origin. The Glorious Revolution, cleared of its religious coloring, is also presented as a struggle of a small nation for local liberty against the imperial state at home and imperial invasion from abroad. "The Whigs were . . . defending some remains of medieval liberty."[35] Chesterton's unwavering thrust was the continuity of England's national life from its earliest Roman-Christian beginnings.

BRITAIN AND AMERICA:
THE ENGLISH-SPEAKING PEOPLES

The real cultural labor of *The Short History* came, however, in the two chapters that deal with the Anglo-American relationship. Chesterton made clear in these chapters that he considered language the key to cultural identity, and language united the British and Americans in the eighteenth and nineteenth century even when war seemed to divide them. Chesterton thus fortified the idea of the "English-speaking peoples" as a cultural alternative to the racial category of "Anglo-Saxons"—an idea that would later be taken up by Winston Churchill to such great effect. "We cannot," Chesterton sets down, "understand the eighteenth century so long as we suppose that rhetoric is artificial."[36] Chesterton's argument is twofold: on the one hand he argues that in spite of illiberal government measures by the British Parliament, the language of the leaders in Parliament never matched their actions; alternatively, he points out that the language of radicals like William Cobbett and Charles Dickens represent more truly British popular sentiment.[37] In a famous passage he acknowledged that "all through the great Whig speeches about liberty, all through the great Tory speeches about patriotism, through the period of Wandewash and Plassy, through the period of Trafalgar and Waterloo, one process was steadily going on in the central senate of the nation. Parliament was passing bill after bill for the enclosure, by the great landlords, of such of the common lands as had survived out of the great communal system of the Middle Ages."[38] Rather than dismissing these speeches as the empty ideological covering the ruling class always gives to its actions, however, Chesterton argued that the reality of language could not be so easily dismissed:

> The English aristocrats of the eighteenth century had a real enthusiasm for liberty; their voices lift like trumpets upon the very word. Whatever their immediate fore-

bears may have meant, these men meant what they said when they talked of the high memory of Hampden or the majesty of Magna Charta . . . Now, before any criticism of the eighteenth-century worthies must be put the proviso of their perfect artistic sincerity. Their oratory was unrhymed poetry, and it had the humanity of poetry.[39]

It was this allegiance to the language of liberalism, Chesterton insisted, that set Britain apart from "the little inland state of the stingy drill-sergeants of Potsdam" and enabled him to end the section with applause for Admiral Nelson as "the incarnation of a spirit in the English that is purely poetic."[40] He takes Nelson's famous last words as a symbol of a cultural connection between England's aristocracy and her Roman-Christian past. "The expression 'hearts of oak' . . . is no mean phrase for the finer side of that England of which he was the best expression. The mere name of oak calls back like a dream those dark but genial interiors of colleges and country houses, in which great gentlemen, not degenerate, almost made Latin an English language and port an English wine."[41]

Nevertheless, Chesterton more enthusiastically celebrated the popular radical tradition in England than the remnants of liberalism surviving in the upper classes. In the concluding lines of his *Short History*, Chesterton took note of the dominant strain of irony in the letters, poems, and memoirs streaming from the trenches. He took this irony as a sign of the vitality of England's liberal spirit. "An illogical laughter survives everything in the English soul" as a sign of the simultaneous belief in human freedom and divine providence.[42] "This is the colour and the character that has run through the realities of English history, and it can hardly be put in a book, least of all a historical book. It has flashes in our fantastic fiction and in the songs of the street, but its true medium is conversation. It has no name but incongruity."[43] Here Chesterton suggests that the language of the people preserves in more robust form what the language of the Parliament tenuously mirrors. The belief in the ineradicable trace of God's image in man is born along through history in this tenacious sense of hope and humor:

That sort of liberty, that sort of humanity, and it is no mean sort, did indeed survive all the drift and downward eddy of an evil economic system, as well as the dragooning of a reactionary epoch and the drearier menace of a materialistic social science, as embodied in the new Puritans, who have purified themselves even of religion. Under this long process, the worst that can be said is that the English humorist has been slowly driven downwards in the social scale. Falstaff was a knight, Sam Weller was a gentleman's servant, and some of our recent restrictions seem designed to drive Sam Weller to the status of the Artful Dodger. But well it was that some such trampled tradition and dark memory of Merry England survived.[44]

Chesterton's narrative was thus a dark, but still recognizably Whig, history of England. The note of Anglo-Saxon triumphalism was gone, but the relish of patriotic pride was not missing.

A Short History of England was a great publishing success and was widely and enthusiastically reviewed, and the press did not fail to note Chesterton's celebration of the "English-speaking peoples" as the hero of his story. The *Saturday Review* wrote, "We love Mr. Chesterton, we could 'hug him' for his real understanding of and sympathy with the rhetoric and the aristocracy of the eighteenth century."[45] The *Glasgow Herald* commended Chesterton for his even-handed enthusiasm for the figures of English history: "The great whom he admires are worthily portrayed, and his appreciations . . . reveal . . . the intensity of his patriotic feeling."[46] The *Nation* too, declared Chesterton "a marvelous rhetorician doing the honours of prose to his enemies. He is forever laying down the whip and inviting the criminals to take their seats while he paints gorgeous portraits of them in all the colors of the rainbow."[47] One reviewer put it succinctly: "Mr. Chesterton's merit is that he tries to understand even unsympathetic things; aristocratic Whigs, for example, and even Puritans." So, while many reviewers could find "no reasonable compromise between the Chestertonian and the official view of English history," they nevertheless found it fitting that the book was published on "the anniversary of the Battle of Trafalgar and the death of Nelson."[48]

THE ANGLO-AMERICAN ALLIANCE

Following up the ideas presented in *A Short History*, Chesterton told an American reporter in an interview in 1917, "I think all sensible Englishmen now sincerely desire a real friendship with America founded on ideas, and not upon fables like the Anglo-Saxon Race."[49] This "real friendship founded on ideas" was made possible, he said, because both nations had been forced by the war to declare a certain allegiance to France, and thereby forced to refuse the myth of a racial struggle between Anglo-Saxons and Latins and to acknowledge a shared classical and Christian European cultural heritage. The entry of the United States into the war, he said, revealed the ultimate bankruptcy of the "subterranean war waged by Germany in America" to gain disciples of "Teutonism." The war had made English and American unity in European liberalism easier to see, he said. In discovering their obligation to European civilization, England and America had turned a "quite colossal corner in history."[50]

Winston Churchill gave this same view of the war resonance in his speech in Westminster on July 4, 1918, when he declared that the Anglo-American alliance appeared to him "to transcend the limits of purely mundane things.

It is a prodigy. It is almost a miraculous event. It fills us with the deepest awe."[51] Chesterton and Churchill both interpreted the war as "a conflict between Christian civilization and scientific barbarism," echoing the understanding that the British public expressed in the silent reaffirmation of the legitimacy of the national struggle and the value of the lives lost in it in countless local war memorials.[52] British popular culture between the wars saw a revival of religious and national piety in spite of the cynicism reflected in the war poets and revisionist histories.[53] This resurgence of patriotism was often expressed in a more profound and somber key, but it powerfully shaped the British understanding of their role on the world stage.[54] The great literary war between the propagandists and the cynics ended in a reworking and reaffirmation rather than a rejection of patriotism. As Chesterton wrote at the end of his history of England, "It is the pathos of many hackneyed things that they are intrinsically delicate and are only mechanically made dull. Anyone who has seen the first white light, when it comes in by a window, knows that daylight is not only as beautiful but as mysterious as moonlight. . . . So patriotism, and especially English patriotism, which is vulgarised with volumes of verbal fog and gas, is still itself something as tenuous and tender as a climate."[55] Chesterton's wartime writing helped to express and preserve the "tenuous and tender" idea that Britain shared in a European Christian tradition that would again be worth defending when it was again menaced in Britain's "Finest Hour" in 1940.

SUGGESTED READINGS

The most influential history of the development of British national identity through the middle of the nineteenth century is Linda Colley's *Britons: Forging a Nation* (New Haven, 1992). The development of British identity in the second half of the nineteenth century can be found in Paul Kennedy, *The Rise of Anglo-German Antagonism, 1860–1914* (Boston, 1980).

The classic account of the transformative effect of World War I on British consciousness is Paul Fussell, *The Great War in Modern Memory* (Oxford, 1975). Samuel Hynes' trilogy, *The Edwardian Turn of Mind* (Princeton, 1968), *A War Imagined: The First World War and English Culture* (New York, 1990), and *The Auden Generation: Literature and Politics in the 1930s* (Princeton, 1976) develops a similar view of the war's impact into a thoroughgoing interpretation of British culture in the twentieth century. The idea that the war marks the end of the tradition of Whig patriotic histories can be found in J. W. Burrow's *Liberal Descent: Victorian Historians and the English Past* (Cambridge, 1981). Works that emphasize the continuity of British consciousness and the continuing tradition of Whig history are Victor Feske, *From Belloc to Churchill: Private Scholars, Public Culture, and the Crisis of British Liberalism* (Chapel Hill, 1996); Alison Light, *Forever England: Femininity, Literature, and Conservatism between the Wars* (London, 1991); and J. M. Winter, *Sites of Memory, Sites of Mourning: The Great War in European Cultural History* (Cambridge, 1995).

NOTES

1. Those authors included Robert Bridges (the poet laureate), James Barrie (the man who created Peter Pan), Arthur Conan Doyle (the author of the Sherlock Holmes mysteries), G. M. Trevelyan (a popular historian), H. G. Wells, Thomas Hardy, and Rudyard Kipling. Samuel Hynes, "The Arts Enlist," in *A War Imagined: The First World War and English Culture* (New York: Bodley Head, 1990), 23–28.

2. Gary S. Messinger, *British Propaganda and the State in the First World War* (Manchester: University Press, 1992).

3. G. K. Chesterton, *Letters to an Old Garibaldian*, (London: Methuen, 1915), 11–12. Italian, French, Spanish, and Dutch translations were published.

4. G. K. Chesterton, *The Barbarism of Berlin* (London: Cassell, 1914), 92. Editions were published in German, French, Dutch, Italian, Spanish, and Swedish during the war.

5. Chesterton, *Barbarism of Berlin*, 92.

6. Chesterton, *Barbarism of Berlin*, 92.

7. G. K. Chesterton, *The Crimes of England* (London: C. Palmer and Hayward, 1915), 156. An American edition was published in 1916 through John Lane Company and a French translation was printed in Paris. See also page 133, "A vague but genuine soul does also possess all peoples who boast of Teutonism; and has possessed ourselves, in so far as we have been touched by that folly. Not a race but rather a religion; the thing exists."

8. Chesterton, *Crimes of England*, 25, 63, 70–75. Describing British government in Ireland, Chesterton wrote, "Germany was not merely present in spirit: Germany was present in the flesh. . . . We should hardly have seen such a nightmare as the Anglicizing of Ireland if we had not already seen the Germanizing of England."

9. Chesterton, *Crimes of England*, 83–93.

10. Chesterton, *Letters to an Old Garibaldian*, 43–44.

11. Chesterton, *Letters to an Old Garibaldian*, 44–46.

12. Chesterton, *Letters to an Old Garibaldian*, 9.

13. Chesterton, *Letters to an Old Garibaldian*, 10.

14. Chesterton, *Letters to an Old Garibaldian*, 13.

15. Chesterton, *Letters to an Old Garibaldian*, 17.

16. *Church Times*, November 9, 1917.

17. "And this difference consists in little more than the assertion that English freedom has never broadened down from precedent to precedent . . . Mr. Chesterton is unable to accept the placid belief of most historians that England has been getting better and better since the first syllable of recorded time; and here the poet is at least as much entitled to his opinion as the scholar." Edward Shanks, *New Statesman*, October 27, 1917.

18. *Daily Chronicle*, October 29, 1917; E. Brett Young, *Liverpool Courier*, November 1, 1917; *Globe*, October 25, 1917.

19. G. K. Chesterton, "The Defeat of the Barbarians," in *A Short History of England* (London: Chatto and Windus; New York: John Lane, 1917), chapter 4, 43.

20. Chesterton, "The Province of Britain," in *Short History* (see note 19), chapter 2, 17–18.

21. Chesterton, "Province of Britain," 20.

22. Chesterton, "Province of Britain," 20.

23. Chesterton, "Province of Britain," 20.

24. Chesterton, *Short History*, 14. Chesterton also described Christian England as "the advance guard of that immense revolt and rout which fled from the failure of the Pagan Empire" in "An Agnostic Establishment," *Nation*, May 16, 1908.

25. Edward Shanks, *New Statesman*, October 27, 1917.

26. Chesterton, "The Age of Legends." in *Short History* (see note 19), chapter 3.

27. Chesterton, "St. Edward and the Norman Kings," in *Short History* (see note 19), chapter 5, 62.

28. Chesterton, "Defeat of the Barbarians," 44.

29. Chesterton, "The Age of the Crusades." in *Short History* (see note 19), chapter 6.

30. Chesterton, "St. Edward and the Norman Kings," 64.

31. Chesterton, "St. Edward and the Norman Kings," 64.

32. Chesterton, "Nationality and the French Wars," The War of the Usurpers," "The Rebellion of the Rich," "Spain and the Schism of Nations," "The Age of the Puritans," and "The Triumph of the Whigs," in *Short History* (see note 19), chapters 9–14,

33. Chesterton, "Spain and the Schism of Nations,"182.

34. Chesterton, "Spain and the Schism of Nations," 184.

35. Chesterton, "Age of the Puritans," 205.

36. Chesterton, "War with the Great Republics," in *Short History* (see note 19), chapter 15, 229.

37. Chesterton, "Aristocracy and the Discontents," in *Short History* (see note 19), chapter 16, 251ff.

38. Chesterton, "Aristocracy and the Discontents," 249.

39. Chesterton, "War with the Great Republics," 230.

40. Chesterton, "Triumph of the Whigs," 228; "War with the Great Republics," 247.

41. Chesterton, "Aristocracy and the Discontents," 248.

42. Chesterton, "Aristocracy and the Discontents," 258.

43. Chesterton, "Aristocracy and the Discontents," 258.

44. Chesterton, "Aristocracy and the Discontents," 258.

45. *Saturday Review*, November 17, 1917.

46. *Glasgow Herald*, October 25, 1917.

47. *Nation,* November 10, 1917.

48. E. Brett Young, *Liverpool Courier*, November 1, 1917; *Public Opinion*, October 26, 1917; *Sheffield Telegraph*, November 29, 1917 (review accompanied by a picture of Nelson).

49. Robert Sloss, "The Future of British-American Relations: An Interview with G. K. Chesterton," *Daily News,* American Edition, November 3, 1917.

50. Sloss, "Future of British-American Relations."

51. See *Winston S. Churchill: His Complete Speeches, 1897–1963,* ed. James Robert Rhodes (New York: Chelsea House Publishers, 1974). "The conviction must be borne in upon the most secularly-minded of us that the world is being guided through all this chaos towards something much better, much finer, than we have ever known. One feels in the presence of a great Design . . . No event since the beginning of the Christian era is more likely to strengthen and restore men's faith in the moral governance of the universe."

52. J. M. Winter, *Sites of Memory, Sites of Mourning: The Great War in European Cultural History* (Cambridge: Cambridge University Press, 1995).

53. Victory Feske, *From Belloc to Churchill: Private Scholars, Public Culture, and the Crisis of British Liberalism* (Chapel Hill: University of North Carolina Press, 1996).

54. Alison Light, *Forever England: Femininity, Literature, and Conservatism Between the Wars* (London: Routledge, 1991).

55. Chesterton, "Aristocracy and the Discontents," 248.

Chapter Fourteen

Barbara Nixon: A Warden's Blitz

Matthew J. Clarcq

For nine straight months, from September 1940 to May 1941, the city of London was bombed by Nazi Germany. Explosives and incendiaries damaged over one million homes and left 1.4 million people homeless. The death toll was even more devastating, with approximately thirty thousand casualties. This was the time Londoners lived through "the Blitz." During the Blitz, warning sirens sounded daily; people flocked to shelters and endured abominable conditions. Through all the confusion, danger, and chaos, the Air Raid Wardens did what they could to assist the people during the bombings.

The Air Raid Warden's job was risky. During a raid, wardens might expose themselves to bombs in order to help civilians—an acceptable, commendable, and even expected action, for a man. Women on the other hand, still had very limited roles, even in the wartime year of 1940. Female wardens were fairly unusual. Women were expected to make tea and sandwiches or at most answer telephones at the command center. Such a role was not enough for Barbara Nixon. Nixon used the position of Air Raid Warden to give active service during the Blitz. Nixon was, in fact, rather nontraditional throughout her adult life. Born in 1908, she was raised in a middle-class family in Cheltenham, Glouchestershire. She entered Newnham College, Cambridge, in 1926 and studied English literature. Immediately after graduation, she joined the Cambridge Festival Theater Company, which included celebrated actors Flora Robson and Robert Donat. Nixon found success in the field despite the underlying connotations of women actors. During her time at Cambridge, she met noted Marxist economist Maurice Dobb and married him in 1931. Her marriage was far from the traditional middle-class ideal. Nixon, dedicated to her profession as an actress, stage manager, and writer for such venues as the

London Theatre, radio, and television, remained in London. Dobb, on the other hand, remained in Cambridge as a lecturer and eventually became a professor of economics. Nixon would spend her next twenty married years seeing her husband on weekends and holidays. Yet her nontraditional background gave Nixon an advantage. Partly because of her profession but more because of her personal inclination, she was not restricted, as many were, by class and gender prejudices of her day. Her educated background, her love for London, and her sympathies towards the lower classes made her want to be an active participant in wartime efforts. When the Second World War broke out and the theaters were closed, Nixon volunteered as an Air Raid Warden.

HONORABLE SERVICE OR ARMY DODGER?

According to the *Times*, throughout the country 750,000 female volunteers were needed in thirty-eight separate roles to prepare for an enemy attack, with special emphasis placed on hospital services, ambulance drivers, and evacuation work.[1] The Air Raid Warden position was ideal for Nixon to assist Londoners actively, particularly the lower classes. Air Raid Wardens, as civil defense workers, were expected to be familiar with their district and its inhabitants to provide the most efficient service. Nixon saw it as a task best suited to her personality. She wrote:

> I joined the Warden's Service because it seemed to me to be the most active and obviously helpful Civil Defense occupation open to women. . . . I wanted an active job; I particularly wanted to avoid being in the position of many women in the First World War—of urging other people to do work they wouldn't think of doing themselves. At that time the ATS [Auxiliary Territorial Service] seemed to be mainly a matter of cooking and cleaning, for neither of which was I either competent or inclined; I found that the AFS [Auxiliary Fire Service] entailed mainly switch-room work and First Aid Posts seemed to me to be too reminiscent of Job waiting patiently for troubles to be brought to him.[2]

Nixon chose to join the Warden's Service at a time when the reputation of wardens was on the rebound. The need for wardens was anticipated at least as early as 1937. When war was declared, thousands raced to volunteer. An official circular stated that a warden "should be a responsible member of the public chosen to be a leader and advisor of his neighbors in a small area, a street or a small group of streets."[3] The key component of the Warden's Service was its essentially local character. Ideally, in the event of a bombing, local knowledge was the most helpful to rescuers. However, the local background of most wardens also opened them to neighborhood criticism, especially during the period of the "phony war" between September 1939 and March 1940 when Hitler seemed to be ignoring the West. With so many men needed in the armed forces, the press was "soon suggesting that the full-timers were overpaid army dodgers."[4] A November 2 editorial in the *Times*, after estimating the yearly wages of Air Raid Precautions [ARP] personnel at over £90 million, asked, "Can a country which must finance large imports of food and raw material afford to run a war on these extravagant lines?"[5] Staging mock incidents for practice did not help convince the public of the need for well-trained and organized wardens. "The spectacle of grown men play-acting in public . . . diminished confidence in A.R.P."[6] Indeed, shortly after the formal declaration of hostilities, the British government began cutting funds to civil defense. "By December, over half the full timers had been fired or had quit in disgust."[7]

The Nazi conquest of Western Europe in early 1940 brought about a reevaluation of the wardens. The possibility of German attacks was more likely and those men presumed to be "army dodgers" were by now serving their country. As the armed forces and war industry claimed more and more of the available manpower, the Warden's Service often took in people who did not qualify for other duty for a variety of reasons, including age, ill health, and gender. Since these individuals could not actively serve in other ways, the public welcomed them as wardens.

Nixon first served the public as a warden assigned in the borough of Finsbury, just north of St. Paul's Cathedral and the Bank of England. Her district included the grounds of City University, headquarters of the Honorable Artillery Company, small shops, and large-scale, world-class businesses. Her area also included a wide variety of residential housing, ranging from the two- and three-story apartments in which Nixon herself lived, to the large scale seven- and eight-story apartment buildings filled with lower-class families. When she first took on the position, Nixon's expectations of her warden duties were rather limited. She expected to report where the bombs had fallen and occasionally check in on the inhabitants of her air-raid shelters. In reality, she found herself not only being the eyes and ears of the civil defense machinery, reporting where bombs had fallen and directing rescue crews to the correct piles of debris, but also putting out small fires, administering first aid, and dealing with unexploded bombs. Equally important to the warden's role was offering moral support and encouragement to those in the shelters. "The warden's visit broke the monotony of the long dreary hours in the shelter. He was regarded as a mine of information about everything from relief, re-housing, to the time of the all-clear, and, if there had been one all clear, whether there

would be another alert that night or the next."[8] Nixon learned nearly all these
skills on the job.

THE BLEAK PICTURE

In many ways, Nixon and wardens in general were unprepared for the pressures and duties of the Blitz. Much of their lack of preparation can be laid at
the feet of the government which in anticipating the bombing of London,
made several erroneous, if understandable assumptions. The most famous
was Prime Minister Stanley Baldwin's statement to the House of Commons
in 1931 that "there was no effective defense against onslaught from the air."[9]
The bombers would always get through and the expected carnage from the
bombing was extraordinarily high. Prewar experts predicted fifty casualties
for every ton of high explosives dropped. These same experts also assumed
that the probable enemy, Germany, would put an enormous fleet of bombers
into the air for a sustained daylight raid against England. After the Nazi
bombing raids on Barcelona in 1938, the casualty figures were raised to
seventy-two per ton. These numbers calculated into fifty-eight thousand Londoners dead in the first twenty-four hours of bombing. Even worse was the
prospect of the enemy dropping poison gas on London. One of the biggest
anticipated problems was how to bury all the dead quickly enough. Those
who did not die faced the prospect of madness. Psychologists publicly stated
that "psychiatric casualties in air raids would tend to fall into two main
groups—the mobile, who ran riot, and the immobile, who were stupefied by
shock."[10] The horrifying prospect of air war led writer Bertrand Russell to
predict that "London would be 'one vast raving bedlam, the hospitals will be
stormed, traffic will cease, the homeless will shriek for peace, the city will
be a pandemonium.'"[11]

   The British government, of course, did not emphasize these stark figures to
the public. In fact, during the "phony war" period, the newspapers published
articles boasting of the power of Britain's antiaircraft batteries and how the
Germans would never make it past the coast. In reality, the government feared
that the bombing would be so terrible the people would demand surrender
or become too incapacitated to carry on. They were particularly worried the
population would become so secure in deep air-raid shelters that they would
refuse to come out. The *Times* reflected the feelings of the government by
claiming, "If the whole nation were really to go to ground like rabbits the
national cause would be buried beyond hope of resurrection."[12] Fear of a possible deep-shelter mentality helped shape the government's attitude toward
the needs and functions of civil defense.

These needs included instruction of wardens, which was rudimentary at best. Official statements claimed all ARP volunteers would be fully prepared by completing up to nine formal lessons.[13] As Nixon reported, after two months as a warden, she was finally called in for training. "We were given several lectures on the smells and effects of the different war gases. We were told of the various standards of shelter protection, authorized by the government. We were taught three ways for dealing with a small incendiary bomb, and we were told that the blast from high explosives travels, like sound, in all directions, and has an outward and suction wave. That was all."[14] Apparently the government did not feel wardens needed to know much more since the bombing effects were expected to be so terrible. From Nixon's perspective, she had to learn her job on the fly, and such an attitude was inexcusable. She later wrote:

> No amount of training can teach you everything, but there should be sufficient to assure you that you know what you ought to do in an emergency. An incident hardly ever goes according to the book; but if you have a thorough knowledge of what you are supposed to do, you are very much quicker at thinking of something else that you can do. My own case is typical of many. I was extremely anxious to be as helpful as possible, but I had hardly any idea of what, officially, I was supposed to do.[15]

So with very little real preparation as to what to expect, London and wardens like Nixon were hit with the Blitz.

THE SHOCK OF THE BLITZ

Although there had been some minor raids on London, the Blitz did not officially begin until September 7, 1940. The target of the raid was the East End of London and the London docks, approximately four miles from Barbara Nixon's district. Although the air-raid sirens sounded and people took to the shelters and could see the fires, those not directly under attack remained disconnected from events. Nixon states, "I went off to Soho for dinner that evening. It was not, technically, one of my nights on duty; but it is surprising, on looking back, that one could have made such a nonchalant miscalculation . . . I was annoyed when the siren went again before we had even reached coffee."[16] The raid continued until dawn with the East End getting most of the punishment, but many other sections of London were hit as well. This first night of the Blitz was the beginning of Nixon's introduction to the full scope of her responsibilities as warden. The people in Nixon's shelters were cold and tired since none had expected to spend more than an hour or two under cover. Many asked Nixon at the end of the night-long raid, "D'you think we'll get another tonight Miss?"[17] Nixon saw this as a distinct and somewhat dangerous turning point. "At last people realized that there was serious war on—a war that meant visible death and destruction, not only newspaper articles and recruiting posters and war memorials. And they did not like the realization."[18]

Since Nixon's district was not being seriously bombed, most of her duties revolved around comforting the people in the shelters. Nixon admitted, "It had not occurred to me that a warden would be expected not only just to poke his head around the door to see if there was anything wrong, but to chat to one and all, and try to cheer them up."[19] Cheering up was necessary and not just because of the realization of a tangible war. Londoners, along with the government and armed forces, were truly caught off-guard by the first attack of the Blitz. Many who once rejected the government-sponsored evacuation scheme prior to the Blitz, now hurriedly left London. Nixon observed, "Clearly, however, a great many of London's population could not leave, and many wives stayed behind to keep alive that strongest tradition of all—the husband's dinner."[20] Cheering the shelter dwellers on a personal level was more of a challenge for Nixon than her fellow wardens. Even though she lived in her own district, most of the people in the shelters were strangers to her. Nixon envied her fellow wardens, who seemed to know everyone by name. The dwellers themselves, however, were very open to her, making Nixon's job much easier. "I soon realized that the mere sight of a tin hat gave people a spurious sense of confidence, and that they were really pleased to see one."[21]

At first, the wardens were, in essence, the only visible sign of support. In addition to a looming sense of being trapped, Nixon found her shelter dwellers to have an increasing sense of abandonment. The poor especially seemed to feel singled out, since it was the poor East End who took the majority of the bombing for the first few days. In her shelter, Nixon heard sentiments quite similar to the ones recorded by American journalist Negley Farson:

"We didn't ask for the blinking war, *did* we?"
"No wonder Germany's not fed up—they've *got* some blinking air raid shelters!"
"My man's in the Army. At Dunkirk, he was, And I'm *here*!"
"We're prisoners of war; that's what we are."
"The official attitude is horrible!"
"No use looking to Labour. They let us in for this war, they did."
"Bloody L.C.C. red tape!"

As Farson saw it, "These people were beginning to lose faith—faith in all degrees of people higher up."[22]

The people's pessimism toward the authorities was linked in some respect to their heightened expectations regarding London's defense. As recently as three days before the beginning of the Blitz, the *Times* ran a story highlighting the efficiency of British antiaircraft guns. The guns' ability to target and bring down German bombers was referred to as almost magical.[23] However, during the first three days of the Blitz, no British antiaircraft fire was used against the Germans. The apparent desertion of London's defenses surely increased public bitterness. Nixon reported, "The loudest cry however, was: where are the guns? Where were these defenses that had been praised as impassable?"[24] Unbeknownst to the man on the street, the government did not allow firing to prevent British night fighters flying overhead from being shot. Since Londoners did not openly know the reason, their sense of abandonment mounted. The government's apparent lack of action ironically fueled its worst fear: the failure of morale was starting to build.

Finally, on September 11, the fourth day after the Blitz began, the night fighters were withdrawn. General Pile, head of London's defense "ordered his troops to blaze away with every ounce of energy they could muster. The resulting hideous noise kept most Londoners awake for most of the night, but they loved it."[25] The antiaircraft fire was ineffective, at most forcing the German bombers to fly a little higher over their targets. In fact, the shrapnel from British shells killed and injured as many, if not more, people than the German bombs.[26] The improvement of morale was palpable. The guns were a sign that the population had not been abandoned to their fate by the government; that they were not going to sit and be bombed without some sort of retaliation. From this point, Nixon observed a remarkable adjustment in the citizens of London.

> Londoners settled down to their strange new life with a dogged equanimity, which was an unspectacular form of genuine courage. Many of the habits of a lifetime were rudely changed; sometimes for the better. Wives, for instance, who suffered from snoring husbands, found allies in the new community life. But where they could stick to old habits, they did, even if the idiom had to be changed. I was standing by a surface shelter one night as a couple emerged. The gunfire was getting heavy and the girl was anxious—"I can't stop now, Tom, really. I must get down to the shelter. Mum will be worrying. But I'll meet you tomorrow, same time, same sand bag."[27]

This is not to say that Londoners now simply accepted their role as passive observers to the conflict. They would soon find other situations to complain about—and justifiably so. At least their morale would never again come so close to breaking.

The start of the Blitz meant a dose of reality not only for Londoners but also for Nixon herself. The lack of action in her own district gave her the time to dwell on her own fears. Primarily, Nixon was concerned with how she would react to the sight of dead bodies. She admitted, "I was terrified that I might be sick when I saw my first entrails, just as some people cannot stop themselves fainting at the sight of blood."[28] Her fears went untested for the first ten days of the Blitz. Then on September 17 while bicycling in a district far from her own, Nixon witnessed the bombing of an apartment building and saw her first casualty. "In the middle of the street lay the remains of a baby. It had been blown through the window and had burst on striking the roadway. To my intense relief, pitiful and horrible as it was, I was not nauseated, and found a torn piece of curtain in which to wrap it."[29] Although she offered her services at the incident, Nixon found herself not much help as she did not know this district. She was reduced to finding blankets to cover the bodies of the dead. After returning to her district, she went on duty as usual. As an aftereffect of the incident, however, the next day she could not recall any of her twelve-hour shift. Nixon's memory loss was an isolated incident, and her educated background led her to draw several conclusions from the experience. First, much to her relief, she knew now that she could control her nerves and was not prone to nausea. For Nixon, this meant she would still be useful even in gruesome circumstances. Second, she realized that wardens were very little use outside their own district. Without the knowledge of the area—knowing where the residents were located at certain times of day, where they slept at night, their peculiar habits—she could not provide rescuers with any information. She also concluded that there was insufficient coordination between separate civil defense services.

> No one had been in charge, and there had been no obvious reporting post. In theory, the warden reported an incident from his Post telephone, the Heavy Rescue Service did the digging and releasing, the Stretcher Party put the victim on a stretcher, the Ambulance loaded and conveyed that stretcher to a hospital. At practice exercises this arrangement worked excellently, but in an actual raid, when it was general[ly] pitch dark, when there were incidents in all directions, when the telephones often broke down, there were frequently a waste of both personnel and time.[30]

SHELTER CRITIC

Seeing the flaws in the government's organization of civil defense, Nixon was more willing to look critically at the government's shelters. The government had tried to provide shelter to as many people as possible. First, they issued the so-called Anderson Shelters. These do-it-yourself shelters made of two curved sections of corrugated steel bolted together were surprisingly effective, providing protection from all but a direct hit. However, they persistently collected rainwater, and the endless bailing made them unpopular, and in some cases, unusable. The government also urged the local authorities to build surface shelters meant to house fifty people at a time, but their shoddy construction and tendency to collapse made people stay away. Unofficial shelters existed under railway bridges. These looked sturdy, but when struck by a high explosive, they became death traps. Sanctioned shelters often occupied the basements of steel-framed buildings, but in many cases they were simply basements with no amenities. The nine shelters in Nixon's district were a good example of the sanctioned type: sturdy, but without adequate sanitation. The government had expected raids to be short and in the daylight. Therefore, fewer people would need to use the shelters and would only occupy them for a short period of time. While Nixon could accept the reasoning at the onset, she believed that once the government had seen how the Germans conquered the nations of Western Europe, they should have understood German tactics. "Again, the Government's argument that it was impossible to provide safety from direct, or very close, hits for the whole population was also tenable if unpopular. . . . But lavatories—lighting—ventilation! For lack of these there can be no excuse. Even if a raid is only going to last an hour, it is still frightening, and a lavatory is essential."[31] In addition to lack of sanitation, ventilation and lack of lighting were basic problems. "In some the atmosphere of dank concrete, of stagnant air, the inevitable smell of bodies, the stench of the chemical closets was indescribable. More than once I had to stop a conversation abruptly and go outside to avoid being sick."[32] Even with these conditions, Nixon admits that hers were some of the best shelters in London.

Nixon felt that people accepted these horrendous conditions because of fear. Their homes were shaky; they had children; they were old and slow; or simply, they were nervous. Too many factors weighed on their minds to simply wait out the attack, so they sought the relative safety of a shelter. While sheltering on the Underground subway platform was initially forbidden, fear made people defy the government and storm the Underground for safety. Initially, the government felt the subway would be necessary for transporting troops and wounded. Especially during the Blitz, once the people had possession of the platform, they refused to relinquish their space. "They unrolled [their bedding] on the platforms, in the passages, even on the escalators and stairways. Once there, the relief from the danger upstairs was so great that they tolerated almost obscene conditions rather than risk being turned out again for making further demands."[33] The government settled for regulations providing space for true users of the service. Eventually, fifteen miles of platforms and tunnels were put to use as shelters. On a record night, 177,000 people were sheltered in the Underground. Although there were still problems with ventilation and sanitation, in general the tubes were warm, dry, well-lit, and made the raids inaudible.

The clamor for more and deeper shelters forced the government to grant the concession of building eight deep shelters, each 80 to 105 feet underground, and each capable of sheltering eight thousand people. Of course, they were not completed until well after the end of the Blitz, but they saw use during the V-1 and V-2 rocket attacks and served as headquarters for General Eisenhower during his preparations for D-Day. In addition to adding more shelters, the government finally did issue some improvements to the existing shelters as well. Between December 1940 and April 1941, during the latter half of the Blitz, six hundred thousand bunks were installed in shelters.[34] The shelter dwellers did not welcome this development as readily as one might think. For one thing, the bunks took up valuable space, making the already crowded shelters even more cramped. For another, by this time, the shelters had developed their own forms of social life, and the arrival of the bunks disrupted this strange sense of stability. Heaters, canteens, and educational programs were more welcomed. These amenities were organized by the Local Authority, which meant that some boroughs received improvements well ahead of others. Nixon's district did not organize these improvements until several months after the Blitz had ended. Nixon saw these programs as more than just a quality of life issue.

> It was an admirable opportunity for truly democratic organization. For the first time, on a large scale, the Englishman left the decaying and often infested home, which is euphemistically called his castle, and mixed with his fellows. There was opportunity for improving the education of the children, widening the interests of the adults, and generally inculcating an understanding of the war, and the need for communal effort.[35]

Nixon's witnessing improvements in the shelters, even at a slow rate, was far more satisfying than answering to the warden's "chain of command." Wardens were under the jurisdiction of the local government, and soon "Town Hall" became the enemy. In her experience, the local authorities did nothing but undermine the reputation of wardens and generally treat them as incompetents. A number of wardens did come from unreliable professions and backgrounds, such as bookmakers and racecourses. While typically such individuals may not have been depended upon during prewar time, during the war, most were quite reliable. In fact, most wardens were skillful at their jobs. The local government's lack of support also served to diminish the confidence at the warden's post itself. "Even the part-timers, who did not suffer so much as the paid wardens, did not find many good words to say for the administration. They did not expect to be thanked for any services they might have rendered, but they certainly resented the suggestion they had remained in the service in order to cadge a uniform, or dodge fire-watching."[36] In some cases, Town Hall was downright callous towards the wardens. Nixon relates the Local Authority's reaction to an incident where a number of wardens had died on duty during a bombing:

> At first Town Hall made no official preparation for the burial of five of their service members—four wardens and one stretcher-party man—killed on duty. We made eight visits to various officials before they agreed to give municipal support to the arrangements the different families had already made. It was not that we ourselves wanted a 'fuss,' but for most relatives anything that can even make a pretence that their irreparable loss was worthwhile, or that it meant something to others as well as themselves, was at least a slight softening of their bitterness. And there was bitterness.[37]

In addition to their lack of support, Town Hall, which was often inefficient and inconsistent, was also ineffective in communicating with their wardens. They seldom acknowledged any of the warden's suggestions or reports, sending them the subtle message that the warden's views and work were of no importance. They also sent out weekly circulars to the posts, often with conflicting orders. When wardens refused to follow the inconsistent orders, Town Hall saw them as defiant. Obviously, Town Hall felt they were justified in their criticisms. Beyond the obvious flaws of inconsistency, the Local Authority also erred by expecting wardens to follow orders without question. The Warden Service was not a branch of the military; Town Hall should not have expected them to respond as soldiers. Indeed, local leaders seemed to fear any kind of independent thought by the wardens themselves. Any effort to improve or contradict instructions from Town Hall was seen as the work of "conscientious objectors and communists. It is hardly surprising that many analogies began to be drawn between the local and the Nazi regimes."[38]

POST 13

In spite of conditions and her dealings with the authorities, Nixon decided to become a full-time warden in December 1940. The transition made sense. After all, she already was working full-time hours. As she wished to remain in London, and all other full-time work would have taken her out of the city, continuing her current position on an official full-time basis was a logical choice. Again, Nixon needed to confront Town Hall, and at first, she was met by numerous objections, including that the borough did not want to hire any more women and then, that they did not employ married women.[39] Finally, after five weeks of wrangling, Town Hall agreed to appoint her full-time warden under the condition that she move to a different post. Willing to accept the change, Nixon's experience as warden was about to be expanded at her new assignment, Post 13.

Post 13 was vastly different to Nixon's previous experience. The contrast of bombing activity was an adjustment itself. While Nixon's former post was lightly bombed, at Post 13,

> Nothing was left. The heart of the largest city in the world was a wilderness. Here and there, desultory trails of smoke curled up; the pigeons had deserted it, no gulls circled over it, the only inhabitants were occasionally, scurrying rats. . . . The silence was almost tangible—literally a dead silence, in which there was no life. It was difficult to believe that this was London whose daily uproar never sank below a steady rumble, even in the small hours.[40]

Within months, what had been the site of world-famous firms would be covered in weeds and wildflowers. The population had quickly developed a healthy respect for bombs and almost always went to the shelters.

The other wardens at her new post were also a stark contrast to Nixon's former position. Post 13 had a reputation of being run by a tough bunch of wardens who did not like women. Nixon was certainly an outsider in this post as all the others had gone to the same school, knew each other's family history, and were loyal to the neighborhood. After an initially cool reception, Nixon finally was accepted as she was. She showed her colleagues she was their equal by not putting on airs and showing she could curse and drink bitter and ale. Slowly she got to know her companions.

> I was always curious to know what people had been or done before the war, but often it was most unwise to ask. Owing to the fact that race tracks, boxing rings and similarly chancy means of livelihood closed down at the outbreak of war, there was a large percentage of bookie's touts, and even more parasitic professions in the CD services, together with a mixed collection of workers in light industry, "intellectuals," opera singers, street traders, dog fanciers etc.[41]

At Post 13, some wardens joined because they thought they would not be called up for some time; others joined because the racetracks were closed; still others had no particular reason at all.

Nixon found that blending with the other wardens was not her only challenge at her new post. She could not get her sense of direction, could not remember who lived in which apartment, and feared she would be no use at all. Her new environment also made her feel less secure. Speaking of her former post, Nixon stated, "Here at least one knew which were the stronger doorways, where the shelters were, and, above all, that if one was missing for an hour someone would start a search."[42]

Like many areas in a battle zone, moments of terror could be followed by long periods of boredom. As an educated outsider, Nixon did not have much in common with the men at Post 13 as their conversations were limited to racing and boxing. From these same men, however, Nixon gained insight to the attitudes of the lower classes towards their wartime experience. She learned a new word: Rucking. "Rucking means a more vociferous and energetic form of grumbling. . . . We rucked about lack of bath tickets after heavy raids and being shorted on food vouchers."[43] This practice gave the wardens something to do during the long hours between raids and gave Nixon an appreciation that although they might be unlettered, her companions' complaints were justifiable.

Grumbling also gave the public something to do in a situation where they were supposed to sit and take the bombing. Common refrains included: "Nobody cares about us. We don't matter; We're the Front Line, we are; I wouldn't mind being the Front Line if there was any other bleeding lines; This ain't no war. My Bert been polishing buttons and scrubbing floors ever since January last." And the inevitable ending, "Oh well, it's the first ten years that's the hardest."[44] Grumbling was so widespread that Nixon only worried when it became absent from conversation. Silence meant a dangerous weakening of spirit. Whether or not the public ever gave in to silent desperation, they put on a very defiant public face. Most prominent were shop owners, big and small, who had their windows blown out. "Impromptu signs became favorite blitz jokes. 'MORE OPEN THAN USUAL' was a common one. 'BLAST' was the most laconic. One pub advertised, 'OUR WINDOWS ARE GONE BUT OUR SPIRITS ARE EXCELLENT. COME IN AND TRY THEM.'"[45]

Common danger seemed to bring Londoners together, no matter what their backgrounds. Nixon's ability to work with the men at Post 13 and make her duration as warden a success may be a reflection of the elasticity that shared peril granted to previously rigid social barriers. Common fears and myths helped bring people together as well. Foremost was the primitive fear of the dark. Affecting everyone, all terrors were delegated to night hours. The relief of surviving until dawn caused Nixon to wax poetic:

> Everything would be possible in daylight, the hydrants would miraculously flow with water again, the Rescue men would be able to lift the heavy piles of concrete. . . . Fifteen minutes after the sound of the last plane had faded into the distance, the all clear sounded. Its ugly high-pitched note screamed triumphantly and, for us, seemed to combine the melody of a French Horn with the pride and exaltation of twenty thousand roosters.[46]

Rumors, myths, and legends likewise helped create common feeling. Most prevalent was the idea that a German bomber could pick out the light of a flashlight from 10,000 feet. "There was also a prevalent rumor that 'they had developed a bomb which could chase you round corners.'"[47] Some rumors obviously remained in circulation because of the lack of education of many Londoners. Nixon reported, "I strongly suspected also that the common phrase "you're only hit by one with your name on it" was in some cases, backed by a miraculous faith that some Ruhr munitions worker actually stamped "Mrs. Perkins, 16 Tichbourn Street," on his handiwork."[48]

Miraculous faith, in another respect, may be what carried London through the Blitz. Nixon herself managed to adjust to and serve Post 13 well. Most Londoners somehow managed to survive their situations the best they could. Even when all the news from the war was uniformly bad, they still carried on. Greece and Crete faced more evacuation, and the Yugoslavs had surrendered to the Nazis. Understandably, frustration mounted since the people had no recourse during the Blitz to strike back in any way. "To be forced to sit down under prolonged bombardment with no hope of retaliation, is the hardest sort of war to fight, unless there is a constant and burning conviction evident. . . . Mr. Churchill's assurance of complete, absolute and final victory was not disbelieved, but it seemed as remote and unobtainable as the traditional pie in the sky—there was no road that led there."[49] That London did not collapse, even with all the confusion and lack of real direction from government officials, national and local, is the most remarkable part of the Blitz.

COMMON GROUND AND SOCIAL CONFLICT

Londoners did find some common ground during the Blitz, but common danger did not mean common experience. Nixon contradicts the comments of many authors and witnesses who claim social boundaries, so rigid in prewar England, were completely broken down during the Blitz. While all of London embraced the symbol of the wisecracking Cockney emerging from the rubble, Nixon found that in some ways class differences still mattered. Maybe some could joke about the loss of their homes and possessions, but in Nixon's experience, they were more likely the rich who, after an attack, had additional resources. The poor, however, most certainly could not laugh so easily. "Most casualties were too stunned to make much noise. But it was something close to hysteria which produced many of the gay remarks, and those who made them might be found a few hours later, sobbing uncontrollably in the rest centers."[50] The contrast of the rich and the poor seemed more blatantly evident during the war, and certainly loss was even more devastating to the lower classes.

> For many of the poor it is a disaster comparable with the loss of life. For many wives, their home had been their life's work. All their energy, all their attention, for

thirty years had gone into polishing, patching and scrubbing; they went without lux-
uries to get the furniture, they spent years paying for it, and now that furniture which
was almost a part of them is a pile of splinters. The face of one woman was purple
with crying, and the tears streamed down her cheeks, but she made no noise.[51]

Beyond the devastation, officialdom, conditions, and publicity always seemed
to favor the wealthy, and the poor felt a growing sense of resentment towards
the upper class, particularly those in positions of authority.

One of the most direct ways the poor interacted with their social betters
was through the Public Assistance Committees (PAC), a division of the local
government which handled the increasingly large problem of what to do with
those made homeless by bombing. Expecting this bureaucracy to be completely sympathetic was unrealistic, but given the fact that the poor residents
of the East End of London had taken the brunt of the bombing and had been
held up as the emblem of British resistance, they should have earned some
respect. Yet the PAC's treatment and attitudes towards these victims vaguely
resembled a scene from a Dickens novel. Essentially, the PAC acted as
modern-day "Poor Law Guardians" from the Victorian workhouses in dealing with those unfortunate enough to have had their lives destroyed by German bombs. Although not the villains of Dickens, the PAC still maintained
the attitude that they should only provide the bare minimum to keep people
alive. Their fear and mentality, of course, was to give the people anything
more, and they would become dependent on the government. Nixon, with her
Socialist tendencies fully intact, was outraged at the treatment people
received from the PAC.

Officials could not rid themselves of the idea that they were dispensing charity, and
it was this attitude that caused even more resentment and anger than the delays . . .
It was seldom a man's own fault that he was out of work, still less was it his fault
that a Nazi bomb had demolished his home and destroyed all his possessions and
means of living. To have his pride trampled as well, by being treated as a beggar
lucky to receive alms, was unforgivable.[52]

Physical conditions were obviously different between the classes, particularly in the availability of water and the luxury to wash. Often the bombing
would disrupt the water mains in Nixon's district. Nixon observed a general
feeling that the wealthy were given priority when it came to repairs. Nixon
stated, "It is impossible to imagine, in advance, how awkward a total lack of
water can be. Candles and lamps can supplant electricity, coal and wood fires
can supplant gas, but the lack of water is inordinately inconvenient."[53] The
lack of water meant, "When the sun shone we sweated, and clean trickles
meandered down our faces; when it rained, one's complexion looked more
like a mud pack."[54] Combined with the fear of being caught unprepared dur-

ing an attack, many lower-class Londoners never took off their clothes. "At Christmas, when raids were lighter, the old lady in the newspaper shop asked me if I thought it was now safe for her to undress; she hadn't she said, had her clothes off since September, and she was so tired."[55] Wealthy residents of London, even if they were without water, had more options, including traveling out of the city where more creature comforts were available.

The media seemed to make class distinctions as well in favor of the rich. The news continuously seemed to overemphasize the disasters sustained by the wealthy, while only mentioning the circumstances of the poor. In March, the Café de Paris was bombed while filled with wealthy patrons. The news made the front page for days. "The same week another dance hall a mile to the east of us was hit and there were nearly two hundred casualties. This time there were only 10s 6d frocks and a few lines in the paper followed by, 'It is feared there were several casualties.' . . . Our people did not mind not being in the news, but the excessive publicity given to the rich and their haunts was, to say the least, tactless."[56] Nixon's sympathies towards the poor made her indignant on their behalf. The people of London were certainly worthy of more respect since they often endured similar, if not more, hardships as the wealthy themselves.

With regret, Nixon saw a lost opportunity to create a stronger democratic community to truly destroy class distinctions. The chance was not exploited for two reasons: the attitude of the people and the active discouragement from the government, especially on the local level. Nixon complained, "The democratic ideal has been degraded only to its negative aspect. Far too many people think that democracy means the maximum of non-interference by the State in their affairs, instead of the maximum interest and interference by them in State affairs."[57] The government could have overcome the reluctance to get involved by trusting the people. In Nixon's view, citizens in London were less isolated, braver, and less selfish during the Blitz. Energetic residents became shelter marshals and wardens, and local councils were elected to represent people.

> What was needed was real co-operation between them all—committees of the shel-
> terers themselves with their marshal, of wardens' representatives and those of the
> local administration. Democracy is more trouble to organize and more cumbrous
> than the totalitarian system. And it is easy to rail at the delays and stupidities of
> committees, but they are the only guarantee against fascism abroad and at home.[58]

Such an effort would certainly have increased morale and the ability of people to bear the stress of the attacks. Instead, local government placed roadblocks in front of this process. Any attempt to complain or organize was frowned upon and participants were labeled Communists. Nixon felt "there were far too many councilors who heaved a sigh of relief when local elections were stopped, and thought that it absolved them from doing anything, or who thought it an excellent opportunity to acquire more personal power, and become local tin gods."[59]

LIFE OF SERVICE

Looking back at her experience, Nixon believed all the more that increased communication between authorities and the people they represented was essential. Nothing less than justification of the war itself and the reasons for accepting suffering were at stake and needed an injection of the democratic ideal.

> It was the lack of a clear and positive ideal, as much as the lack of armaments, that made the dark days of 1939–1941 so very dark. The destruction of one man and his group of henchmen alone could scarcely justify a war in which millions are to be killed. It is the destruction of a vile and sub-human system that can be the only justification. And for that, understanding, not slavish acquiescence, is needed. We are fighting for democracy—the only way to do that thoroughly is to understand it, and to understand it one must be able to see evidence of it in every walk of life, in factories, in shelters, in CD services and in the local government itself.[60]

The suffering and missed opportunities Nixon observed during the Blitz intensified her commitment to the people of London. Following the Blitz, she became an instructor and helped rectify some of the problems she found in her own training. In 1943 she published *Raiders Overhead; A Diary of Wartime London*, detailing her warden experiences during the Blitz. In her book she took the opportunity to criticize the civil defense system, particularly regarding the lack of water, poor shelters, and rehousing. On the positive side, she made allowances that improvements had been made in all areas by 1941. She was also unqualified in her praise of the system for its general coordination in getting reinforcements to hard-hit areas and its ability to keep a communication system cobbled together no matter what damage had been done during the previous raid. After the war, she returned to her first love, the stage, and eventually spent five years working in British television before settling down with her husband in Cambridge. That is not to say that Nixon abandoned public service. Barbara Nixon served the Finsbury Borough Council for seven years and on the London County Council from 1946 to 1950 as a Labour member. She was particularly proud of her work related to creating housing for those who had been victims of the Blitz.

SUGGESTED READINGS

The actions and courage of the people of London during the Blitz have rightly
attracted the attention and admiration of journalists, writers, and historians
since before the end of World War II. The first introduction of Americans to
the plight and courage of Londoners came through radio broadcasts. Some of
those broadcasts are collected in *In Search of Light: The Broadcasts of
Edward R. Murrow, 1938–1961* edited by Edward Bliss (New York, 1967).
Early historians of the Blitz continued Murrow's emphasis on the courage on
Londoners. Some examples of these earlier works are Constantine FitzGib-
bon, *The Winter of the Bombs: The Story of the Blitz of London* (New York,
1958); Asher Lee, *Blitz on London* (London, 1960); and Leonard Mosley,
Backs to the Wall: The Heroic Story of the People of London World War II
(New York, 1971). A shift in the historiography began with Angus Calder,
The People's War: Britain, 1939–1945 (New York, 1969), which concerned
itself with the opinion and experience of the common person, not just official
reports and newspaper stories. Updated studies written under Calder's influence include Philip Ziegler, *London at War, 1939–1945* (New York, 1995);
and Robert Mackay, *The Test of War: Inside Britain, 1939–1945* (New York,
1998). Eyewitness accounts were published during the Blitz and have since
been reprinted. Some of the most interesting are Barbara Marion Nixon,
Raiders Overhead: A Diary of the London Blitz (London, 1980) and George
Sava, *They Stayed in London* (London, 1941). For a study of a single day of
the attacks see David Johnson, *London Blitz: The City Ablaze, December 29,
1940* (Chelsea, Michigan, 1990). A balanced study of the wartime experience
of women can be found in Gail Braybon and Penny Summerfield, *Out of the
Cage: Women's Experience in Two World Wars* (New York, 1987). For a traditional look at political and military events leading up to the Blitz, see Telford Taylor, *The Breaking Wave: The Second World War in the Summer of
1940*, (New York, 1967) and Laurence Thompson, *1940* (New York, 1966).
Uri Bialer, *The Shadow of the Bomber: The Fear of Air Attack and British
Politics, 1932–1939* (London, 1980) examines the national psyche that led to
the tremendous over-estimation regarding bomber effectiveness. Perhaps one
of the most radical reinterpretations of the Blitz is Clive Pointing, *1940: Myth
and Reality* (Chicago, 1990), which charges that the British government,
knowing they were financially bankrupt, handed over control of the war and
their future destiny to the Americans.

NOTES

1. "Women to Drive Ambulances," *Times*, February 8, 1939, 9g.
2. Barbara Nixon, *Raiders Overhead: A Diary of the London Blitz*, (London: Scolar,
1980), 8.

3. Angus Calder, *The People's War: Britain, 1939–1945*, (New York: Pantheon Books, 1969), 195.

4. Calder, *People's War*, 68.

5. K. G. B. Dewar, "The ARP Problem," *Times*, November 2, 1939, 9f.

6. Dewar, *"ARP Problem,"* 67.

7. Calder, *People's War*, 68.

8. Nixon, *Raiders Overhead*, 162.

9. Philip Ziegler, *London at War, 1939–1945*, (New York: Knopf, 1995), 11.

10. "Civilian Morale in Air Raids," *Times*, January 5, 1939, 9d.

11. Ziegler, *London at War*, 11.

12. "Civilian Defence," *Times*, March 2, 1939, 15b.

13. "Shorter Anti-Gas Training," *Times*, March 23, 1939, 8d.

14. Nixon, *Raiders Overhead*, 10.

15. Nixon, *Raiders Overhead*, 32.

16. Nixon, *Raiders Overhead*, 13.

17. Nixon, *Raiders Overhead*, 18.

18. Nixon, *Raiders Overhead*, 18.

19. Nixon, *Raiders Overhead*, 17.

20. Nixon, *Raiders Overhead*, 22.

21. Nixon, *Raiders Overhead*, 17.

22. Calder, *People's War*, 179.

23. "Defending Ports from Air Attack," *Times*, September 4, 1940, 2b.

24. Nixon, *Raiders Overhead*, 20.

25. Calder, *People's War*, 168.

26. Calder, *People's War*, 168.

27. Nixon, *Raiders Overhead*, 23.

28. Nixon, *Raiders Overhead*, 25.

29. Nixon, *Raiders Overhead*, 26.

30. Nixon, *Raiders Overhead*, 31.

31. Nixon, *Raiders Overhead*, 55.

32. Nixon, *Raiders Overhead*, 55.

33. Nixon, *Raiders Overhead*, 56.

34. Calder, *People's War*, 186.

35. Nixon, *Raiders Overhead*, 66.

36. Nixon, *Raiders Overhead*, 166.

37. Nixon, *Raiders Overhead*, 148.

38. Nixon, *Raiders Overhead*, 166.

39. Nixon, *Raiders Overhead*, 74.

40. Nixon, *Raiders Overhead*, 78.

41. Nixon, *Raiders Overhead*, 82.

42. Nixon, *Raiders Overhead*, 81.

43. Nixon, *Raiders Overhead*, 92.

44. Nixon, *Raiders Overhead*, 106.

45. Calder, *People's War*, 174.

46. Nixon, *Raiders Overhead*, 121.

47. Calder, *People's War*, 177.

48. Nixon, *Raiders Overhead*, 66.

49. Nixon, *Raiders Overhead*, 155.
50. Calder, *People's War*, 188.
51. Nixon, *Raiders Overhead*, 138.
52. Nixon, *Raiders Overhead*, 148.
53. Nixon, *Raiders Overhead*, 122.
54. Nixon, *Raiders Overhead*, 147.
55. Nixon, *Raiders Overhead*, 42.
56. Nixon, *Raiders Overhead*, 103.
57. Nixon, *Raiders Overhead*, 167.
58. Nixon, *Raiders Overhead*, 167
59. Nixon, *Raiders Overhead*, 170.
60. Nixon, *Raiders Overhead*, 170.

Chapter Fifteen

Mothers First: Onitsha Women Battle the Government in Colonial and Postcolonial Nigeria, 1956–1964

Anene Ejikeme

African women are typically portrayed as totally lacking in autonomy, the objects of patriarchal control by husbands and fathers, victims to be pitied. Students are surprised to discover that the largest demonstrations by women ever recorded in history took place in Africa. These occurred during the 1929 Women's War in colonial Nigeria, which involved tens of thousands of Igbo women. This chapter examines another mass movement by Igbo women on a much smaller scale at a later date. The focus of this essay is the demonstrations orchestrated by women in the important commercial town of Onitsha between late 1956 and early 1957 and again in 1964 to protest educational initiatives by the regional government. The demonstrators organized under the rubric "Catholic women," but the chief factor uniting these women was not religious affiliation but their identities as mothers. Although the political actions of "Catholic women" in Onitsha in the years just prior to and after independence did not approach the scale of the Women's War, these confrontations between women and government are significant because they indicate women's continued desire and ability to organize to address those issues which were of concern to them.

These demonstrations by Catholic women in Onitsha were remarkable because they transcended the chief line of political demarcation in late colonial and postcolonial Onitsha, that of separating the indigenous Onitsha Igbo (the so-called "sons" and "daughters of the soil") from non-Onitsha Igbo "strangers." The demonstrations united a broad section of women in a way that recalled non-Christian women's formations such as *umuada* ("daughters of the lineage") or *inyemedi* ("wives of the lineage") that transcended age and economic status, and in the case of *inyemedi*, place of origin. Onitsha and non-Onitsha women, elite and nonelite women, as well as women who were not even officially Catholic joined forces to challenge proposals by the nationalist male leadership. The women organized as mothers, concerned to protect the welfare of their children against government proposals that they deemed put their children's future employment prospects in jeopardy.

ONITSHA'S SOCIOPOLITICAL SYSTEM

Onitsha, situated on the River Niger, is an Igbo-speaking community in southeastern Nigeria. The Igbo, one of the three largest linguistic groups in Nigeria, appear frequently in anthropological literature: they are a favorite example of "acephalous" political organization because, prior to colonial rule, the majority of Igbo lived in what social scientists describe as "village democracies." Onitsha was one of the exceptions to the norm of Igbo village democracies. The Onitsha sociopolitical system was a monarchical system in which titles and age-grades featured prominently. In the nineteenth century, Onitsha operated what is typically described in the literature as a dual-monarchical system in which the male *obi ("king")* and the female *omu ("queen")*, neither spouses nor siblings, presided each over their own separate cabinets. The *omu* and her councillors regulated the central market and determined the terms of trade.[1] Today Onitsha elders continue to recall the names of fabled merchants of the nineteenth and twentieth centuries, women such as Mgbogo Ifeajuna and Madam Emejulu.

Gender was, and continues to be, an important principle of social organization in Igbo communities: women joined together as *umuada* and *inyemedi*. Daughters especially exercised a significant degree of power within their lineages and villages, but even wives, as a corporate group, could make their opinions matter. For example, no funeral could be performed in Onitsha without the assent of the daughters of the lineage. As indicated above, the *omu* and her cabinet regulated the market. Trade was seen as a primarily female sphere of activity. The *omu*-ship became defunct in the last quarter of the nineteenth century when Omu Nwagboka died in 1886 and no successor was named to the throne; from then until now Onitsha has had only a male monarch. Scholars disagree on the reasons for the demise of the *omu*-ship. There is no agreement whether the European presence played any role in the demise.[2]

EUROPEAN ARRIVAL IN ONITSHA

Onitsha's location on the Niger River made it a center of trade, which attracted merchants from other parts of Africa as well as Europe. The earliest Europeans to establish a presence in Onitsha were traders and missionaries who arrived there in the middle of the nineteenth century. Economic imperatives coupled with moral arguments had led the British Parliament to abolish the Atlantic slave trade in 1807. The end of the slave trade resulted in a shift toward legitimate enterprises: commerce, Christianity, and civilization (the so-called 3Cs). A priority was the penetration of the hinterland in an effort to forge direct links with the producers of palm oil. Several expeditions sought to map the full course of the Niger River. Success finally came with the efforts of the Lander brothers who in 1830 discovered that the Oil Rivers was indeed the mouth of the Niger. However, full exploration and an expansion of trade inland in towns such as Onitsha would be delayed until Europeans learned how to protect themselves from malaria through the use of quinine around mid-century.[3]

The first missionaries to preach the Christian message in Onitsha belonged to the Protestant, British-based Church Missionary Society (CMS). Founded in 1799 in London by a group of Anglican clergymen and laypeople, the CMS was one of numerous missionary societies to be established throughout Europe and North America in the late eighteenth and early nineteenth centuries. The CMS Onitsha mission was established in 1857 by African missionaries, led by Samuel Ajayi Crowther, the Yoruba liberated slave who later became the first African Anglican bishop. While Ajayi oversaw the Onitsha mission and others throughout Southern Nigeria, the day-to-day operation at Onitsha was in the hands of Sierra Leonian–born descendants of ex-slaves.[4] A Catholic mission (RCM) was set up in Onitsha in 1885 by French missionaries of the Holy Ghost Congregation in 1885, just a year before the trading company, the Royal Niger Company (RNC), was granted a Royal Charter by the British government to "administer" the territories along the Niger. The stated mandate of the Holy Ghost order was "the regeneration of the black race."[5] The history of the Holy Ghost Congregation and the Church Missionary Society in Onitsha was, as may be expected, one of intense competition and rivalry.[6] Relations between the British company and the French missionaries at times were tense and, ironically, the Frenchmen expressed joy in 1900 when Onitsha formally came under the authority of the British Colonial Office and the RNC charter was rescinded. The French missionaries were often accused by the RNC, not without some justification, of seeking to bring Onitsha under the influence of France.

While careful to cultivate the friendship of the Onitsha elite, the early

Catholic missionaries focused their resources and proselytization efforts on those at the bottom of the social hierarchy: slaves, abandoned infants (multiple births or those born with deformities), and refugees from the local community. Freeborn persons and even the elite did convert and associate with the mission, but the disenfranchised were disproportionately represented among the ranks of the early converts. By the turn of the century, with colonial rule now established under the auspices of the British government rather than the RNC, the position of Christian converts and mission vis-à-vis the local population began to be radically transformed. Association with the mission conferred certain benefits; for example, the mission-educated were exempted from *corvée* labor for the government.[7] Also, the colonial regime required a supply of literate subordinates and this led to a great deal of interest in the mission school from the early years of the twentieth century. The Catholic mission in Onitsha especially enjoyed great popularity because it provided education in English, the language required for employment by government and merchant firms. In keeping with a basic tenet of Protestantism, the CMS missionaries in Onitsha insisted that local converts ought to be able to read the Bible in their mother tongue, and thus literacy in Igbo was emphasized over English in the early years in CMS schooling. This meant that many of those who saw mission education as the necessary first step in acquiring a job in the new labor markets preferred Catholic education to Protestant education. It should be pointed out, however, that the Protestants certainly did not abjure English literacy completely; until the middle of the last century, the Protestant mission dominated the post-primary field, where instruction was exclusively in English.[8]

TRANSFORMATION OF SOCIAL AND ECONOMIC STRUCTURES IN ONITSHA

Colonial rule naturally spelled changes in the political landscape of the town: now it was no longer local elites who claimed ultimate authority, but British officials. The onset of mission education and colonial rule also transformed social and economic structures in Onitsha. Over time, women completely lost their primacy in trade. Before the nineteenth century was over, the *omu*-ship had ceased to exist, and by the early 1930s women were being rapidly displaced by men, a visible proportion of them non-Onitsha, as the key merchants in Onitsha.

Engaging in mercantile activity was not the preferred occupation for Onitsha men in the colonial period. In the nineteenth century, Onitsha trade had been seen primarily as a female sphere of activity. With the onset of waged employment, Onitsha men who had received missionary education moved into the wage sector. Working for the government and, later, becoming a professional (law, medicine) were the favored options for those who were able to pursue the requisite education. The early stages of this education were acquired usually in a mission school as almost all Western-style education in colonial Nigeria was provided by Christian missionary organizations. Those who were mission-educated and literate in English were able to acquire wage-paying jobs in the new sectors. The first decade of colonial rule witnessed the appearance of a new elite in Onitsha, consisting of those who were mission-educated, literate in English, employed in wage labor, and relatively affluent.

One characteristic of this new elite class was its maleness. Women were completely absent from the salariat in the first two decades of the twentieth century. It was not until the 1930s that a class of women began to emerge that was defined simultaneously on the basis of its elite status as well as its Catholic identity. The arrival of missionary Catholic nuns to Onitsha in 1928 bore directly on this development. Prior to *circa* 1930 the women who dominated Onitsha's social hierarchy were the wealthy merchants. A small percentage of the girls who graduated from the convent school went on to train as teachers and nurses. Those who became professionals clearly belonged to an emergent class, but even those who had spent only a few years in the convent schools acquired literacy in English and/or other accoutrements of "ladylike" behavior, such as serving tea and sandwiches, and could marry men who, on the basis of their own jobs and aspirations, belonged to the new elite.

Ex-Catholic schoolgirls who attained the status of "Teacher" or "Nurse" enjoyed a great deal of social prestige. Social elites typically form networks exclusive to themselves, as indeed does any group of individuals that seeks to foster a sense of communal identity. In the period before the 1930s, for example, wealthy merchant women formed exclusionary social clubs. Catholic nurses and teachers formed associations restricted to elite women of similar background. Some of these groups were directly sponsored by the mission hierarchy; in other instances the women themselves took the initiative. In all cases, the Catholic mission hierarchy insisted that only women "in good standing" should be admitted to these new social functions and formations. Thus, in the period before the mass mobilization of the fifties and sixties with which we are concerned, Catholic women's organizations can be divided into two types. There were associations which were open to all the pious (and necessarily thus "in good standing") and there were organizations that were limited to those who were both pious and members of the new elite, for example, the "Legion of Mary" in which the members were all female teachers.

NATIONALIST STRUGGLE IN NIGERIA

The backdrop to the activism of Onitsha Catholic women in the fifties and sixties was the nationalist struggle, and later, the early years of independence. Nigeria's road to independence was marked by the gradual devolution of powers to regions beginning in 1946 with the creation of three semiautonomous regions, which set the stage for the protests discussed here. The end of World War II was a major turning point for Britain as well as its colonies. The impact of the war on political developments in the colonial world has been the object of extensive study. India, the jewel in the crown, and Pakistan became independent just two years after the war ended, with Burma following a year later. In 1957 Ghana became the first African state to regain its independence.

During the war, nationalist leaders in the colonies had suspended their pro-independence agitations and thrown their support behind the metropole in the battle against Nazi Germany. Thousands of Nigerians, as well as troops from all over the British Empire, fought for Britain. At the end of the war, Britain found itself in straitened financial circumstances and in a world now dominated by the American and Russian superpowers, which claimed to be opposed to colonial domination (although both were themselves colonial powers). The Atlantic Charter, signed by Roosevelt and Churchill in 1941, had proclaimed that the parties "respect the rights of all people to choose the form of government under which they will live; and they wish to see sovereign rights and self-government restored to those who have been forcibly deprived of them." Historians have argued that Churchill signed the Charter under pressure from Roosevelt. Only a year after signing the Atlantic Charter, Churchill made his famous statement that he had not become the King's First Minister "in order to preside over the liquidation of the British Empire."[9]

Following the war, nationalists again began to agitate for political power. The colonial government in Nigeria embarked on a policy of greater regional autonomy combined with "Nigerianization," which essentially called for the placement of "qualified" Nigerians in positions formerly reserved to expatriates. The upshot was intense interregional competition, and the regional governments focused on educational policy as the gateway to success within the new dispensation. Postwar nationalism in Nigeria thus wore an exceedingly regional face. The nationalist ferment was marked by such intense interregional competition that the political scientist Larry Diamond has concluded, "The decades preceding Nigerian Independence had featured conflict within the nationalist movement far more intense than anything it had waged against British colonial rule."[10]

INCREASE IN REGIONAL AUTONOMY

The postwar period ushered in an accelerated pace in the inclusion of Nigerians in positions of decision making and authority. The 1946 Richards Constitution displaced the twenty-four-year-old Clifford Constitution, which had established a legislative council that included a handful of Africans with extremely limited power and no autonomy. The Richards Constitution remained in effect until 1951 when it was replaced by the Macpherson Constitution, which in turn was substituted by another constitution in 1954. The Richards Constitution created three regional Houses of Assembly for the north, east, and west. It was widely criticized by nationalists because they had played little role in its formulation, and the constitution was presented almost as a *fait accompli*, and more importantly, it failed to give Africans much participation in the governance of the country. The 1951 Macpherson Constitution created a federal House of Assembly and extended the powers of the regions. Each region was to appoint its own minister of education, for example. Although the regions were free to make educational policies, the purse strings were still controlled at the center.[11] Barely two months after communal riots in the northern Nigerian town of Kano left thirty-six people dead, the 1953 Constitutional Conference took place in London.[12] The 1954 Constitution gave even greater powers to the regions. According to I. F. Nicolson, this step [was] dictated by the desire of the political parties in each of the regions to be masters of their own regional machine, in preparation for the forthcoming struggle for power in an independent Nigeria . . .[13]

EDUCATION LAW OF 1956 AND UNIVERSAL PRIMARY EDUCATION

In 1956 the Eastern and Western Regions were granted internal self-government. That same year the National Convention of Nigerian Citizens (NCNC) government passed an education law announcing that the following year the Eastern Region would embark on a policy of universal primary education (UPE). UPE must be seen in the larger political context of the times. Although it was the Education Law of 1956 that enshrined UPE, the first suggestion that such a program was in the works in the east came in a speech by the minister of education in 1953.

The devolution of powers in the form of Nigerianization and the creation of autonomous regional governments fostered tremendous interregional conflict. When the Western Region of Nigeria announced in 1952 that it would embark on its own universal free primary education program, it was only a question of time before the Eastern Region announced a similar plan. For decades, the Yoruba of the Western Region had led the country in the numbers of high school graduates, college graduates, and professionals. In 1921, for example, there were 14,000 "educated" Yorubas and only 4,900 "educated" Igbos.[14]

> Until the mid-1930s the overwhelming majority of higher positions in the African civil service and in business firms were held by Yorubas. . . . By 1945 the gap [in education and high status employment] between Yorubas and Igbo was virtually closed.[15]

The pursuit of education was not a function solely of interregional competition. It is important to recall that in the fifties education was widely seen as a panacea, especially with regard to the "emerging nations." These states were particularly concerned with "catching up" with the "developed" world. Politicians and experts the world over endorsed the ideals of universal primary education. Education was to uplift both the individual and the state. Education was seen as a necessary requirement for "progress" and "modernity." Article 27 of the United Nations Universal Declaration of Human Rights states, "Everyone has a right to education. Education shall be free, at least in the elementary and fundamental stages. Elementary education shall be compulsory." From its very inception in 1946, UNESCO called for every signatory state to be held accountable for achieving this goal and at General Conferences in the 1950s, UNESCO consistently upheld the principles of UPE.[16]

The UPE scheme of the government of the Eastern Region proposed that, from January 1957 on, all *new* grant-receiving schools would be owned by the local government. Missions would be free to open new purely private schools that did not receive government grants. Those mission schools already in operation, which continued to be owned by the mission, would remain eligible for grants in 1957 but not in later years. The aim of the plan was to stop the expansion of mission schools, building in their place local council schools, which were to be nondenominational. The government sought control of education in order to rationalize the provision of schooling. Under the system currently in place some communities had no school while others had two or more. The placing of schools often had more to do with interdenominational rivalry between different missions rather than community needs.

One might ordinarily expect that UPE would be acclaimed and noncontroversial. This was not the case because some feared that UPE would mean the lowering of standards and thus impact negatively the future employment prospects of their children and wards. Of course, not everyone opposed UPE.

In fact, as stridently as some opposed it, others were just as adamantly in favor of the new scheme. Schools that were to be free of both fees and the imperiousness encountered in mission schools appeared extremely appealing to some. Missionaries could be high-handed in their treatment of their converts and neophytes, with some priests reigning over their parishes like feudal lords. People who were known to be "public sinners," for example, were refused sacraments. Some priests slapped and reprimanded adult teachers in public. A set of regulations issued to priests in 1952 reminded them, "It is forbidden under pain of suspension reserved to the Archbishop to strike anybody *in or near the confessional* (i.e., to strike with hand, foot or any instrument)."[17]

CAMPAIGN AGAINST UNIVERSAL PRIMARY EDUCATION

UPE supporters insisted the government had a right to determine how to disburse public funds; opponents challenged the idea of public funds and maintained that these were taxpayers' monies, and they threatened the NCNC, the party that controlled the regional government, with defeat at the polls. In late 1956, Catholic lay leaders established an organization, the Eastern Nigerian Catholic Council (ENCC), the object of which was to campaign against the UPE proposal. Although at least one woman was a founding member of the ENCC, and other women were active in the organization, all the leadership positions were occupied by men. Women organized another forum, one that was exclusively their own, the Catholics Eastern Women Association (CEWA). The leaders of this organization were women active in pious organizations such as St. Anne's, the Catholic lay group led by certificated teachers. CEWA was not as formally organized a body as was the ENCC; it had, for example, no constitution and no chaplain. Although these deficiencies were no deterrents to mounting effective resistance, the fact that CEWA did not have a chaplain raises questions about its relationship with the church hierarchy. All officially sanctioned groups in the Catholic church are appointed a spiritual adviser; if CEWA had no such provision, that would appear to indicate that the group did not have the official (or public) approval of the Church hierarchy. Another possibility is that the CEWA neither sought nor was given a spiritual adviser because the group was organized on an informal basis.

CEWA mounted a massive letter-writing campaign. Women were directed to write four letters: two to Nnamdi Azikiwe, the Premier of the Eastern Region; one to the Queen; and one to the British Minister for the Colonies. The women of each of the four parishes in Onitsha were required to send

twelve sets of letters on behalf of twelve different communities outside Onitsha. CEWA was intent on bringing down the minister of education, and
"Akpabio must go" became a rallying cry. Akpabio was minister of education. The first demonstration of Onitsha Catholic women and sympathizers
occurred on November 17, 1956. On that day five hundred women disrupted
a meeting of the Onitsha Urban District Council and submitted a petition stat-
ing their preference for schools run by missions. The police were called in to
protect the members of the council. Less than two weeks later, police were
again called upon to subdue a crowd of "women—all Catholics—[who] are
demanding that the council should not take over the management of Catholic
schools when the universal primary education scheme comes into force next
January."[18]

Catholic lay women leaders, along with ENCC male leaders, toured the
region, speaking against UPE, issuing press releases, distributing propaganda
leaflets, and collecting signatures on petitions. The press was rife with talk of
"crisis precipitated by Catholics." In early December 1956, Azikiwe, Premier
of the Eastern Region, made a special trip to Onitsha and declared in a speech
there that "the right of Roman Catholic parents to choose the school which
their children would attend was fundamental." The premier also informed the
crowd that "All public and private schools built before 1st January 1957 will
not charge fees, but shall be eligible for grants-in-aid [i.e., government fund-
ing], other things being equal."[19] The visit by Azikiwe mollified protesters,
who interpreted his statements as refutation of those made by the minister of
education that any expansion of mission schools would not be funded by the
government.

Early in 1957, just before the new school was set to begin, Onitsha women
demonstrators resumed their agitation, issuing petitions to the premier and to
the minister of education accusing the Ministry of favoring the CMS in the
granting of financial aid to schools. The Onitsha branch of CEWA declared
January 15–25 as "Action Days for Women." In the end the women achieved
their aims: the concessions granted by the government assured that the Catholic authorities in Onitsha were allowed to enroll all the children whose parents
wished them to register in Catholic schools.

The women activists who had been calling for the dismissal of the minister
of education must have felt especially elated by his transfer from the Ministry
of Education. Six other Catholics received cabinet appointments, a noticeable
increase over the 1954 cabinet in which there had been only one. Prominent
Protestants considered the makeup of the new cabinet "capitulation" to the
Catholic mobs. Even the ban on the opening of new private Roman Catholic
mission schools was effectively rescinded: in April 1957 the Ministry of Education authorized the opening of Catholic schools in Onitsha. Catholics con-

tinued to provide schooling for more children in Eastern Nigeria than any other group, government included. The initial fears in 1956–1957 that UPE would mean the end of government grants for mission schools did not come to pass. By 1959 even some of the new "private" schools that opened in 1957 were receiving government grants.

After independence in 1960, education remained an important site of contestation. Nationalists believed that one way to encourage a stronger "national" (in reality, regional) identity was by reducing the sectarianism which characterized the educational system, and to this end, in 1964, the government proposed a common religious syllabus. It was this call by the government for a common religious syllabus that brought Onitsha Catholic women onto the streets in 1964. The actions of 1964 followed very much the model established in the late fifties, bringing together a very broad coalition of women who organized again under the rubric "Catholic women." Women feared that a common religious syllabus was simply the first salvo in the struggle to wrest schools from the missions. Again the fear was that such schools would not attain the quality of Catholic schools.

On March 24, 1964, Onitsha Catholic women, along with women from other parts of the archdiocese as well as the Owerri archdiocese, again burst onto the political stage to express their displeasure at a new government educational initiative to modify the religious instruction in schools. The March on Enugu, in which about two thousand women took part, was the most dramatic demonstration by women in the region since the Women's War of 1929. The image of women of all ages, including ones with babies in their arms, running in all directions as they were tear-gassed by police continues to stir strong emotions in Onitsha.

Many women made the journey to Enugu, the regional capital, with young children; some were pregnant. At the House of Assembly the women turned the grounds into a picnic site as they ate their breakfast and waited for the Speaker of the House to address them. While the women waited patiently, the House met and dispersed, and police surrounded the protestors. Pandemonium erupted as the police moved in on the women, spraying them with tear gas. Demonstrators ran helter-skelter. As the women fled, the police apprehended nine protesters who were subsequently placed under arrest.[20]

The demonstration in 1964 appears to have included an even broader spectrum of "Catholic women" than those in 1956–1957. Some of the marchers, as already noted, were pregnant or took along their young children. But the involvement of older women, beyond child-bearing age, was pivotal: it was they who swelled the ranks of protestors. Many, perhaps most, of these women were unbaptized. The women's actions in 1964 were spearheaded by the ENCC Women's Wing, an organization formed in Onitsha in 1961. It is particularly noteworthy that the ENCC Women's Wing came into existence in 1961, i.e., following the achievement of political independence. This is because these women were motivated by issues of concern to them, irrespective of whether it was British colonial officials or Nigerian nationalist leaders at the helm. Again the women could claim victory: the government reluctantly abandoned the proposal to institute a common religious syllabus.

CONCLUSIONS

The demonstrations mounted by Onitsha women between 1956 and 1964 to challenge the proposals by the government with regards to education brought together a broad coalition of women, united by a common desire to protect the future employment prospects of children, grandchildren, and other wards. Of the large numbers of women who demonstrated in Onitsha, not all were baptized Catholics. Many were elderly women who had either been barred from baptism or had elected not to be baptized but sent children to Catholic schools. There were also younger women (women in their thirties and forties) as well as newly married young women with varying affiliations to the Catholic Church. These demonstrations were remarkable occurrences for several reasons. First, they are the first documented large-scale demonstrations of any kind in Onitsha that united the indigenous and nonindigenous. Secondly, and even more significantly, in contrast to previous groupings of Catholic women, such as the Legion of Mary and other pious associations, these movements joined women who belonged to the Catholic elite and whose status within the Church was thus acknowledged as "regular" by the Catholic hierarchy with women who had never been even nominally Catholic. While it was the literate elite of Catholic women who wrote the letters and petitions, it was women who were not recognized by the Church hierarchy as Catholic who swelled the ranks of the protesters.

Although British colonial rule generally was unable or unwilling to acknowledge female officeholders, these demonstrations affirm the willingness and ability of women to mount mass action in order effectively to challenge policies they felt were not in their best interests.

ACRONYMS

ASON   Archdiocese of Onitsha Archives
CEWA   Catholics Eastern Women Association
CJAS   Canadian Journal of African Studies

CMS	Church Missionary Society
ENCC	Eastern Nigeria Catholic Council
NAE	National Archives, Enugu, Nigeria
NCNC	National Convention of Nigerian Citizens
RCM	Roman Catholic Mission
RNC	Royal Niger Company
UPE	Universal Primary Education

SUGGESTED READINGS

For a broad overview of the history of Nigeria see Andrew Roberts, ed., *The Cambridge History of Africa, Vol. 7: c. 1905–c. 1940* (Cambridge, 1986) and Michael Crowder, ed., *The Cambridge History of Africa, vol 8: c. 1940–c. 1975* (Cambridge, 1984). More specialized studies of education, the work of the missionaries in Nigeria, and women's political activity include David B. Abernethy, *The Political Dilemma of Popular Education: An African Case* (Stanford, 1969); James S. Coleman, *Nigeria: Background to Nationalism* (Berkeley, 1971); Felix K. Ekechi, *Missionary Enterprise and Rivalry in Igboland, 1857–1914* (London, 1972); Nina E. Mba, *Nigerian Women Mobilized: Women's Political Activity in Southern Nigeria, 1900–1965* (Berkeley, 1982); Vincent A. Nwosu, *The Laity and the Growth of the Catholic Church in Nigeria: The Onitsha Story, 1903–1983* (Onitsha, 1990); and Fernando Valderrama Martinez, *A History of UNESCO* (Paris, 1995).

NOTES

1. For a general discussion of the *omu*-ship, see Kamene Okonjo, "The Dual-Sex Political System in Operation: Igbo Women and Community Politics in Midwestern Nigeria," in *Women in Africa: Studies in Social and Economic Change*, ed. Nancy J. Hafkin and Edna G. Bay (Stanford: Stanford University Press, 1976). For the *obi*-ship in Onitsha, with some discussion of the *omu*-ship, see Richard N. Henderson, *The King in Every Man: Evolutionary Trends in Onitsha Ibo Society and Culture* (New Haven and London: Yale University Press, 1972).

2. See Helen K. Henderson, "Onitsha Women: The Traditional Context for Political Power," in *Queens, Queen-Mothers, Priestesses & Power*, ed. Flora Kaplan, (New York: New York Academy of Sciences, 1997) and Nina E. Mba, *Nigerian Women Mobilized: Women's Political Activity in Southern Nigeria, 1900–1965* (Berkeley: Institute of International Research, University of California, 1982).

3. A broad overview of the British Empire can be found in Niall Ferguson, *Empire: The Rise and Demise of the British World Order and the Lessons for Global Power* (London: Allen Lane, 2002).

4. The classic history of the CMS history in Nigeria is J. F. Ade Ajayi's *Christian Missions in Nigeria, 1841–1891: The Making of a New Elite* (Evanston: Northwestern University Press, 1965).

5. The standard history of the Holy Ghost Congregation (or Spiritans) is Henry K. Koren's *To the End of the Earth: A General History of the Congregation of the Holy Ghost* (Pittsburgh: Duquesne University Press, 1983).

6. On rivalry between Catholic and Protestant missions in Onitsha, see Felix K. Ekechi, *Missionary Enterprise and Rivalry in Igboland, 1857–1914* (London: Frank Cass, 1972).

7. Corvée labor is forced unpaid work, usually for construction of public works such as roads.

8. Again, this can be attributed to the larger project of the CMS missionaries. Their goal from the very outset was the creation of a "native" clergy.

9. Ferguson, *Empire,* 346.

10. Larry Diamond, *Class, Ethnicity and Democracy in Nigeria: The Failure of the First Republic* (London: Macmillan, 1988), 74. Sylvia Leith-Ross, who spent many years in Nigeria as a colonial officer, made a similar point in her memoirs. Speaking of the 1950s she wrote: "Often one read with growing anger an article full of sneers and insinuations, only to discover with relief when the last sentence was reached that it was aimed at a rival political party, not at us." Leith-Ross, *Stepping Stones: Memoirs of Colonial Nigeria, 1907–1960* (Boston: Peter Owen, 1983), 139.

11. It was the following year, 1952, that the Western Region announced it would implement universal, free, compulsory primary education. The compulsory component of the program failed to materialize for the same reason that UPE in the east was to be abandoned: money. James S. Coleman, *Nigeria: Background to Nationalism* (Berkeley: University of California Press, 1971), chapters 12–15; James O'Connell, "The State and the Organization of Elementary Education in Nigeria: 1945–1960," 113–131 in *Education and Politics in Nigeria,* ed. Hans N. Weiler, (Freiburg: Rombach, 1964).

12. E. C. Amucheazi, *Church and Politics in Eastern Nigeria, 1945–1966: A Study in Pressure Group Politics* (Lagos: Macmillan Nigeria, 1986), 46.

13. I. F. Nicolson, *The Administration of Nigeria, 1900–1960: Men, Methods, and Myths* (Oxford: Clarendon Press, 1969), 280.

14. The educated included all those who had completed Standard Six. Standard Six was the top grade of primary education.

15. James S. Coleman, *Nigeria: Background to Nationalism* (Berkeley: University of California Press, 1971), 331–333.

16. Fernando Valderrama Martinez, *A History of UNESCO* (Paris: UNESCO, 1995). See also "Final Report" issued by the Conference of African States on the Development of Education in Africa, Addis Ababa, May 15–25 (Paris, 1961).

17. "Archdiocese of Onitsha. December 1952. "Revision of Regulations," File: Mission, Education Room, ASON.

18. "500 Women March on Councillors," *Daily Times,* November 19, 1956, front page. Nina Mba gives a figure of two thousand demonstrators for the November 17 demonstration. Mba, *Nigerian Women Mobilized,* 123.

19. "Minister of Education Clarifies Universal Primary Education Scheme," *News From Eastern Nigeria* [Government bulletin], NAE.

20. Charges against the women were later dropped, a development they celebrated as another victory. The women were represented by Catholic lawyers on a gratis basis.

Chapter Sixteen

Margaret Thatcher:
The Woman and Her Times

Mark Garnett

Margaret Thatcher (born 1925) was the most notable British prime minister since Winston Churchill. Leading her Conservative Party to three consecutive general election victories (1979, 1983, and 1987), she implemented radical policy changes that affected almost every area of the nation's life. As a result, she aroused strong feelings, inspiring fierce and enduring loyalty in her followers but also provoking hostility even within Conservative ranks. In November 1990 she was removed from office after a vote of her own parliamentary party.

Even if Thatcher had not been Britain's first female prime minister and the first politician in the democratic era to win three consecutive general elections, she would have been noteworthy. More than any of her predecessors, whether from the left or the right, she was influenced by political ideas. Her idiosyncratic brand of individualism provides the main focus of this essay, which is divided into two main sections. The first examines Thatcher's personal background, showing how this influenced her political thinking. The second section asks whether Thatcher's personal outlook really did strike a chord with voters or whether her views were unrepresentative of the country she governed for eleven years. In closing, there will be some suggestions about the best way of understanding the nature of her legacy in British politics and society.

THE MAKING OF A POLITICAL LEADER

Margaret Thatcher's admirers and opponents rarely agree, but they are at one in recognizing the importance of her upbringing. They all assume that her outlook was heavily influenced by her childhood experiences and in particular by the "Victorian Values" espoused by her father. Years later she drew encouragement from ideological think tanks, notably the Institute of Economic Affairs (IEA), which attacked collectivism from a more academic perspective. But there was no question of "converting" her to economic liberalism; she had never believed in anything else.

It is important, though, to avoid oversimplifying Thatcher's ideological development and thus distorting the nature of her impact on British society. She gave repeated tributes to the memory of her father, and she certainly used the language of "Victorian Values" in many of her speeches. Even so, as prime minister she presided over a society which few Victorians would have relished, and she showed little sign of dissatisfaction with the dominant trends of modern British life. It is possible to argue that while the views of Thatcher's father played a crucial role in shaping her, there was a negative reaction as well as a degree of assent. Indeed, had Thatcher been a faithful custodian of the Victorian flame, she might never have been elected to Parliament, let alone elevated to the highest office.

Alfred Roberts (1892–1970) owned and worked in a grocery store, which was reasonably prosperous. In the Lincolnshire market town of Grantham, he was a fairly well-known and influential man. Margaret, his second and favored daughter, was three years old when he cemented his status by winning a seat on Grantham's town council. For twenty years he was chairman of the Finance and Rating Committee—a key budgetary post within the council.

Roberts had run for office as an independent candidate, but, as John Campbell has shown in the first truly comprehensive biography of Thatcher, his ideas marked him as a thoroughgoing liberal in ideological terms.[1] In this he was typical of many small businessmen. Religion reinforced Roberts's political views. He was a Wesleyan Methodist—the most aspirational and middle-class branch of that divided church—who took his commitment to the extent of regular lay preaching. His creed was simple, and he upheld it with complete conviction. Its main elements were hard work, duty, self-respect, thrift, and dedication to one's immediate family. It would be a mistake to describe Roberts as a blinkered individualist, who felt that (as his daughter once memorably put it) "there is no such thing as society." Charity was also encouraged. Yet Roberts drew a crucial distinction. If people had fallen into difficulties despite trying to live by the doctrine of "self-help," it was only right to offer them some support. The case was different for those who expected assistance without effort or demanded it as a right. Thus Margaret remembered that her father had little sympathy for the unemployed workers from the northeast of England who passed through Grantham in 1936 on their "hunger march" to London.[2]

Roberts believed that if taxation had to be levied on hard-working local people, they had a right to expect constant vigilance from their elected representatives. There was no justification for extravagance with other people's money. Young Margaret certainly absorbed this lesson from her father. As leader of the Conservative Party she saw the reduction of state expenditure as her chief goal, and her attempt to redistribute the burden of local taxation in favor of the affluent led directly to her departure from office in 1990.

The influence of Alfred Roberts went further than the positive inculcation of ideas. Little attempt was made to expose his daughter to any potential sources of alternative views. Roberts was not the most sociable of men, and he was far from being an intrepid traveler. He never took Margaret abroad. He was an enthusiastic reader in his youth, and in her memoirs Thatcher attributes her own literary interests to his example. Yet her cultural tastes were resolutely "middlebrow." Her favorite poet, Rudyard Kipling, had hidden depths; but most people read him as a straightforward propagandist for the British Empire, who knew how to write in everyday language.

If she was unduly sheltered from unsettling ideas, it is doubtful that Margaret Roberts felt any deprivation. But as John Campbell has argued, it would be a mistake to accept at face value her reminiscences of a happy childhood. In particular, she seems to have resented the conspicuous consumption of other young people, while her own family frowned on such fripperies even though they could afford the occasional luxury.

This is a point of the utmost significance in explaining Margaret Thatcher's subsequent career. She had never been encouraged to think for herself—or at least, she grew up thinking that there was no reason for examining her ideas since they were self-evidently right. But no one could insulate her from the social changes of the interwar period in Britain. This saw the beginnings of a consumerist culture, fueled by new techniques of mass production. However, Alfred Roberts was not the kind of man who rushed out to purchase the latest labor-saving device. In a revealing interview many years later, Thatcher admitted that "the one thing I really wanted was a nice house, you know, a house with more things than we had."[3]

It is extremely doubtful that Thatcher could ever have recognized her desire for the mechanical conveniences of modern life as a significant breach in the "Victorian" code of values, which she had been taught by her father. Yet self-denial was not the least important of those values; it can be seen as a distant echo of the view that the possession of riches amid specious temptations is a trial for the soul. Rising living standards for those in employment during the interwar period complemented the previous work of Charles Darwin and the carnage of the Flanders fields between 1914 and 1918 to undermine what was left of the original rationale behind self-denial. If British people were still thrifty, it was no longer as part of a strategy for bolstering self-worth, underpinning a confident belief in a heavenly reward beyond price. Where it was practiced at all, saving was now purely instrumental for strictly secular purposes; self-worth was to be attained through possessions. In sharing this view Margaret Thatcher was a child of her times; by contrast, her father represented a mode of thought that was dying away in a world of hire-purchase, mortgages, and consumer durables.

Probably disagreement on this point helped to distance Margaret from her father. Notwithstanding her later eulogies of his memory, after her marriage in 1952 she saw relatively little of him. Alfred's evident disapproval of her husband might have arisen from Denis Thatcher's previous divorce, but as a more affluent businessman he was also in a position to fulfill Margaret's dreams of domestic comfort. The couple did not flaunt their wealth; but equally they never betrayed any disapproval of those who did. Significantly, Margaret later loosened her ties with Methodism. Admirers stress a continuing streak of Christianity in her outlook, and her speeches drew freely on religious sources—the parable of the Good Samaritan being a special favorite. But the requirements of the flesh were always prioritized over spiritual concerns. For practical purposes the adult Margaret Thatcher might just as well have been an atheist.

At Oxford University between 1943 and 1947, Margaret studied chemistry. True to her father's precepts, she worked hard; but the subject was unlikely to nurture her limited powers of critical reflection. The fact that she joined the University's Conservative Association (OUCA) is partly a testament to her political ambitions—she was far less likely to win a place in Parliament as a representative of the declining Liberal Party, let alone as an independent like her father—but it also shows that the Conservative Party was now widely acknowledged as the natural home for ideological liberals who wanted to concentrate their energies in the fight against the "socialist" Labour Party. Her organizational skills ensured that she eventually became President of OUCA, although there is no evidence that she was personally popular in what was still a socially exclusive body.

This effortless rise cemented Margaret's feeling that despite her relatively humble background she really did belong with the Conservatives. That conviction was reinforced by her idolization of Churchill, the symbol of defiance against Germany. Having never visited the European mainland, she could be forgiven for taking a wholly negative view of the Germans; her only exposure to them had been air raids on Grantham, which had been targeted as a minor industrial center. But Margaret also shared Churchill's emotional attachment to the British Empire; indeed at one time she had hoped to work within the Indian civil service. Presumably this devotion to Britain's historical destiny was absorbed through her reading of Kipling. It was still evident in her political speeches, long after Britain had begun to disengage from her empire. An ability to overlook the obvious symptoms of national decline was another key feature that Margaret shared with her contemporary Britons, along with an admiration of America that was a by-product of her consumerism and a reflection of her gratitude for the part they had played in the war. Those who heard Thatcher speak on the supposed "special relationship" would have shared the common British delusion that the only reason for U.S. participation in the struggle against the Axis powers was a pure, disinterested love of freedom.

The election of a Labour government in 1945 also played an important formative role for Margaret Roberts. Indeed, it is not too fanciful to argue that Labour's continuation of wartime rationing after the end of hostilities allowed her to divert her resentment against her father's penny-pinching into a more constructive political channel. Self-denial for the young woman was even more of an irritant than it had been when her father had inflicted it on her as a child, since this time personal sacrifices were being demanded by the impersonal state. In fact, Labour's economic policy was at least partly based on "Victorian Values"—asking British citizens to defer their own consumption in the name of the long-term goal of restoring the country's credit as an exporting nation. This cut no ice with Margaret Roberts, who was invigorated rather than repelled when the Conservatives began to campaign on behalf of economic freedom as a tactical ploy against Labour. In fact, her own party had originally brought in rationing along with other restrictions on individual liberty; but this inconvenient fact was easily forgotten as the new government prosecuted its "socialist" program of nationalization. For a while she was out of step with the majority of voters, who returned Labour to office with a slender majority in the 1950 general election. But in the following year the growing desire for a return to consumerism brought Churchill back to Downing Street.

As so often, events conspired to confirm Margaret in her youthful beliefs. While the collectivist mood slowly dissipated among the electorate as a whole, the party she had joined gave a platform for those who had always resisted it. She was thrilled by her first experience of a Conservative Party conference, in 1946, which demonstrated the aggressive "libertarian" mood among many grassroots members. A foreign observer of that gathering, Bertrand de Jouvenal, encountered one "militant" who told him, "I ask for nothing better than to fight for the individual against the encroachments of the State."[4] The fact that Britain's state-coordinated effort during the war had just saved the nation from fascism seems to have escaped both de Jouvenal and his interlocutor. It also eluded Margaret Roberts, although it deeply impressed fellow Conservatives like Edward Heath. Heath and other male Conservatives of Margaret's generation were also unrepresentative of British opinion because their experience of commanding troops from all sections of society persuaded them of the need for policies that transcended the sectional interests traditionally associated with their party. Heath also recognized the need for European unity, having reflected on the devastation in continental towns and cities. By contrast, Margaret Roberts, like most of her fellow Britons, was further alienated from the European mainland, which seemed only a source of stagnation and potential conflict while the United States offered freedom and economic opportunity.

Thus by the time that she was selected to stand for election in Dartford in 1951, the hallmarks of the future prime minister could be discerned in the twenty-seven-year-old Margaret Roberts. The fact that she was relatively young and good-looking drew unusual press attention to her campaign—and since she proved herself an able candidate in a seat which her party had no chance of winning, the coverage she earned was invariably positive. She showed many of the qualities that make a notable—rather than a brilliant—politician. What made her unusual—apart from her sex—was that she was entirely devoid of skepticism, about herself or her country. She could recite her views with the same certainty as her father because she had never encountered a person who would offer alternative suggestions—or rather, if she did meet a potential antagonist, she was now confident enough in her abilities and her outlook to smile sweetly and avoid any discussion. This highly partial education in the realities of life ended up being a major advantage for Thatcher as her career progressed; the sense of mission arising from her ideological certainty was extremely helpful in debate and probably fueled her legendary physical stamina.

Even so, in 1951 her equipment for future battles was incomplete. Her outlook on life might have been shaken had she failed to find a partner who was affluent enough to satisfy her material needs, while providing quiet reassurance that her political views were infallible. Meeting Denis Thatcher satisfied both of these requirements; the fact that the couple had twin children in August 1953, allowing Margaret to feel that she had performed her key marital duty in one fell swoop rather than enduring two time-wasting pregnancies, added a gratuitous bounty from providence.

THATCHER AND THE BRITISH PEOPLE

Between her election as MP for Finchley in 1959 and her emergence as Conservative leader in 1975, Margaret Thatcher proved her mettle as a politician within a party that had never been welcoming to dynamic women. It had, though, recognized the presentational advantage of allowing at least one "token" woman at a time into its higher echelons. Thatcher took full advantage of this tiny chink in the glass ceiling. For three years after October 1961 she served as a junior minister in the Department of Pensions, and after the Conservatives returned to Opposition in October 1964, she held a variety of front-bench posts. As Education Secretary between 1970 and 1974 in Edward Heath's government, she showed her administrative capabilities and was surprisingly pragmatic at a time when her department was something of an ideological battlefield. After the Conservatives lost power in February 1974, she enhanced her reputation as a doughty opponent of the Labour government when morale within her own party was low. Yet her victory over Edward Heath in the 1975 Conservative leadership contest was still a major surprise. A detailed discussion of her rise is beyond our present purpose. Suffice it to say that luck played a greater role than it had for any previous Conservative leader; but then again this was only the second time that the position had been filled by election, and none of Thatcher's successors in the post has commanded anything like unanimous support.

While Thatcher was climbing through the Conservative ranks, her country was being transformed. The 1960s saw a series of blows for the old "establishment," notably the 1963 Profumo scandal that gave the impression that the ruling elite only differed from "ordinary" people because of a greater gap between its prescriptions and its habitual practices.[5] The liberalizing measures of the so-called "permissive society" are often hailed as the hallmark of a mature democratic civilization. Yet for all the well-meaning attempts to trigger off a public debate, particularly via the relatively new medium of television, the various participants tended to resort to sloganeering. Thatcher herself sometimes articulated views that encouraged her supporters to think that she was against "permissiveness." Whatever her real views, she certainly benefited from the peculiar, Janus-faced individualism of the 1960s, which produced a significant constituency of aggrieved voters. These individuals were alienated by the emerging blend of economic intervention and social toleration in government policy. Feeling betrayed by the existing political classes, they were looking for an outsider to voice their concerns; Thatcher was ready to fill the role when more orthodox candidates proved unwilling to challenge the Conservative Party establishment.

Even if Thatcher was deluded about the postwar situation facing Britain at home and abroad, this was an asset rather than a hindrance at a time when the country had no desire to face harsh realities. So, for example, people wanted to be told that their country could be great again, by someone who really believed it—even if by 1979 they had a sneaking suspicion that the glory days were over. Thatcher was ready to supply that rhetorical fix. In her mind-set, Britain's decline had been more apparent than real. The retreat from the empire had been driven by socialists, beguiled by a wrong-headed belief in the "brotherhood of man." While her predecessors had wrestled with the transition from superpower status to the role of a constructive moral influence in the world's councils, Thatcher just wanted Britain's voice to matter, regardless of what it happened to be saying at any given time and even if the international community regarded it as a puny echo of the United States. In this respect, she was probably in tune with the majority of her compatriots. She won plaudits at home and abroad for her pugnacious approach towards the Soviet Union, and for many Conservatives her status as a national heroine was secured by her determination to reclaim the Falkland Islands from the Argentinean invasion of 1982. This mood was even shared by Opposition leaders, although they recoiled at her attempt to invoke old imperial glories after a conflict that she had helped to bring about through her cuts in Britain's defense budget.

Thatcher also spoke for the majority in taking a rigid line on industrial relations, backing a series of legal reforms that tilted the balance of power in the workplace strongly in favor of management. The British trade unions had once been highly popular; indeed they had reflected the dominant postwar ethos because most of their leaders dedicated themselves to securing better living standards for their members. But now that the "working poor" had almost disappeared, strikes were regarded as unwelcome interruptions in the flow of goods and services—such as the laws prohibiting Sunday trading, which Thatcher also reformed. With their memories of the early 1970s, Britons thought that industrial stoppages could only be ended by settlements that caused the cost of living to rise. Thatcher thought that trade unions in themselves could not cause inflation; her economic dogma taught her that this phenomenon resulted from increases in the money supply. Yet even if their antipathy arose for different reasons, it was enough for many voters that Thatcher hated the unions as much as they did.

British consumers also wanted to enrich themselves without feeling guilty about those who were excluded from the rise in living standards. Alfred Roberts had taught his daughter to distinguish between the "deserving" and "undeserving" poor, and this was one "Victorian Value" from which she never swerved. Thatcher genuinely believed that only the feckless could truly be in need of the necessities of life. The welfare state ensured that the unemployed would be maintained at subsistence level until such a time as they showed the necessary initiative to reequip themselves for the marketplace. Hence she could reassure voters that there was no need for guilt and accuse her critics of "drivelling and drooling" about the poor while opposing the very measures that would allow them to drag themselves out of poverty through their own efforts. Many state benefits were cut (though not so much as Thatcher would have liked). In the meantime, the maximum rate of direct taxation (only levied on a proportion of the highest incomes) was reduced from a punitive 83 percent to 40 percent—a level that was much lower than the wildest dreams of economic liberals in 1979. Tax cuts, rather than expenditure on Britain's crumbling infrastructure, absorbed much of the proceeds from the reserves of oil in the North Sea.

Thatcher undoubtedly garnered electoral support through her open antipathy towards immigrants. A more reflective politician might have hesitated before stepping into this field because her parliamentary constituency of Finchley in North London contained a relatively high proportion of Jewish immigrants, and critics noted that her stance contradicted her loud advocacy of freedom in other respects. However, Thatcher thought that skin color was far more important than cultural differences or the dictates of intellectual consistency. She was satisfied that the only significant cultural difference between the Jewish community and Britons of earlier provenance was that Jewish people better exemplified an economic ethos which she would have liked to spread more widely. Probably most Britons would have found her insufficiently anti-Semitic. But this they were willing to forgive, so long as she shared their belief in tough restrictions on immigrants from the West Indies, (black) Africa, and Asia.

Finally, although Thatcher became prime minister at a time when traditional gender roles in Britain were dissolving, she made no attempt further to complicate the situation by standing forth as a champion of women's rights. Only one other woman ever served within her cabinets, although several female MPs at the time thought they deserved ministerial rank. In her domestic arrangements no professional woman could have been less subversive as a role model. Rather, she reinforced the old lesson that freedom was available to all, provided that they could pay. A nanny was brought in to attend to her children when they were young. But like many British women of her class, Thatcher continued to uphold housewifely ideals, even after she became prime minister. She was not averse to rustling up a meal for her husband and close aides after wading through several boxes of official papers or during the composition of a crucial speech. In short, she epitomized the ambiguity of gender roles in Britain in the wake of the supposed sexual revolution rather than helping to negotiate a new settlement of this momentous question.

THATCHER'S LEGACY

When asked what changes her premiership had wrought in Britain, Margaret Thatcher famously replied, "Everything." Now that more than a decade has passed since her downfall, the old divisions reemerge in contrasting assessments of her legacy. Her admirers look back on the 1980s with undisguised nostalgia, while people who dislike contemporary life in Britain tend to attribute all the country's woes to her eleven years in power.

Opinions will always conflict about the economic record of Thatcher's governments, which presided over two deep recessions on either side of a prosperous period that some commentators hailed as a "miracle." In particular, the world still awaits some concrete evidence to support her assertion that low rates of direct taxation increase incentives for hard-working people, rather than reducing the incentive for the rich to exert themselves. Equally, while "Thatcherites" insist that Britain has seen the rebirth of an entrepreneurial culture since 1979, capitalists still seem to be risk averse. Thus the privatization of state-owned utilities under Thatcher was characterized by the under-valuation of assets, so that shareholders were handed overnight profits. Many of them cashed in their gains at the first opportunity. But although the idea of getting rich quickly, with minimal effort, was far removed from her father's approach, it was perfectly compatible with the British ethos in the 1980s and far beyond. The bare statistics suggest that the effect of privatization on the economy as a whole has been highly beneficial, especially since loss-making enterprises are no longer a drain on the taxpayer. Yet some of the later privatizations, notably that of the railways, remain deeply unpopular.

The fate of Thatcher's rhetorical drive for a moral renaissance of Britain seems less equivocal. In an important chapter for a book published just before she fell from office, the political scientist Ivor Crewe produced telling evidence to suggest that this "crusade" had failed. On all the important counts, opinion surveys showed that the experience of life under Thatcher had actually increased the popularity of the things that were damned by her father's philosophy. For example, at the time of the 1979 general election which brought her to power, the proportion of people who advocated more spending on public services was exactly the same (37 percent) as those who wanted taxation to be reduced. By September 1986 the proportion who wanted tax cuts was down to 9 percent; 68 percent wanted an increase in spending on public services.[6] Despite this significant finding, the proportion of voters favoring the Conservatives was almost the same at the 1987 general election as it had been in 1983—just over 42 percent. Nevertheless, in Parliament Thatcher's party had a majority of 122 over all of its opponents.

The rebellion among Conservative MPs, which led to Thatcher's fall in November 1990, suggested that the contradictions within her thinking had been exposed. It was commonly argued that the Poll Tax—which meant that dukes paid the same amount for local services as the people who collected their garbage—provided the final proof that she was "out of touch" with ordinary voters. Significantly, her successor John Major had suffered the kind of hardships that are visited on ordinary people—including unemployment. His more emollient image undoubtedly helped the Conservatives to win the 1992 general election.

However, after that fleeting moment the Conservative Party disintegrated into faction fights, fueled in part by Thatcher from her new berth in the House of Lords. After all the talk of national revival after the Falklands War, it became apparent that Britain was still a middle-ranking power faced with a choice between integration within Europe and cooperation with the United States. For Thatcher, who had never felt the need to confront the true lessons of two World Wars, this was not a choice at all; for her, Americans were Britons with a slightly different accent, bigger cars, and much greater freedom from government intervention. Although at first Major talked as if he wanted to be open-minded on the question of Europe, he eventually sensed that, on this question as elsewhere, the "out of touch" Thatcher had the majority of Britons behind her. During the 1997 election campaign that ended his premiership and cast the Conservatives out of power for the foreseeable future, Major failed to present any constructive vision of Britain's proper role in the world.

Ironically, Major's government was also lumbered with a reputation for corruption in financial dealings and laxity in personal morality. There had been numerous examples of a decline in the standards of public life during the Thatcher years, but most voters had been too busy in the shopping malls to notice. In Thatcher's mouth, "Victorian Values" had been about economic activity; as a code for private life, it rarely extended beyond a preference for the traditional family—and even that was contradicted by tax reforms in the 1980s, which removed the financial incentive for marriage. Her view was that personal conduct was only to be condemned if it conflicted with the dictates of economic rationality; here, too, the majority of the public was on her side of the argument.

A THATCHERITE "CONSENSUS"?

In assessing the legacy of any individual, the obvious difficulty is to distinguish developments that might have happened anyway, whether or not one particular person existed. We have argued here that Thatcher articulated the views of an existing strand of opinion in Britain. In addition, many of Thatcher's policy ideas chimed in with more general trends in world politics, mainly associated with the recession induced by the oil shock of 1973–1974. Finally, the story of British politics in the 1980s contains continuity as well as change;

for example, the welfare state survived as a legacy from the "collectivist" era.

But while rejecting Thatcher's claim to have changed "everything," it would be just as mistaken to start downgrading her personal role or to underestimate the differences between the Britain of 1979 and the country that marked her departure with such mixed emotions in November 1990. Leaving aside all the statistical battles, Thatcher certainly helped to produce a distinct shift in the terms of public discourse (or "the climate of opinion"). She might not have changed many minds, but she encouraged many of the people who agreed with her to speak up. Most notably, by 1990 those who advocated action by the central state as the automatic remedy for any economic problem found themselves sidelined, just as believers in the free market had been for most of the earlier postwar period.

Over the eleven years of Thatcher's premiership, other party leaders began to recognize the potency of the electoral coalition she had assembled. They accepted that in 1979 there had been an urgent need to reform Britain's trade unions and that although voters were reluctant to ask for more tax cuts, they were more than happy with the bounty they had already received. Thus even before he became leader of the Labour Party in 1994, Tony Blair had pledged that her union policies would not be reversed, and in 1997 he guaranteed that there would be no increase in the basic rate of income tax.

In short, by 1997 Labour's senior figures had become active participants in what can be described as a Thatcherite "consensus." In Tony Blair, Britain currently has a prime minister who resembles Thatcher in many ways. Like Thatcher, he has been able to secure parliamentary majorities well out of proportion with his popularity because the opposition is in disarray. At home he has persisted with privatization, even at the risk of annoying traditional Labour supporters, and he has shown even less regret about the growth of social inequality than Thatcher ever did, despite his membership in a party which was founded to advance the interests of working people. More than anything, Blair wants to avoid giving the impression that prosperous Britons should ever deny themselves anything. The most significant difference is that Blair is capable of clothing the substance of Thatcherite policies with compassionate rhetoric, which his predecessor never tried to master.

Yet initial enthusiasm for Blair's "caring" image soon dissipated, suggesting that the persisting contradictions within Thatcherism are of more than academic interest. Even without the additional tensions created since September 11, 2001, British society is still torn between the desire to prosper and consume and a hankering after a more relaxed way of life. There has been a political price, too. Surveys reveal an electorate that has limited respect for politicians in general. The more they describe themselves as mere "servants of the people," the more inclined are their constituents to accept their humble self-evaluation. Politicians have become convenient scapegoats for voters; in their well-publicized frailties, they are no different from the people who attack them. Their loss of esteem is part of a general fashion for denigrating public servants, who are condemned whenever they deviate from traditional values but also derided for following them at a time when other people are feathering their nests through dubious practices. The attitude can be attributed directly to "Thatcherism," which worked on the crude assumption that everyone is self-interested and that professions of concern for others are invariably synthetic.

It might be argued that the law of unintended consequences means that all politicians who hope to change their country are bound to leave a legacy on both sides of the balance sheet. On this view, Thatcher's critics only have more to say because she changed so much more than most. Yet a different perspective is equally plausible. For them, the negative consequences of Thatcher's policies might have been "unintended"—but only because Thatcher herself lacked the grain of skepticism that would have alerted her to the dangers. Thus Thatcher's inability to doubt—the product of her upbringing—explains why some admire her to the point of idolatry, while others will never give her credit for anything.

SUGGESTED READINGS

The volume of literature on "Thatcherism" is some indication of the significant impact on Britain of Conservative governments between 1979 and 1990. The following is merely the tip of an enormous iceberg. A useful account written from a sympathetic viewpoint is Shirley Robin Letwin, *The Anatomy of Thatcherism* (London, 1992). From the opposite perspective, Ian Gilmour, *Dancing with Dogma* (London, 1992) is a hard-hitting critique by a former cabinet minister. Key aspects of policy are ably addressed in Simon Jenkins, *Accountable to None: The Tory Nationalisation of Britain* (Harmondsworth, 1995); and David Smith, *The Rise and Fall of Monetarism: The Theory and Practice of an Economic Experiment* (Harmondsworth, 1987). There are excellent studies covering a range of subjects in Dennis Kavanagh and Anthony Seldon, eds., *The Thatcher Effect; A Decade of Change* (Oxford, 1989). John Campbell's *Margaret Thatcher* (*Volume One, The Grocer's Daughter* [London, 2000]; *Volume Two, The Iron Lady* [London, 2003]) is an exhaustive, brilliantly compiled biography with an objective flavor; Hugo Young's *One of Us* (London, 1989 and subsequent editions) is admirable but much more antagonistic. The authorized biography being written by Charles

Moore will exploit private papers, but it will be difficult to supersede the judgements provided by Campbell and Young. Thatcher's own two-volume memoir published as *The Path to Power* (London, 1995) and *The Downing Street Years* (London, 1993) is informative but understandably tends towards self-justification.

NOTES

1. John Campbell, *Margaret Thatcher: Volume One, The Grocer's Daughter*, (London: Jonathan Cape, 2000), 11). This chapter is heavily indebted to Dr. Campbell's judicious and well-researched book.

2. Campbell, 16-17.

3. Campbell, 24.

4. Bertrand de Jouvenal, *Problems of Socialist England* (London: The Batchworth Press, 1949), 22.

5. The "Profumo Affair" was a political scandal in Britain in 1963 involving the then Secretary of State for War, John Profumo, and a showgirl named Christine Keeler with whom he had a brief affair. Keeler had also had a relationship with an attaché at the Soviet Embassy, raising concerns that Profumo had fraternized with a Soviet spy.

6. Ivor Crewe, "Values: The Crusade that Failed," in *The Thatcher Effect: A Decade of Change*, ed. Dennis Kavanagh and Anthony Seldon (Oxford University Press: Oxford, 1989), 246.

Index

About the Contributors

Myriam Boussahba-Bravard lectures in British political and social history in the Department of English Studies, University of Rouen, France. Her main research interests are suffragism and female employment, 1870–1939. She currently works on Teresa Billington-Greig, feminist and political writer in the Edwardian period.

Grayson Carter is an associate professor of church history at Fuller Theological Seminary Southwest in Phoenix, Arizona. He has written extensively on aspects of eighteenth- and nineteenth-century English religious history, including *Anglican Evangelicals: Protestant Secessions from the Via Media, c. 1800–1850.*

Matthew J. Clarcq is an assistant professor at Niagara County Community College in Lewiston, New York. He specializes in Modern Britain, paying particular attention to the mid-twentieth century. He is currently researching the efforts of Britain and the United States to organize and create a military unit whose purpose was to protect and repair art and architecture in Italy during the Second World War.

John R. Davis is a reader in modern European history at Kingston University, United Kingdom. His books include *Britain and the German Zollverein* and *The Great Exhibition*, and he has written articles on many aspects of nineteenth-century British and German history and Anglo-German relations. He is currently working on a book entitled *The Victorians and Germany.*

Anene Ejikeme is an assistant professor of history at Trinity University in San Antonio, Texas. She specializes in African history.

Amy M. Froide is an assistant professor of history at the University of Maryland, Baltimore County. Her publications include *Singlewomen in the European Past, 1250–1800*, which she coedited with Judith M. Bennett, "Old Maids: The Lifecycle of Singlewomen in Early Modern England" in *Women and Ageing in British Society since 1500*, and a monograph entitled *Never Married: Singlewomen in Early Modern England*.

Mark Garnett is a lecturer in politics at Lancaster University, United Kingdom. He is the author of several books on the contemporary British Conservative Party, including *Keith Joseph: A Life* with Andrew Denham, *Whatever Happened to the Tories?* with Ian Gilmour, and *Splendid! Splendid! The Authorized Biography of Willie Whitelaw* with Ian Aiken.

June Hannam is associate dean (research and staff development) and reader in women's history in the Faculty of Humanities, Languages and Social Sciences, University of the West of England, Bristol, United Kingdom. She is the author of *Isabella Ford, 1855-1924, Socialist Women: Britain, 1880s–1920s* with Karen Hunt and several articles on socialist and feminist politics in Britain in the late nineteenth and early twentieth centuries. Currently she is working on Labour Party women MPs and the meaning of their politics between the world wars.

Susan Hanssen is an assistant professor of history at the University of Dallas. She is currently working on the public reception of G. K. Chesterton's work in Britain and the United States.

Michael Huggins is a senior lecturer in the Department of History and Archaeology at the University of Chester in the United Kingdom. He has also lectured in history at the Institute of Irish Studies, University of Liverpool. He won the Beckett Prize in Irish History in 2000 for his doctoral work on agrarian combinations in prefamine County Roscommon and has written a monograph, *The Secret Ireland* (forthcoming) based on his dissertation. He is currently researching the relationship between Irish nationalism and Chartism.

Frances Knight is a senior lecturer in church history and head of the Department of Theology and Religious Studies at the University of Wales, Lampeter. She is the author of *The Nineteenth Century Church and English Society* and several articles on the history of Anglicanism in England and Wales since 1800.

Timothy Larsen is an associate professor of theology at Wheaton College, Wheaton, Illinois. He is the author of *Friends of Religious Equality: Nonconformist Politics in Mid-Victorian England*, *Christabel Pankhurst: Fundamentalism and Feminism in Coalition*, and *Contested Christianity: The Political and Social Contexts of Victorian Theology*.

Caroline Litzenberger is an associate professor of history at Portland State University, Portland, Oregon. She has written extensively on English religious history, including *The English Reformation and the Laity*.

Eileen Groth Lyon is an associate professor of history at the State University of New York at Fredonia. She is the author of *Politicians in the Pulpit* and several articles on modern British religious and political history.

D. A. J. MacPherson teaches history at the University of Sunderland. He has published widely on the history of women in nineteenth- and twentieth-century Ireland, including in the journal *Eire-Ireland*. He is currently researching Irish women's migration to the northeast of England, 1870–1970.

David Savage is professor emeritus at Lewis & Clark College in Portland, Oregon. His area of specialty is British colonialism and the history of education in British India. His most recent publications are "Evangelical Educational Policy in Britain and India, 1857–60" and "Missionaries and the Development of the Colonial Ideology of Female Education in India."

W. J. Sheils is a reader in history at the University of York, United Kingdom. His books include *The Puritans in the Diocese of Peterborough, 1558–1610*; *Restoration Exhibit Books and the Northern Clergy, 1662–1664*; *The English Reformation*, and (with S. Gilley) *A History of Religion in Britain: Practice and Belief from Roman Times to the Present*. He is a past editor of *Studies in Church History* and the author of numerous articles on English Reformation history.

Eric G. Tenbus is an associate professor of history at Central Missouri State University, Warrensburg, Missouri. He is currently working on Roman Catholics and the education of the poor in late nineteenth-century England.

Andrew C. Thompson is a college lecturer in history at Queens College, University of Cambridge. He is the author of "Popery, Politics, and Private Judgement in Early Hanoverian Britain" and a monograph, *Britain, Hanover, and the Protestant Interest: 1688–1756* (forthcoming).